the
emptiness
of our
hands

a lent lived on the streets

phyllis cole-dai
and
james murray

pinhole photography by
james murray

authorHOUSE

1663 LIBERTY DRIVE, SUITE 200
BLOOMINGTON, INDIANA 47403
(800) 839-8640
www.authorhouse.com

Digital prints of any or all of the photographs in this book are available upon request. Please contact James Murray by email at Jamesgm4@yahoo.com.

First published by AuthorHouse 08/30/04

ISBN: 1-4184-3329-2 (sc)

Library of Congress Control Number:2004094449

Printed in the United States of America
Bloomington, Indiana

This book is printed on acid-free paper.

For more information, please contact Phyllis Cole-Dai, 712 6th Street, Brookings, SD 57006; or James Murray, Box 572, 3 Petticoat Hill Rd., Williamsburg, MA 01096.

This book is a work of non-fiction. To protect the privacy of individuals, all personal names have been changed, except for those of the authors' friends and relatives, and those of public figures whose identities would be impossible to conceal. Some personal and location details have also been altered.

A portion of the proceeds from the sale of this book will be donated to programs that benefit homeless persons.

First edition printed by AlphaGraphics, Sioux Falls, SD, 2003.

To all of us,
that we might learn,
through the tender and tough tutelage of Spirit,
to be more present to one another

We must love one another or die.

—W. H. Auden

acknowledgments

James and I are immensely grateful to all of you who offered us unconditional and generous support during Lent and Easter Week, 1999. There isn't space enough to identify all the particular forms your assistance took, but in reading your name below, please be assured that we remember.

For special thanks we wish to single out a few people on whose dependable and skillful help we constantly relied while on the streets: Mary Sartain, who collected, organized and stored our little scraps and bundles of notes; Ellen Puckett and Sarah Reeder, who quickly developed James's negatives so that he could gauge the progress of his work; Gwyn Stetler, who helped inspire this journey and was for us a witness, and a rock, throughout; our families, who, walking with us in spirit, were always there to listen when we phoned; and most of all, Phoebe Walker and Jihong Cole-Dai, who loved us enough to let us go.

Blessings to you, and then, to all of these sweet souls: Maggie Atkinson, Nancy and Spence Badet, Alice Barbera, Rick Bauman, Atlee and Winnie Beechy, Phyllis Berman, Gordon and Lucy Bixel, Mary Brennan-Hoffman, Marcia Broucek, Patti Carrigan, Elliot Charrow, Barry Cole, Carol and Lynn Cole, Dave Cole, Dortha Cole, Father George Deas, Bob and Joan Deaton, Tim Durham, Jody Dzuranin, Patsy Ernsberger, Dan Everly, Melanie Ewing, James Ford, Bob Gillespie, Peter Gold, Nick Gumprecht, Ann and Jack Harris, the Hellraisers, Bill Hill, Sharon Johnson, Bernie Khunsman, Judy and Rob Limekiller, Donna Link, Beth Lonn, Diane and Ron Mattox, Michelle Mau, Dorotha Mengert, Pat and Paul Miller, Theda Oberholtzer, Ami Peacock, Betty Persons, Sandra Ritchie, Susan Ritchie, Barbara Ryan, Christie Sabol, Deya Murray, Eileen Murray, Jerry Murray, Sandy Murray, Scot Murray, Jack Schwarz, Ron and Doris Seward, Peg and Fletcher Shafer, Jamie Smith, Warren Smith, Madelyn Snyder, Ryan Snyder, Max and Marjorie Stacy, Jerry Strine, Tyler Studds, Chuck Thomas, Cheryl Throwe, Marela Trejozacari, Ethel Umble, Linda and Norman Walker, Ruth Wood, the photography department of Kenyon College, the Dublin Unitarian Universalist Church, the Columbus and Marion spirituality groups, and the Westerville Senior Citizens Center writing group.

Our thanks to all who shared in our noontime meditations, whether you actually came downtown to the Statue of Peace or joined us in spirit from a distance, as (we later learned) did various individuals and communities of faith in Ohio, Indiana, Illinois, Michigan, Kentucky, North Carolina, New York, Connecticut, Maine, New Mexico and California. However you became aware of our undertaking, you helped sustain us, and more so the homeless people in and beyond Columbus, Ohio, with your prayers, good will and the strength of collective intention.

We're also indebted to the many strangers in Columbus who, without knowing who we were, gifted us in uncountable ways while we were on the streets. Among them we especially lift up our homeless neighbors along the Scioto River; staff members of the Agora, the Five Loaves Bakery, and the Interfaith Hospitality Center; the Take It to the Streets organization; the cooks and volunteers in the food lines at Central Presbyterian Church and the Holy Family Soup Kitchen; the workers at JOIN and The Place to Be; the lenient librarians at Main Library and the tolerant employees of McDonald's and White Castle; the congregation and staff of St. Joseph Cathedral; and various staff members in city shelters.

We deeply appreciate the counsel that was so graciously provided by Maura Casey, Jay Erickson, Susan Ritchie, Jack Schwarz, Gwyn Stetler, Amanda Stewart and Tyler Studds, all of whom served as critical readers for our manuscript-in-progress. You helped bring this book to life.

Finally, we wish to acknowledge Bernie Glassman Roshi. In the stream of inspiring events eventually leading us to the streets, your book *Bearing Witness: A Zen Master's Lessons in Making Peace* was the last and most compelling. With our hands at gassho, we offer you, in humblest gratitude, the words of Bashō, the Zen poet of seventeenth-century Japan:

> The temple bell stops
> But I still hear the sound
> Coming out of the flowers.

This list of acknowledgments is long, and could be endless; nothing was insignificant. We apologize to anyone whose name we've failed to include. Sometimes bounty overflows the baskets.

We offer to all of you, and to every reader, the Hebrew blessing of a Jewish friend who graciously sent us off on our Lenten journey: *Yashir koach*. *"May you grow in strength."* May your souls forever bear witness to that unnameable Mystery in which all life has its being.

contents

illustrations

prologue

I will take with me the emptiness of my hands
What you do not have you find everywhere
—W.S. Merwin

From February 17 through April 4, 1999, James Murray and I lived voluntarily on the streets of Columbus, Ohio. This period of forty-seven days, beginning on Ash Wednesday and ending on Easter Sunday, coincided with the Christian observance of Lent and Holy Week.

James and I didn't go out on the streets to satisfy idle curiosity, or to experience a strange new world. We didn't go out to find answers to questions, solutions to problems. We didn't go out to save anyone, or to hand out donations of food and blankets. We went out for one primary reason: to be as present as possible to everyone we met—homeless person, volunteer, university president, cop. In other words, we set out, in our own way, to love our neighbor as ourselves, with eyes open, minds open, hearts open, hands open as wide as they could be, not ignoring potential risks but not looking for trouble either. Doing so, we were reminded just how difficult the practice of compassion can be, not only because of external obstacles and distractions, or physical hardships, but even more because of our own judgments, assumptions, fears and desires, all of which harden our regard for and behavior toward other people.

James and I have been told, more than once, that spending Lent on the streets of Columbus was a crazy thing to do. But then worthwhile things do often seem a little out of the ordinary, and they change you in ways you could never have imagined. Still, let us be clear: James and I are not thrill-seekers. No thirst for adventure drove us to do this. It's more like Annie Dillard says in her poem "I Am Trying to Get at Something Utterly Heartbroken." "This is not a thing that I have sought," she writes, "But it has come across my path and I have seized it." An apt description. The Thing—the calling, if you will—comes, and you realize, deep down, it's come for you, and you can't turn your back, or toy with it; it demands you take it up with single-minded passion, even though you never asked for it, or even want it, now. It's here, and it's yours. You don't ask why it has come, for who would know the answer, and besides, the why doesn't matter. You trust the Thing totally, and that's enough. Finally, you don't ask how you'll survive it, if the Thing is hard, and will break your heart—now is not the time for asking that, but for telling your husband that this is what you've been given to do. And because he understands you, and loves you, and is a remarkable man, he says, "If this is what you have to do, what can I do to help?"

The Thing "came across my path" on a hot day in August, 1998. At the time, I'd been living and writing in Columbus for thirteen years. James, a dear friend and gifted photographer with whom I'd collaborated the previous year, was just finishing his studies in religion and art at Kenyon College, an hour north of the city. By chance, he and I had a meeting scheduled the afternoon of that August day. When during that meeting I announced my intention to go to the streets, explaining my reasons as best I could, he seized the Thing, too, said, "Can I go?" As he later confessed, the words escaped his mouth before he realized, but he didn't want to take them back, even though at the time going to the streets seemed less his calling than mine. Over the previous year, he'd watched the issue of homelessness tapping me on the shoulder again and again, taking on faces, names, stories; deeply affected, I'd been waiting to see where it all would lead. Now, suddenly, the Thing had appeared to me in full, and was pulling me toward the unknown heart of the city.

The unknown is the crucible of the human spirit; if we give ourselves to it with faith, inevitably we undergo a change, and little by little the world changes with us. This is why James wanted to go with me. He didn't know what it would mean to be truly present on the streets, where every security has been stripped away, and he didn't know what would happen if he tried, but try he would.

James and I share Christian roots (his Roman Catholic, mine Methodist) as well as a deep appreciation for eastern philosophy and meditation. We also share an intuitive sensibility, and an abiding interest in spirituality and art. Other than that, and our both being anglo, we're not much alike. Thirteen years younger than I am, James is a sturdy six-foot-four inches tall, with shoulder-length curls; I'm a slender five-foot-six, with straight hair bobbed short. James grew up in a New York City penthouse near Central Park, attending private schools and spending weekends on Long Island; I was raised on a hog farm in northwest Ohio. James is a bold extrovert; I'm more inward and cautious by nature. James loves looking at life through a lens; I avoid cameras, and make love to the world through language. All these differences, however, meant little that hot day in August, and still do; in general, we're both more concerned with what people hold in common than what sets them apart. So when James offered to accompany me to the streets, I gladly accepted. Now, on the other end, I know I wouldn't have lasted, in body or spirit, had he not gone along.

Eventually James and I decided to leave home on the first day of Lent, the traditional Christian season of self-examination and fasting; if all went as planned, we would return home on Easter, the springtime festival of resurrection, of cosmic renewal. This liturgical backdrop would provide a rich spiritual context for what would probably be the most raw experience of our sheltered lives. We had no doubt those forty-seven days would be incredibly tough. Just how tough we rarely speculated, not wanting to shadow-box with what-ifs and could-happens.

Over the ensuing months, we made certain promises to each other. While on the streets we would, first of all, try to avoid staying in homeless shelters, since we didn't want to take up beds. Second, we wouldn't tell anyone exactly why we were out, since the truth would color every interaction. If questioned, we would simply be vague or evasive; we would directly lie only if it was necessary to prevent harm. Third, we would each do whatever we could to support and protect the other. Finally, either of us could quit at any time. If one of us left the streets, the other would be free to follow, or not.

James and I naturally considered chronicling our time on the streets through his photography and my writing. Our artwork could be a companion on the streets as it was elsewhere in our lives, challenging us to greater awareness. Someday the work might shape-shift into a book that other people could grapple with, wring some blessing from, but we didn't dwell on that possibility. The last thing we wanted to take to the streets was a confused mix of motives. Come Lent, we would go to the streets prepared to pick up the pencil, to shoot the picture, but we would actually do so only if it helped us be present. Only if it proved another way to love our neighbor.

Our biggest artistic question was how James would manage the camera work without being conspicuous. The answer was soon clear: pinhole photography—a method so basic that even grade schoolers can learn. If James carried certain supplies onto the streets, he'd be able to build crude cameras from boxes or cans scavenged from dumpsters. James and I both liked the symbolism of recycling trash into cameras, plus the pragmatism was unbeatable: whenever James took a picture, he'd appear to any casual observer simply to be holding a box.

While basic in its method, pinhole photography isn't easy. It's imprecise, frustrating, time-consuming guesswork, much more complicated than the ethical code James would follow in his shoots. That code consisted of two fundamental rules: No taking photographs of people, since he couldn't ask their permission; for the same reason, no taking photographs of shanties or other makeshift homes.

While on the streets James arranged every so often for one of his photographer-friends to pick up his exposures, take them to a darkroom and develop them into negatives. Once he returned home, he transformed the best of those negatives into black and white pictures. The images turned out as bleary and rough as our experience of the streets.

Our first night on the streets was—to be frank—hell. It so traumatized us that we were tempted to quit and go home; paradoxically, however, it also convinced us that we were exactly where we had to be, doing what we had to do. And part of what we would have to do, if we somehow managed to remain, was produce the book that until then had been merely a shadowy prospect. We would have to speak up. Of this, we were now certain. If only in a limited way, the book could portray how being without a real home can devastate the human spirit—after a single night, we already had some sense of this. Then, too, perhaps the book could inspire its readers to reflect on their own ability to be more present, more compassionate, in their small corners of the world.

I asked James if he would help me write such a book, and he graciously agreed. Photographer turned storyteller. It wasn't easy after we came off the streets to make sense of our fragmented notes, scribbled whenever and wherever we'd had the energy and the paper. Nor was it easy, in fleshing out the notes, to relive the hardship all over again. Thanks, James, for the gift of your perspective. Thanks, too, for entrusting me with the editing of your words.

An ordeal doesn't mean much until it begins to lighten a little; till then, you're just in shock, or in pain, dragging beneath its weight. Though James and I came off the streets in early April, 1999, we couldn't muster the heart to write about them until the very end of October. By then, he'd moved from Ohio to Connecticut. States apart, the two of us were alone, for the first time, with the fullness of the Thing, grappling with it even as we were still struggling to get our energy back, still suffering panic attacks, still trying to readjust to the pace and perks of "ordinary life."

Now, finally, the book is done. We've tried to be as loyal as possible to what we remember. But however true it might be, this story is also a fiction; less a recital of objective facts than a montage of perceived events, snatches of conversation, dream remnants, scraps of ideas, fleeting impressions. The fragments are more organized, their language more polished, than they should rightfully be. That's for your sake. If we didn't make the Thing intelligible, you might give up reading. This is your advantage over James and me; on the streets we had no narrator to help make things sensible, or sane.

Perhaps you know Columbus. Perhaps you know the artsy Short North, trendy German Village, the impoverished Bottoms, blue-collar Whitehall, affluent Bexley, the downtown around Broad and High, Capitol Square with its Statue of Peace. Perhaps you know how the golden crown of the LaVeque Tower lights up the skyline at night, or how the Olentangy and Scioto Rivers unite at the heart of the city like long-lost lovers. Perhaps you know how gloomy and gusty Columbus winters can be, wind chills often dropping well below zero; then, of course, spring—some years it's here barely a week before the hot humidity of summer swallows it whole.

When James and I hit the streets, Columbus was the nation's fifteenth-largest city, with 1.5 million residents in the metropolitan area. With a booming white-collar sector, it had rock-bottom unemployment, yet the poverty rate was rising. Many people in the working class struggled to rent, let alone own, a home; a minimum-wage worker had to put in at least eighty-three hours a week to afford even a modest two-bedroom apartment. Whether such an apartment would be available was another matter. The number of affordable housing units had dwindled as the city had grown—an estimated 22,000 additional units were needed. This lack of affordable housing, together with deepening poverty, had been largely responsible for the dramatic increase in the city's homeless population (as across the United States) over the previous two decades.[1] The number of people sleeping in Columbus shelters had doubled just in the 1990s. Often the shelters were filled to overflowing. Additionally, there was a substantial street population, though its size was understandably difficult to judge (estimates ranged all the way from 150 to 1000 per night). Finally, an unknown number of people was living temporarily with friends or in other unstable housing arrangements, a very common occurrence.[2]

No one can say with any certainty how many people in Columbus were living without homes during Lent, 1999. Let's say, simply, that there were too many. Even one person would have been too many, but to quote the director of the Community Shelter Board, Columbus had practically "a small city" of homeless people.[3] If all the "small cities" of people experiencing homelessness in this country around that time had been consolidated, we'd have had a virtual metropolis: an estimated two million in 1998,[4] about the same number of people as were living within the city limits of Philadelphia and Boston combined.[5] All the more tragically, one in every four of these persons was a child.[6]

Then as now, homeless persons in Columbus tended to be individuals who had suffered a temporary setback, such as loss of employment, relationship problems or eviction. Contrary to popular belief, while many of these persons suffered from mental illness or chemical dependency, they did so only at around the same rate as the general population.[7] However, use of alcohol and drugs did seem to be the strongest single predictor of whether a person who was temporarily without housing would become chronically homeless.[8] James and I ended up spending most of our days and nights among chronically homeless persons, especially those residing on the banks of the Scioto River.

Columbus was more tolerant of its homeless population than were some other cities in this nation, where efforts to criminalize homelessness often violated basic human rights. Of the fifty largest U.S. cities, thirty-eight per cent had recently initiated crackdowns on homeless people—for example: having the police dump them at the city limits; giving them bus tickets out of town; arresting them if they refused to be transported to a public shelter; passing ordinances against begging or sleeping (or even "covering oneself with a blanket") in a public place, sitting on the sidewalk, and so on. More than half of the fifty cities studied had conducted police sweeps simply to remove homeless people from public view.

According to a source in the city sheltering coalition, Columbus also had an unspoken policy of trying to keep homeless people out of sight. This unspoken policy had made its way into several anti-homeless ordinances, including one against sleeping in public parks. Nevertheless, the city was also seeking constructive ways of addressing the perceived needs of the homeless population. Its "Rebuilding Lives" plan, meant to move chronically homeless men out of shelters into permanent housing linked with job training and support services, has been hailed as a national model. But whether real change, and compassionate change, is happening in Columbus, only time will tell.

All of this is background to the pages that follow. It's part of the Lenten sidewalks you'll be walking with James and me, part of the Lenten food you'll be scavenging from dumpsters. It will be there in your shivers, your insomnia, your sweat, your stink, your longings, your limp. Let it sink in. Let it settle into the marrow of your bones, like a disease, and hope for recovery.

If you do this, you'll be ahead. When James and I hit the streets on Ash Wednesday, 1999, we weren't aware of any homeless statistics or policies. We were scarcely aware of any services (shelters, soup kitchens, clinics) available to homeless persons. We'd made few efforts, through research, to prepare, wanting to go out as thousands do each year in this city who suddenly have no place to call home and must stumble their way through the not-knowing.

About the only serious inquiries James and I made beforehand were into ourselves. As earnestly as we could, we dragged up into the light of day all the things we'd ever heard, or believed, about homeless people; all the stereotypes and prejudices and assumptions, not even sure how they'd become part of us—*Homeless people are dumb, lazy, on the streets because they want to be, mentally ill, violent, lucky not to have any responsibilities, inarticulate, dirty, rude, mostly male, mostly black, mostly drunks and addicts, many of them Vietnam vets. . . .* These were the things we "knew" best—not that a homeless woman could be so lonely she'd ride up and down in a shopping mall elevator, just to be close to other human beings; or that a young man, unable to cope with the tragic deaths of his wife and infant daughter, would abandon his home for the streets, intent on destroying himself.

Before you read further, James and I invite you to reflect on what you think you know about homeless people; on what you believe it's like to live without a real home. Be honest.

Now, lay all that aside, if you can. The Thing's about to cross your path. Empty your hands, and seize it. Let it lead you out the open door, away from the comforts of your sheltered life, from your usual sense of what's necessary, and real, and meaningful, and good. Go with it where you might never have gone alone, not that you might be entertained there, or even find wise answers to hard questions, but because there are people—*lives*—at stake. Dare to exist in the in-between, that place where nothing is secure, and everything is significant, if you'll allow it to be; a place where you can see most anything and, in good faith, do almost nothing except feel a shattering, and sometimes a mend; a place where you think and think and think and still, in the end, know precious little but for the fact that you've been where you've been, and anguished there, and were scarred—and now, on the other side, if you've been lucky enough to return home, you have no regrets at all, just much work to do.

the

emptiness

of our

hands

a lent lived on the streets

into the

between

day 1: wednesday, february 17

doors

I've walked through thousands of doors in my life; left some of them standing wide open, closed others, locked my share. But I've never walked through a door quite like this one—my own front door, a plain slab, not very thick and not very heavy but looking sturdy as steel on this brisk, gray morning—and I've never pulled a locked door securely shut behind me, as I'm about to do now, without a key resting in my pocket or under the doormat so I can easily go back inside. Today there'll be no easy way back in, no easy changing of the mind. Only the leaving. . . .

Ash Wednesday: what T.S. Eliot called "the time of tension between dying and birth." I pause just over the doorsill, James behind me on the porch, my gloved hand clinging to the knob. It's a little after 8:00 a.m. Jihong's already left for work, as if this were just a usual day in our marriage; Phoebe, James's girlfriend, has started for her home in Connecticut, as if this were just the end of another too-brief visit. They couldn't bear to stay here at the house and watch us go, and we couldn't bear to leave them behind, so they were the first out the door, just after the four of us had made our parting, borrowing the strength of ceremony. In a small bowl we'd combined wood ash from the fireplace with the finer, sweeter ash of incense collected from the meditation room. Then we'd marked each other, as Cain is said to have been marked by God before setting out into the unknown, better to learn the keeping of his brother. The faint dust marks, so tenderly imposed on the skin of our foreheads, were our sign of belonging—to each other, to this set-apart time, and to a world that covers us with the dust of sufferings and miracles alike.

Now I look over my shoulder at James, hand still full of knob.

"Are we ready, Irishman?"

His body visibly braces: he feels the edge. Who empties his bags, rather than packs, before a long, hard journey? He breathes deeply, all he can do, bright tears staining his cheeks. Then his eyes lock mine. "Okay," he says firmly. "Ready."

I step down, tug the door home, test the lock. Ready or not, the thing's done.

miles

Between the front door of my suburban home and the heart of Columbus, where most of the city's homeless population is found, stretch fourteen miles of pavement. A long march into Godknowswhat. It's all James and I can do, the first block, to put one foot in front of the other. Reality is setting in: For the next forty-seven days, we won't have any material comforts of home—no thermostat to turn up, no refrigerator to raid, no lights to switch on, no bed to sleep in, no toilet just across the hall, no morning shower, no clean clothes in the closet, no locked doors. We won't have the intangibles of home, either—especially the sense of belonging. What we will have, for sure, is fear. Uncertainty. Struggle.

Still, as our stride picks up and hits a rhythm, an inexplicable lightness of spirit sets in. Perhaps it's the gift of deep conviction, or maybe, after months of anticipation and sometimes dread, it's just plain relief that we're finally underway. We laugh, even, at James's scruffy first beard, sprouted just for the occasion.

At a traffic light we stand waiting. People stare at us from stopped cars. We smile back. The eyes glower, glance away. Ten minutes from home, already we're perceived as different, it seems. Is it because of our clothes? We're dressed for winter. I wear two old pair of long underwear, worn blue jeans, knitted leg warmers, thermal jacket, pullover sweatshirt, Jihong's ski sweater, heavy overalls, and a down coat, blessed with many pockets, which a friend had intended for the Salvation Army. Two pair of gloves for my hands, three pair of wool-blend boot socks and insulated boots on my feet, and finally, for my head, two knit hats and a neck warmer. Only the boots are new.

In my pockets I carry little: a baggie of vitamin C tablets; my driver's license for identification; a card with emergency contact information; a love note from Jihong ("This is me," it begins, "when you are out and about"); a photograph, given me by a friend for good luck, of a Native American mask he'd carved from wood. On a cord around my neck, two amulets from other friends, along with my wedding ring. These lie over my heart.

Over his long underwear (a Christmas present from Phoebe, so she could be close to him every day on the streets) James wears wool pants, thin turquoise trousers, turtleneck, wool army sweater, hooded sweatshirt, and hooded coat, beige with furry brown lining, a style from the seventies. Old boots, two pair of socks. Hat and mittens. His pockets hold a toothbrush, emergency information, ID and vitamin C. Around his neck, two amulets from friends and a ring identical to one Phoebe wears. Over his shoulder, a medium blue duffel that contains, along with an extra pair of gloves and socks, the supplies he'll need for pinhole photography: flat black spray paint, electrical tape, masking tape, 5"x7" photo papers, lightproof film-changing bag, black storage bags for exposures, and a pocket tool kit, about the size of a credit card. This tool kit, a gift from his father, James prizes mainly for its

6

two-inch knife and three-inch rule, which he'll use to build cameras.

The temperature is in the low thirties. Snow begins to fall, light flakes like so much ash, drifting, never reaching the ground.

Within a half hour we both start to chill as sweat saturates the clothing next to our skin. I scrounge in a trash bin for a large plastic bag, peel off some outer layers of clothes and stuff them in, then search the ground for a stout stick. As a child I listened, spellbound, to my grandparents telling stories about depression-era hobos. Now, bag propped over my shoulder on the stick, I'm the spittin' image of one.

A couple of miles east along the busy commercial strip of Route 161, then we turn south along High Street, the yellow brick road that leads directly into the heart of the city. We've entered Worthington, an affluent historic suburb with a colonial New England feel. Its brick sidewalks are clean and even, its houses distinguished, its grounds carefully landscaped. We pass through the village green on the main square. City workers are trimming tender young trees with long-handled pruning shears. James and I identify with the trees.

teeth

A sign outside a dentist's office reminds me that I need to acquire a toothbrush and paste. No time like the present. Leaving James on the sidewalk, I go inside the building, heart pounding. I don't know what it is to be a beggar. I've never been someone to readily ask for help. Now I'm offended by my pride.

I remove my hat. The receptionist scowls. Clearly she'd rather not deal with me. Smiling, I request her kind assistance. The scowl deepens. "I'll have to check," she says, face turning red, and abruptly leaves her desk. Muffled voices confer behind a door.

I smile, no longer caring what happens. It's been enough, just to try.

Waiting for me outside, James has ventured around back of the dentist's office, where he finds several dumpsters. Trash receptacles like these will be our cupboards and closets for the next one-and-a-half months. Neither of us is a stranger to scavenging for hidden treasures at flea markets and thrift stores. But out here we'll be rummaging in trash, and by necessity. For food, especially. As soon as this morning's pancakes have worn off, we'll be scrounging for discarded leftovers. Expired goods. Spoilage. Anything for a meal.

Curiosity lifts the lid on the underside of a dentist's world: empty supply boxes, used rubber gloves, crinkled plastic wrappers and warning labels, wadded tissues. James's first taste of dumpster diving is about as appealing as getting his teeth cleaned.

Back inside, the receptionist finally returns. Somehow now she's smiling.

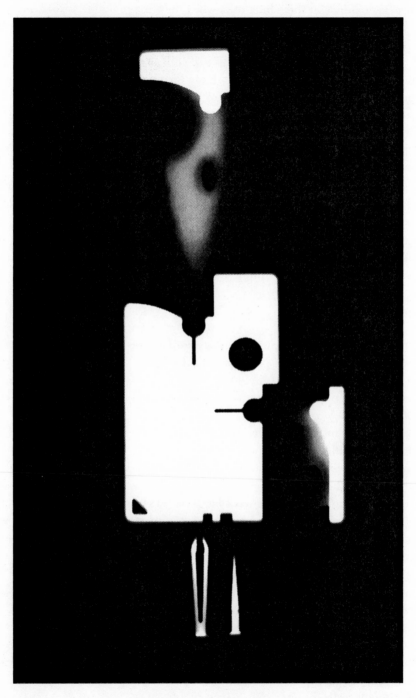

James's tool kit, in pieces

Beaming, almost. She hands me a brand-new Oral-B toothbrush and two thin sample packets of Crest, then wishes me well. Rejoining James outside, I wonder at the change in her.

On the sidewalk, a half-eaten Granny Smith apple. James and I each relish a bite before we toss away the core.

sesame street

Cookie Monster, wedged in a chainlink fence. Strange place for a toy; far from Sesame Street.

A row of dumpsters is barely visible behind a pharmacy across High. They're a hundred yards out of our way, but on a hunch we cross the street to check them out.

At first glance the largest bin, though full, seems empty to our needs. Then I burrow down. "Cookies!" James exclaims, at the sight of the plastic package, still half full. Beneath it, twenty more packages, still sealed in their wrappers, twenty-four chocolate-chip cookies in each. Laughing, James and I dance an awkward jig in our heavy boots, shouting, "We have food!"

While munching down, we stuff all the packages into a large trashbag. James heaves the load over his shoulder, and we're off. From here on, we mark our trail down High Street with cookies, dropping packages at bus stops, on benches, on tenement steps. The giving is energizing.

"'C' is for cookie," sang Cookie Monster, "That's good enough for me!"

diamonds

Around noontime, we take a break at Whetstone Park, just behind a neighborhood branch of the Columbus Metropolitan Library. With Worthington, the Graceland Mall area and residential Beechwold behind us, we've entered popular Clintonville, with its Roaring Twenties housing. Not far ahead lies the Ohio State campus scene. Then there'll be a stretch of tumbledown rowhouses, storefronts and abandoned buildings, then the artsy Short North, and finally, downtown.

I collapse, backs of my legs burning, on a bench beside a baseball diamond. Field one, out of four.

Chawing on cookies, James gravitates toward home plate. Then, suddenly, he takes off running the bases. With the recent light snow and cold rain, the base path is muck. Rounding first, his left foot slip-slides under his right—he catches himself, barely, from a full-body sprawl. Then, as I cheer him on, he kicks up mud on a full-tilt slog to second base, third, and, at last, home again. *"Safe!"* our best umpire voices yell.

phyllis cole-dai and james murray

eyebrows

We meditate in the library's garden, desolate in winter. Seated on a bench, cold settling into our bones, we shiver but aren't in a hurry. It's essential, in these moments, to remember why we're on the streets: to be as present as possible to our surroundings and everybody we meet; to be present without judgment, without pity. Silently, I renew these intentions. Then, focusing on my breath, I gradually let go of thought—my questions, my worries, my plans, my fears—till at last there's only the breath, moving in, moving out. In, out. In. Out.

This is life. So simple. Just this.

After a while I feel more rested, and strangely fortified, too, as though by a company of unseen helpers, wise ones who know what it means to live with a heart as open as a clear blue sky, as passionate as the summer sun, as patient as rain on rock. *How I want to live that way.* A Zen saying burrows into my quiet, becomes a prayer: "May I walk hand in hand with you, ancestors, the hair of my eyebrows entangled with yours."

The empty garden is full.

born-agains

Mid-afternoon, maybe four miles from downtown, we get our first hazy view of the city skyline. We think of having to nest somewhere tonight amidst steel and concrete. Emotions surge. We crawl forward.

Soiled royal-blue pants hang over the rim of a trash can—34" long, James's size, with permanent creases. Just in the last mile or so, James wondered aloud whether he might need a fourth layer for his legs after the sun goes down; the temperature is already dropping. Gratefully now he stuffs the pants into his duffel, just as we're approached by a middle-aged anglo walking a dog.

The man introduces himself as Pete, a born-again. "D'ya need any food?" he asks.

"Yeah," we say, famished.

He leads us to a storefront mission a block away, unlocks the door. A Better Way, the place is called. He directs us to sit down on folding chairs, then disappears into the back. When he returns, he's carrying a grocery bag. Canned goods bulge against white plastic.

"How long ya been out?" he asks. "Not long, I guess." He looks pointedly at me, says, "Are you born again?"

"Yeah," I say, meaning something quite different from what he does. His concern for my soul is touching, but I'm not interested in debating religion.

I'm interested in the contents of that grocery bag.

"How 'bout you?" Pete says to James. "You born again?"

"I'm a spiritual person," James says.

"In other words," Pete says, "you're *not.*" He looks both of us up and down. Finally he announces that he suspects James is on the lam, and I'm a person in deep pain, needing to be healed. Jesus is the answer. It's not too late. A Better Way has the power to help us change, if we'll only come back for Bible study and worship. They'll even feed us dinner, Pete says.

James and I stand up to go. Pete hugs us, sniffing James, presumably for liquor, then hands me the grocery bag. We thank him, sincerely, and hurry out the door.

Sidewalk inventory: one can government-issued peanut butter, one can boiled potatoes, two cans tuna, one can chicken and noodle soup, two cans pork and beans. We're rich—and very lucky that James has a tiny can opener in his tool kit.

nesting

4:00 p.m., downtown. On a bench outside the huge Nationwide Insurance building, worldwide headquarters, we celebrate our arrival in center city with a feast of cold beans and dumpster cookies dipped in government peanut butter. Businesspeople walk briskly past, paying us no mind. We remove our boots and prop up our sore stockinged feet, trying not to think about the blisters.

Rest is short, though. We need to find a place to spend the night, homeless shelters being a last resort. Instinct soon draws us west, toward the Scioto River, where we scout possible sleeping sites.

Low spreading evergreen bushes surround a large office building between Front Street and Civic Center Drive. Exploring the bushes we spot a number of human nests, some abandoned, others seemingly still occupied, given the backpacks and other possessions lying around. This area feels right. We choose a deserted nest, then begin to scavenge the nearby streets for plastic, cardboard, foam, anything we can put between the cold, hard ground and our hope for sleep.

Once our beds are ready, we have leisure time. To get warm we hike over to Main Library, where in the past I've sometimes noticed (apparently) homeless people reading newspapers, browsing the stacks, using the computers. James drowses at a table. Across from him I write on the back of a poster-size print pulled from a dumpster earlier in the day: "Signing of the Treaty of Greene Ville, August 3, 1795." A famous painting, by Howard Chandler Christy. Chief Little Turtle is surrendering to General Mad Anthony Wayne,

11

concluding another war conducted by the U.S. government against the native inhabitants of this territory. White pioneers had been hungry to settle the land, so the government drew a map, charted a line, and forced the Miami, Chippewa and Potawatomi, among others, to move to the other side.

Today, in Columbus, it's not farmland our leaders are after. It's a brand-new professional hockey arena, a relocated Center of Science and Industry, an expanded Veterans Memorial hall, revitalized business in the old Franklinton neighborhood—on it goes. All this development is taking place just across the river from downtown, in an area where several homeless shelters are situated. The shelters may be closed down or re-established elsewhere in the city: the picture's not yet clear. Lines are still being drawn. Homeless people, whom one civic leader has called "bums, winos and druggies," don't fit into the developers' plans.

quarters

Leaving the library, we stop by Grant Hospital to see if it hosts any Twelve-Step meetings. James, who is in recovery, would like to find one soon. He assures me that he isn't afraid for his sobriety; he just wants to be with people who won't stare at him and judge. "Besides," he grins, "there'll prob'ly be donuts and coffee."

The woman behind the reception desk is aloof. "No meetings here," she says, when James asks.

"D'ya maybe have a phone book so I could look up the number for Central Office? Maybe they could tell me where to go."

In a huff the woman pulls out the White Pages. James quickly looks up the number, scribbles it down on a slip of paper. "Could I please use your phone?"

"There's payphones over there," she frowns, gesturing over her shoulder.

James stares at me helplessly; neither of us has change for a phone call. "Thanks anyway for your help," he tells the woman. We turn to go. "Wait—" she says suddenly, then reaches down for her purse, retrieves two quarters. Somehow she's smiling, now.

picnic

James and I lounge atop a hot-air vent behind a warehouse, eating a dinner of cold canned tuna and soup, with more cookies and peanut butter for dessert. Closing his eyes, James says playfully that he almost feels like he's at the beach. Tropical. But instead of salt air, the faint smell of laundry exhaust.

12

intoxication

Our little nest in the bushes, we notice now, is on the grounds of the Ohio Departments Building (ODB), one of many state government buildings in the downtown. We lean against its gray western wall as the sun sets over the Scioto. Engraved on the frieze high above us:

THEIR SACRIFICE GUARANTEE OF POSTERITY

FREEDOM   OPPORTUNITY

The calm is intoxicating. We almost forget our weary bodies.

We jot notes. We speak of high things: how we might get to know the street people living among the bushes, and share with them our little store of food, and all of us watch out for one another. Streetlights shimmer gold on the river.

We bed down in the bushes around 9:00 p.m., as best we can tell, wearing no watches. "Whaddya wanna do in the morning?" James asks, as we're settling in under low, prickly branches.

"Morning seems so far away. Let's wait and see. Yashir koach, Irishman."

"Yashir koach."[9]

the state

No sleep for me. I feel trapped. Under the low evergreens there's hardly room to move, even to lift my head. I bear it as long as I can, then instinct takes over. My body erupts into frantic struggle, and I blunder up and out of the bushes, escape into air, stand panting under an indifferent moon.

I bed down again some thirty feet away from James, in a gap between the bushes and a wall of the ODB. Here I'm more comfortable, able to move freely, but since I'm more exposed, I'm also much colder, even wearing my many layers of clothes. Drawing my legs up to my chest, I tuck in my head and exhale long and hard into my coat, time and again, as if blowing up a balloon. It's no use. There's no getting warm.

Hours go by. I toss and turn in shivering exhaustion.

Suddenly I hear footsteps—

Quiet—quiet—

More steps on the pavement—coming my way—

Don't make a sound—
A mag light shines down, blinding me. I shield my eyes.

"Come outa there, now!" A male voice.

Slowly my eyes adjust. The voice belongs to a state trooper, middle-aged, black. He demands a form of identification, then radios a dispatcher, checking for outstanding warrants. As we await the report, I ask the trooper for the time.

"Around midnight," he says, kindly enough. "Why aren'tcha in a shelter?"

"I prefer not to be, thanks."

"If you hadna been rustlin' around, I wouldna known you was here."

By now, James has wakened to shivers and voices. He listens closely as the trooper questions me. Occasionally the beam of the trooper's mag light falls on the bushes where he lies, motionless. He wonders if he's been spotted; if he should just crawl out, give himself up.

He decides to wait.

My warrant check is clear. I feel a strange relief, as if it could have been otherwise.

"This property belongs to the state," the trooper says, crisply now. "You gotta move on. If you stick around, I'll have to arrest you for loitering."

Who's the state if not the people? But let it go. The man's just doing his job. Move now, and quick, or James'll get rousted, too.

The streets of downtown are empty, and dimly yellow. Completely spent, very much alone, I'm filled with foreboding. *Don't go where there isn't light.*

James is still hidden in the evergreens, hoping he won't be made. But once I've left the premises, the trooper's mag light sweeps directly to his face.

"Come outa there," the trooper says. "Lemme see your hands. Do ya have any weapons?"

"No, sir."

"Base," he radios, "I have a male caucasian, approximately 6'2", under some bushes, close by the woman. . . . Do you have any identification?"

James scrounges for his driver's license.

"If you don't have any outstandin' warrants," says the trooper, "I'll letcha go with a warning. This is state property. You can't sleep here."

"Yes, sir."

"Why aren'tcha in a shelter?"

James shrugs.

"Yeah, that's pretty much the same answer *she* gave," he says, pointing in the direction I'd gone.

"Couldya please tell me what time it is?" James asks, gathering his duffel and the food bag.

14

"Almost 12:30," the trooper says.

James moves out, shivering and in a daze.

I'm nowhere to be seen.

parking

On the very top level of the Riffe Center parking garage, hidden between stacks of construction materials, I try for sleep. It doesn't come. I'm just too cold; starting to shake uncontrollably.

My body needs warmth, my body needs rest—the part of me that is flesh and blood realizes this, and begins to feel an urgency, even desperation. Yet the part of me that is mind is strangely detached from what's happening, as if convinced this is just an episode in a bad dream, and soon there will be a waking up.

Meanwhile, James trudges the streets of downtown. He's new to the city. What a way, what a time, to orient himself. He crosses through a major intersection at the slowest pace he's ever walked. No traffic. No pedestrians, but for him. Unsettling.

His eyes search constantly for any sign of me. Misery, wishing for company.

A ramp to a parking garage looks inviting. James takes a couple of steps up the incline before two security guards turn the corner and wag their heads.

man of god

I decide to risk sneaking from the parking garage into the Riffe Center. Once inside, I might be able to catch some sleep in a janitor's closet or backstage in one of the theaters. I shuffle toward the door. *Anyplace warm. Anyplace out of the way—*

"Stop right where you are!"

A uniformed guard, out of nowhere. Another black man; in his twenties, maybe. He radios in to the security detail, reporting my trespass, then says with seeming reluctance that he'll have to escort me down to street level.

On our way down the man tells me his name is David. He draws out his wallet. "This is all I got," he says, handing me three dollar bills. "If I had more, I'd give it to ya."

"I don't need money," I tell him, trying not to sound ungrateful. "I just needa place to sleep."

"When a man of God tries to give ya somethin'," David declares, "ya *don't* say *no.*"

sanctuary

Where to go now?
Mind is numb. Legs are lead.
Where to go—
A church. All I can think of. The closest one I remember is on Capitol Square, due east of the Ohio Statehouse, right in the heart of downtown.

Trinity Episcopal, the sign reads; corner of Broad and Third. I circle the building, trying the doors. Every one is locked. I circle again, this time inspecting the building for a bit of shelter. Finally, on its south side: a nook between two jutting walls, just wide enough, with my knees slightly bent, to sit in sideways. The stone church is cold against my back, the ground frozen beneath me, but I feel relatively safe. It's refuge enough.

I draw my line. If somebody tries to roust me from this spot, I'll refuse to go. "This is a sanctuary of God," I'll tell them, "and I will not be moved."

Meanwhile, unknown to me, James has arrived on the grounds of the Ohio Statehouse, just across the street from the church. A pine tree on the east side of the capitol offers him the promise of shelter, but he hesitates. At least one state trooper is probably patrolling the square. If James is caught again on state property, he's off to jail. Two strikes, you're out.

His eyes take in a scrolling bank sign: *1:23 am. . . .24°. . . .*

The tree tempts. Thick cover, its lowest branches drooping, skirting the ground like a full gown.

He crawls under.

The thick, dead grass around the tree trunk is matted down; obviously he won't be the first person to have lain here. Fatigue covers him like a blanket. Pillowing his head on pine needles, he fades off.

teasers

Mustn't sleep. Battling hypothermia. Every few minutes I stand up, stamp my feet like a child, run in place, do squats, jumping jacks, fire-breathe from my belly, begin to feel warmer. Sit down again and try to meditate. Sing in whispers. Talk to Jihong. Watch for change in the eastern sky, any hint it's lightening. Cloud cover reflects city lights, paints the sky a pale orange-rose, like dawn. Cruel tease. *Mustn't sleep.*

Under his tree at the Statehouse, James shivers awake, needing to relieve himself. No time for modesty, no thought for propriety. He does his business between the tree and a concrete wall, then hurries down the hill to the sidewalk. "Gotta move," he says to his sore, tired body. "Gotta get warm."

2:47 am, according to the bank. He doesn't wait for the temperature to

16

scroll by. He knows it's dropped. He doesn't want to know how much.

Eventually he returns to the hot-air vent where he and I ate dinner. Small comfort, now. The blasts of heat make the night around him feel even colder.

ice

French bakery next door to the church—called Au Bon Pain—means "good bread," probably, but looks like "good pain"—

Nonstop shivers—ribs ache like I've cried for days—

Blow into gloves—no fast way through the night—each minute ice—*just endure—no way around but through—*

James—still asleep in our nest? Other people in the bushes—rousted?

santa maria

James walks aimlessly. In his exhaustion, not afraid anymore. Numb. His legs, his joints are wood, don't want to move; marionette limbs without a puppeteer.

Lights ripple on the Scioto River. Beneath a bridge, a homeless person lies wrapped in blankets, suitcase wired to one leg. Not far away, a replica of the Santa Maria, flagship of Christopher Columbus, half frozen in ice at its mooring. The original never made it home.

bread

I stand outside the night-forsaken bakery—exhaust vent above me—lukewarm air swirls down—smells yeasty sweet—I salivate—

James, wandering through a grid of alleys behind the State Supreme Court, discovers some bread in a dumpster, whole wheat and white. The wheat's soggy, so he tosses it back. He stares hungrily at the white in his gloved hand, but finally he throws that back, too, doesn't know why.

A wider alley, now. Halfway down, a stray cat lunges. James jumps back, terrified, suddenly aware. This is no place to sleepwalk. He heads back to his tree.

sympathies

Bakery light switches on—

Maybe get inside now—use bathroom—beg hot water—nap—please—just till they open—

In kitchen, man in white—back turned—fussing with oven—clock—red digits—*5:25 maybe—can't see—*

Rap on window—man glances around—shuffles over—peers through windowpane—

Raise arms at sides—open wide—*harmless—*

Gesture for drink—*please—*

Man's face fills with disgust—arms wag hard away—he turns on heel—back to kitchen—

Pace by window—fifteen minutes—half hour—back and forth—*ignore me again—decide—not to help—again—*

no sympathy—for you—

somewhere else

James huddles against his tree trunk—the sky, dull orange between sagging branches—almost dawn, he's hoping, but no, the bank clock says *no, hours to go*—no way to speed the night—

He stands up—shakes legs, rolls head, swings arms—Where's Phyl, he wonders—

Morning—coming—

Oh, he thinks—to wake up—somewhere else—

glory

no more—too cold—

Bank across alley from bakery—no guard at lobby desk—*maybe—please—*

Fast—through revolving door—wall of heat—head swims—knees buckle—hands reach out—*steady*—sink to marble floor—

Across the lobby, a plate glass wall—*glory*—McDonald's across Broad Street, its lights on—*open!*—six o'clock, must be—*night—finally—over—*

day 2: thursday, february 18

survivors

(**mcdonald's on broad street, early morning.**) I beg a cup of hot water at the counter, then collapse at a corner table in the back of the restaurant, head in hands. All around me, voices—loud, husky, hoarse, yawning, nervous; at

18

first, to my dull senses, they're no more than ghosts of sound, but finally I'm warm enough to hear, and I gather myself enough to look up, amazed that I'm not alone. Maybe a dozen people, men mostly, all apparently homeless. Teenage to elderly; anglo, black, latino; some scruffy like me, others neatly groomed or in the process of cleaning up, slipping in and out of the restrooms to wash, shave, comb their hair.

A white guy asks me for 25¢. I slip him one of David's dollar bills, money from the man of God. The rest I'll save for James. I don't know what shape he'll be in when I find him. Whenever I find him.

Another anglo, fifty-ish, immaculately dressed, with his belongings piled on the seat beside him, tosses me a copy of yesterday's Ohio State Lantern.

A young latino asks if he might join me. Over his coffee cup he tells me his problems, trying to reassure himself that he can make it. "The sun's comin' up," I tell him. "Try to take one day at a time." Out here, no cliché.

"That's exactly the attitude, miss," says a graybeard across the aisle.

"We gotta have faith," agrees the latino. "I'm innocent, you're innocent, and a loving God wouldn't *do* this to us. When we're the most cold and tired, God's right here with us. That's what I believe."

He tells me how difficult it is to have patience, to hang in day after day after day, when you don't get enough sleep. "Some nights," the man sighs, "it's just too *cold* to sleep." Sometimes, when he's desperate for a little rest, he's tempted to make up a crisis in order to get admitted to a mental hospital. "But then," he says, "they might decide I'm nuts and keep me."

angel

Once the sun's up, I leave McDonald's to search for James, hoping against the odds that he'll still be where we camped, outside the ODB. Stepping into a stream of work-bound pedestrians, I'm swept down the sidewalk along Broad, across High, and past the Riffe Center, where I'm startled to pass by David the security guard—so near I might have touched him, and then gone, carried away in the opposite direction. His face, still so kind—no, I didn't dream him. *Angel.* I float.

arms

(mid-morning.) Two hours later, I'm limping up State Street toward Main Library. James wasn't at the ODB. He wasn't at the hot air vent. He wasn't anywhere along Front Street. He wasn't anywhere. The library, about to open, is my last hope, for now. I don't have it in me to walk much more, the street keeps sliding sideways—

But, oh, there he *is*—those two long arms, those two long and skinny arms, waving wearily outside the front entrance—

Even from two blocks away, I can see that he's grinning. I thrust my arms into the air, triumphantly pumping my fists. Irishman made it through the night.

wichita

(**main library, mid-morning.**) Periodicals section, third floor. I'm not writing because I want to. I need to sleep—Godknows—but for some reason I can't. James, seated across from me, has his head down on the table like a schoolboy; said he might have slept a total of four hours last night. I envy him that. I envy him, sleeping now.

Just behind me, a homeless man is slumped over in his chair, snoring into a magazine.

When James and I compared nights, we realized that we'd been separated by less than a hundred yards, pine tree to church. Tonight, having learned our lesson the hard way, we'll stay in city shelters. Before we try again to sleep on the streets, we'll have to find some blankets and a more tolerable place to bed down.

My eyes skim a rack of newspapers, catch the lead headline from Wichita, Kansas: "How Secure Will You Be?"

blankets

Around 10:30 a.m. James and I part ways to track down some blankets, or beg money with which to buy them. At a men's shelter James offers to buy one for $2, the remaining money from my man of God. The staffer sees COLD stamped on James's forehead and says, with a touch of regret, "Sorry, our blankets aren't for sale."

Meanwhile, mid-morning business is slow at The Place to Be, a café housed in the basement of Trinity Episcopal Church, only steps from where I'd drawn my line in the night hours. I ask several employees behind the counter for money, assuring them I'll spend it on blankets. "Sorry," they say, "we can't help ya, but shouldncha be stayin' in a shelter? It's too *cold* to be sleepin' out there."

Wearily I drag myself back up the steps to street level. Icy snow is falling, now. A bank clock reminds me that it's nearly time to meditate at the Statue of Peace, on the Broad Street side of the Statehouse. Before leaving home, James and I had decided to meditate there for a half hour each day at noon, with friends and relatives welcome to join us at a distance.

Slow as pain I start shuffling toward the capitol grounds, only to be

20

Main Library, front view

stopped by shouts. One of the café employees, a young anglo sporting a baseball cap and full white apron, trots up behind me, thumbing through his wallet. "Here"—breathless, he hands me a $10 bill—"maybe you can getta blanket at a thrift store. Maybe get yourself somethin' to eat, too."

Tears.[10]

initiation

(ohio statehouse, noon.) Wings outstretched, cape billowing, gown flowing long, the angel is in mid-stride, her face determined and strong. Her right hand, raised triumphantly overhead, holds a leafy olive branch; her left hand steadies a shield, tip resting on the ground. At least twelve feet tall, cast in bronze and installed on a granite base, she was unveiled on June 26, 1923, a tribute to the Ohio men, Grand Army of the Republic, who had fought in the Civil War, as well as the women who had labored in support of them. The inscription: "Let Us Have Peace."

In the shadow of the angel, a number of our friends. In their presence James and I break down, weep, cling. This close mingling might attract attention (Statehouse visitors and street people don't often hug), but we don't care. Today, at least, we need the comfort of touch. There's no meditation; only the tears, and the effort to speak, to somehow assign words to a night unlike any we've ever experienced. Initiation, we begin to call it.

I ache for Jihong, but he's teaching his chemistry class at Ohio State. Maybe it's best that he's not here to witness what's already become of me.

budget

Our exhaustion plain, our friend Gwyn urges us to go to the Agora and try to get some sleep. Located across the Scioto River, a fifteen or twenty-minute hike west of the Statehouse, the Agora houses not only a socially concerned Mennonite congregation but also a day-center for homeless families operated by the Interfaith Hospitality Network, which Gwyn directs. Homeless families can stay all day at the center, receiving assistance from social workers; then, in late afternoon, they're bussed for the night to makeshift living quarters in synagogues and churches around the city.

On our way to the Agora, James and I stop at a Volunteers of America thrift shop. Earlier James had scouted the blankets, afghans and comforters hanging on its racks. Now he points out a wool blanket. Heavy. Full-sized. $2.99. This morning, it was beyond our budget.

That was then. This is now.

I lay the $10 bill on the counter.

looking up at the Statue of Peace

agora

(**the agora, early afternoon.**) We arrive footsore and ready to drop. Two staffers, whom Gwyn has apparently told about us, hurry to set up cots in a small meeting room. "Thank you, thank you, thank you." James falls headlong onto the nearer cot, not caring at all that his big feet hang well off the end. Two deep exhalations, and he's out cold.

The staffers cover us both with blankets, pull the blinds, turn off the lights, and close the door against the crying of babies, ringing phones, the shrieks and laughter of children, adult voices in the hallway, the click and clatter of a typewriter, a tv's drone. . . .

the bottoms

In thirty hours I haven't slept more than one, but I can't relax. Maybe I'm high on adrenaline, maybe on the sugar from all the cookies I've devoured. A vegetarian at home, I usually don't eat many sweets. Now my body feels toxic.

After much fitful, frustrated tossing, I finally give up on sleep. Leaving my cot, I wander out front to Five Loaves, the Agora's café. Its profits support the church's many socially concerned ministries.

Rebecca, a youth minister, is behind the counter, taking her turn serving pastries and sandwiches. During a lull in business, she tells me that she feels called by God to work with the teenagers in this neighborhood. "The Bottoms, that's what they call it," she says. "Thirteenth-poorest white ghetto in the country. Mosta the kids here don't know it's a good thing to eat three meals a day, or get lotsa sleep, or wear clean clothes, or go to school, or even have parents who love 'em. They've never had it, never seen it, never been taught, so how would they know?" Rebecca shakes her head. "The kids don't have any dreams," she says. "They think it'd be a great life, growin' up to work at McDonald's."

A customer appears at the register. I retire to a small table to write. Yesterday afternoon, in Main Library, drafting on the back of the Treaty of Greene Ville, I composed. Ink flowed. Themes were sustained, sentence structure was varied, word choices were deliberate. My handwriting, while never elegant, was quick, slashing, confident; here and there, a flourish.

Today, though, I scribble. Like a young child I grip my pencil, found yesterday at the baseball field, too tightly. I bear down so hard *(was that only yesterday?)* that my fist smears lead. My marks on the paper are crude. My thoughts clot in simple sentences, abrupt phrases, single words. I struggle to spell ("*It doesn't* look *right*—"). I abandon punctuation. *Just get it down.*

Style belongs to somebody else. *Whatever will help you remember.* Concern for diction, obsolete. *Or forget.* The page glares white. *Don't tell me to stay between the lines.*

Sitting at the next table is Peggy, a social worker on coffee break. Over the distance between us she tells me the story of Isaac, a homeless child, five years old. Last summer she was trying to arrange permanent housing for his family and employment for his parents. Then, in September, Isaac was struck and killed by a car near the Methodist church where his family was being sheltered for the night. Soon after, his family disappeared, hasn't been heard from since. She still grieves.

Before she returns to work, Peggy kindly buys me a huge deli sandwich, a bowl of vegetable soup, and a bag of potato chips. I'm hungry as a dog, but the feast will have to wait till James wakes up.

numbers

3:00 p.m., standing at an Agora payphone. In my hand are the phone numbers of two homeless shelters, one for men, one for women. Before James and I hit the streets, a contact on the staff of a city shelter had recommended we call these numbers if we ever needed a place to spend the night. We'd be taken care of, few questions asked.

James and I had hoped never to use these numbers, not wanting to take up the beds. Still, our contact had told us not to worry, there would always be enough space for those in need; that no matter how crowded the city shelters, nobody would be turned away, especially in inclement weather.

I drop my quarter and dial. On the fourth ring, somebody at the women's shelter picks up. "Call back around six," a husky female voice tells me. "We'll know then if we have room for ya."

If we have room.

James calls the men's shelter when he wakes up, around 4:30. The guy on the phone tells him that if he wants a bed for the night, he'd better come right away.

Right away. If he wants a bed.

The men's shelter is located way back across the river, but James can walk the distance. I, on the other hand, will have to catch a bus to the women's shelter—*if* they tell me I can come. Should they turn me away, my options will be severely limited. To my knowledge, most city shelters serve either single men, families, or individuals battling addiction. Where to go if you're female, childless and sober?

I accompany James as far as High Street. There, as we say goodbye, I smile a little, force myself to sound optimistic. "My bus fare out to the shelter will be $1.10," I tell him. "You're gettin' off cheap."

"I don't like leavin' without knowin' for sure you're in."

"I know."

He waits for words. Finally he says, "My instincts tell me you'll be okay."

"We'll both be okay."

"Why don't we meet at McDonald's on Broad," he suggests, "first thing in the morning?"

"I'll be there," I say, giving him a tight hug. "Yashir koach, Irishman."

shelter

(men's shelter in the downtown, late afternoon.) Outside the shelter, guys loiter, smoke and shoot the bull, a loose crowd of cliques and loners. James sidles through them, then walks past the security guard stationed at the front door and gets in line at the reception desk. Straight ahead, a room painted baby blue, a passage of scripture barely legible on the wall; rows of hardwood pews face a battered podium and a big-screen tv. Some men are watching a third-rate movie. Others are milling about, restless.

Instantly James is nervous.

A new guy, he's told to register. He fills out an information form and signs a contract, agreeing among other things not to have alcohol, drugs or weapons on the premises. To complete the paperwork, the intake staffer asks him basic questions, all of which he answers vaguely.

"Why ya here?" the staffer wants to know.

"Separated from my girlfriend," James tells him, as true an answer as he can think of, and the staffer marks the Relationship Problems box under Cause.

After the interview James is searched by a security guard. When asked to surrender any weapons or sharp objects on his person, he takes out his tool kit and hands over its miniature can opener. Somehow he never thinks to mention its two-inch knife.

He won't be told where he's to sleep till 9:00 p.m. Hours to go.

In the blue room he claims a spot in the very back pew, chucking his duffel underneath. Now, from all around him, time presses in, turning thick, quicksand pulling him down. Whenever he makes eye contact with somebody, he nods a "Whassup," trying to appear more relaxed than he feels. Some men creep around the room as if in pain. Others dart like water bugs. Many are just lounging in the pews, like James, each keeping close watch on his own suitcase, satchel, backpack, pile of plastic bags.

Meanwhile, I'm still on High Street. I drop another quarter on the women's shelter, calling an hour earlier than I'm supposed to, unable any longer to endure the wait. I hold my breath as the phone rings. Finally, an answer; the same voice. "We've got room," the woman says. "C'mon over." She tells me which bus to take, which stop to get off. "The location of this shelter is confidential," she says; a protective measure, since many of the residents have been battered by husbands and boyfriends. "Don't tell anybody—*anybody*—exactly where you're goin'."

During the half-hour bus ride I meet Sweetness, a smiling, middle-aged black woman who's been staying at the shelter. She's tremendously excited, having just made arrangements to rent an apartment. "Soon I'll be in my own place. Girl, I can't wait!"

"How's it been," I ask her, "livin' at the shelter?"

"You'll wanna watch your *p*s and *q*s, girl," she warns. "Somma them women's tough customers. Had to be, to survive."

ad-libbing

(**women's shelter, early evening.**) Name, most recent address, age, social security number, marital status—so many questions. . . . After two strenuous days without sleep, I can scarcely digest the intake staffer's words. Now and then her voice is drowned out by bantering and laughter, weeping, petty accusations and arguments, a tv turned up loud. Some women keep to themselves. Others crowd the cluttered desk where we're seated with complaints, requests, demands.

The staffer studies my driver's license. "Why aren'tcha livin' anymore at this address?" she asks, almost shouting now to be heard, and I don't know what to say. "So sorry," I murmur. "So tired. Can't think." She tries to help me by reading down a standard list of reasons women become homeless: financial problems, eviction, unemployment, domestic violence, divorce, separation—

"*That's* it," I say, inwardly cringing at the doublespeak, but at least it isn't an outright lie. "My husband and I are separated."

"Why's that?"

"It's sorta hard to talk about."

She doesn't press.

The staffer escorts me up a flight of wooden steps. Unlocking a door, she leads me into a suite of three rooms and a bathroom. Situated in one corner of the main room is somebody's ad-libbed home: a set of bunk beds, cracked wall mirror, busy dresser, and shabby chair tossed with clothes. The rest of the room is empty except for a small sofa, well past its prime, and a few twin-sized mattresses scattered on the floor for temporary "overflow girls" like me. The two far rooms, quite cramped, are for longer-term residents who are making a gradual transition to more permanent housing. Apparently the shelter is a hive of suites like this one.

The shower, I learn, is for resident use only. What I wouldn't give to laze under the showerhead, water steaming hot, but as an "o-girl," I'm obviously at the bottom of the pecking order and can't risk breaking the rules. Not on my first night, anyway. Grateful for a bit of soap lying on the sink, I take a spitbath and wash my hair, toweling off with my sweaty long johns. Then I scrub out my underwear and socks, lay them out to dry.

Spreading the rest of my clothes over one of the mattresses on the floor, I lie down on top ("the best way to keep somebody from stealin' `em," Sweetness had advised) and cover myself with the wool blanket from Volunteers of America. At last, for the first time in days, I drift toward sleep.

Then, chaos—

Angry shouts—feet running up and down the stairs—women in and out, in and out the door—a rowdy fight downstairs—glass breaking—

I yank the blanket over my head.

el diablo

(men's shelter in the downtown.) A dirty, potbellied latino, barely five feet tall, lightly touches James's shoulder, as if they're old friends, and through a heavy accent invites him outside for a cigarette. James doesn't smoke but somehow can't say so. He rises to follow. The latino points to James's duffel, indicating he should bring it along.

The two are watched intently as they go, though the stares are furtive. Most of the men, James noticed earlier, won't acknowledge the latino's presence. The latino disapproves of them—his eyes tell it—and his disdain, if nothing else, seems to have made him an outsider. Now the men are probably wondering who James is, what his alliances are.

He steps from the shelter into night.

"Your first time here?" the latino says, and James nods, amazed it was so obvious. He reaches out his hand, introducing himself. The man returns a firm grip. "Manuel," he says, laying his free hand over his heart.

A wrinkled brow, a round unshaven face, lackluster eyes, Manuel has the look of somebody grown used to despair. Forcing a cigarette into James's hand, lighting it before his own, he begins to unburden himself. He complains in a mumble about the other men in the shelter, switching rapidly between English and Spanish. James struggles to understand, to respond. Their conversation deepens. Soon Manuel is confiding problems with his marriage, his finances; an entire life in turmoil. Finally James says, "Manuel, what keeps ya goin'? D'ya believe in God, or—?"

The man swells with emotion. "I believe in God," he replies, but—" a long pause— "El Diablo es El Diablo." The Devil is the Devil. This much, James understands.

Manuel draws on his cigarette, shakes his head, then looks up at James. Suddenly, his eyes fill with tears. "I can *cry!*" he exclaims. The tears spill over, slide all the way down to his jawbone before he wipes them away.

first-timing

James, having reclaimed his old spot in the back pew, asks guys sitting around him where to get food, where to do laundry. One-word replies mostly. A few pews up, a black man wearing a Kelly green cap and matching down jacket turns around and says, "This your first time here?" James nods. "Don't worry 'bout it," the man says, dismissively.

Manuel paces.

A blond anglo, built like an offensive lineman, plops down nearby. He appears to be around James's age—a rare thing; at twenty-three James may be the youngest man here. After some chit chat, the blond guy leans in, asks James if he has any weed. "Naw man," James says. "Wanna smoke some with me?" the fellow says. James shakes his head.

The guy says, "Ya gonna stay here?"

"Yeah, if they let me."

"Well, I'm just here to getta bus pass. Been livin' in the basement of a building out east—some guy lets people stay there. Ya leave there by bus first thing in the morning, and ya can go back there at night, if ya want."

James doesn't know what to make of this information. It sounds sketchy. Homeless people living in somebody's basement? After getting bus passes from a city shelter? It doesn't make much sense, but out here, James muses, nothing much does, so far.

overflow

(**men's shelter in the downtown, late evening.**) After four hours of waiting and a food-line meal, James is told the shelter is full. He and nine other men, including the offensive lineman, will be transported to an "overflow shelter" on the city's east side. Since no buses run to that part of town this late at night, a staffer orders two taxis.

At 10:30 p.m. the cabs drop the men at a rec hall in a city park. The entire building is dark except for the dim red light radiating from two EXIT signs. Once inside the doors, the men proceed down a flight of stairs, then through a steel door, and finally down three more steps into the basement. This, James figures, must be the place the big blond had been talking about.

After signing more papers in a small staff room, James pulls a flimsy collapsible cot from a depleted stack and paws through a pile of ratty blankets till he finds one his nose can tolerate. Then, on to the largest room in the basement—the sleeping room, which is wall-to-wall men, maybe seventy in all; little space left for latecomers. Three rows of cots, set side by side, run the entire length of the room, separated by narrow aisles. The men's cots are only inches apart.

"Whassup," James says to his neighbor, unfolding his cot in tight rank, stowing his boots and duffel underneath. The cot droops so low, the duffel bulges against its vinyl sheeting.

His neighbor, who introduces himself as Bob, seems in a daze. An ugly red gash extends from his hairline down the left side of his nose to his upper lip. "Car crash," he says, when James asks. "Been in a coma the last three days. Just came out of it today. I'm from outa town. Totaled my car. Nowhere else to go."

Bob sounds bewildered, almost like he'd rather be back in the coma than staying here. Looking at him, James wonders how many other men with physical ailments might be sleeping tonight in this shelter. Chances are, some of them have serious infectious diseases, like tuberculosis or hepatitis.

"This place is worse than the state pen," gripes the new guy settling in on James's right.

James digs down in his duffel, takes out a copy of The Big Book, borrowed for the night from the downtown shelter. "Whatcha got there?" Bob asks, his voice weak.

"I've hadda problem with alcohol," James explains. "This book's about recovery. It's helped me out alot." Bob nods, as if he can relate.

James flips to a page, tries to focus, the sour stench of blankets and bodies turning his stomach. He reads the same paragraph three times. Finally he sets his book aside and tries to relax, his body tense as a Wall Street nerve.

The lights go out.

life as

overflow

day 3: friday, february 19

wake-up calls

(men's overflow shelter, bexley.) "Five-thirty! You're outa here!" barks the staff. Fluorescent lights flicker on. The air fills with shouted commands, the grumblings of exhausted men. James lifts his head, eyes screwed in a squint, trying to get his bearings. One whiff reminds him not to inhale through his nose. He forces his body up, instructs it to dress, fold cot, toss blanket on the pile.

As a staffer distributes bus passes for their trip back into the downtown, the men are herded outside. Together they slouch toward the bus stop, some distance away. No loitering. The overflow shelter is located in Bexley, a wealthy suburb; the residents want all the homeless men transported from the rec center before sunrise. At least, that's the scuttlebutt. Last night, after the lights went out, one of the guys piped up, said, "Shit, since we're sleepin' in Bexley, maybe tomorrow we'll *all* get rich!" Everybody laughed, a little.

Waiting for the bus, men still half asleep lean down to the pavement, pick up old cigarette butts, relight them for a single drag. Morning extroverts curse the cold, shifting their weight from one foot to the other, trying to keep the blood flowing. Homeless calisthenics. James hunches his shoulders, stamps his feet, breathes clouds. Lights flicker on in nearby mansions. Crows caw. The sky begins to brighten.

(women's shelter.) "Gotta get up! It's six o'clock!"

I peer at a backlit figure in the doorway, say, "Yeah, okay, thanks," and roll over, covering my head with my blanket. "You gotta leave in *one hour*," warns the voice. "You and the resta the o-girls." The door bangs shut.

I stay on my mattress. Not much primping to do.

At 6:30 I'm rousted again, this time by a staffer who whispers my name and shakes my toes gently through the blanket. I feel like a child being wakened for school, early on a dark winter morning. "You're a mother," I murmur.

The staffer sighs, moves on.

morning commute

James isn't actually homeless, but from the disgusted looks he's getting as he moves up the aisle behind the other men, the people on this bus believe he is. He hurries to find a seat. No special section for our kind, he thinks to

33

himself; we're scattered all over the bus.

Up front a homeless man gives up his seat for an elderly woman. He stands, she smiles. James feels a little warmer.

The bus running the route near the women's shelter is early. My new friend Sweetness, walking with me and the other women on the snow-dusted sidewalk, sees it coming, grabs my arm, and together we run slipping and sliding for the stop. Once on board, I fumble for fare: another $1.10 into the downtown. The money in my pocket, courtesy of the café worker, is dwindling fast. I ask Sweetness how she manages the fare every day. Rather than answer me directly, she lets me know that one-day bus passes are available, for free, at a place called JOIN.

"Men," she complains, "*they* get bus passes at *their* shelters, no problem. Not us. They think long's we got cootchy coo, we can always get the money we need. That's what they think. `S not right."

Downtown, at the bustling intersection of Broad and High, Sweetness and I get off the bus, exchange quick goodbyes in the flurrying cold. "Just be positive, child," she says (when we first met I was "girl," but now I'm under her wing). She gives my arm a squeeze. "If ya *want* help, you'll *find* it. God bless."

staying

(**mcdonald's on broad street, early morning.**) James's appearance after his first night in the men's shelter is shocking: heavy dark circles under his eyes, face sallow and swollen from tiredness, head and shoulders sagging. Through exhausted tears he tells me the story of his stay. Then, at the end, a burst of hysterical laughter—

"What are we doin', Phyl? This is nuts."

"Do you wanna end it?"

He grows quiet. Shakes his head. Not a "no," exactly; bewilderment.

"I'm broken, Phyl."

"I know." *How to tell him you're sorry, you never expected, never wanted, the streets to hurt him like this?*

His hands gesture helplessly. "I feel like I've lost big pieces of me, and it hurts like hell."

"Whaddya feel like you've lost?"

"I don't know. . . . Trust, maybe. Trust that I'll survive. Trust that I won't lose my mind. . . . I don't know. Maybe I just wanna believe that my life matters more than it seems to, out here."

For a while we don't speak. Can't speak. Then James wipes the tears from his eyes. "What about you? How was your night?"

I tell him about Sweetness, the shelter, the noise, the fighting. Apparently an o-girl was thrown out for assaulting a staffer. She won't be allowed to return.

"My biggest worry is the bus-fare," I say then. "It'll cost more than two dollars a day, gettin' out there and back."

"Last night I heard there's a women's shelter, here in the downtown, where if ya tell 'em you're battered, you can stay, no matter what."

"I'm not gonna lie, James."

"Figured you'd say that, but had to tell ya anyway. Any cuts on your face, you're in."

"Whaddya want, an excuse to beat me up?"

We laugh. It feels good to laugh, even at a lame joke.

"So you're doin' okay?" James says.

"Much better than yesterday. Gettin' some sleep helped."

"Gonna keep goin'?"

I nod. "But if *you* need to quit, that's okay. I understand."

"Just be sure to quit for the right reason—that's what we said, comin' out."

"Yeah. Right now, I gotta stay. I'm where I gotta be."

James smiles weakly. "Count me in."

Manuel, a new friend from the men's shelter, stops by our table, suggests that James try to hire on at the factory where he works. "Maybe," James says, his tone noncommittal. His lack of enthusiasm obviously puzzles Manuel, whose frown seems to say, "D'ya know what hangin' out'll do to ya?"

illusions

(downtown, mid-morning.) An uncanny connection seems to exist among street people. You may not know each other, but you easily recognize each other. Maybe it's the scruffy clothes that give you away, or maybe the hollow pain in your eyes; more likely, it's the way you walk, down and heavy, like a constant ache. The backs of the legs complain. You don't hurry unless you have to. You fill your steps.

So much walking. So much walking in straight lines. Sidewalks: right—left—up—down. Streets: this way—that. Doors: in—out. Suddenly the world's a grid; life, unswerving conformity. Spirit in a straitjacket.

Already I feel light-years from home, and lost, even from Jihong. I see him everywhere—turning the corner, entering a building, getting on a bus. Always he disappears. My mind puts him there, real enough, then, the next instant, erases him without a trace.

I so want to speak to him face to face, to touch his cheek, to be held by him and hold him close, yet I doubt I could, even if I had the chance. That

35

where he is and where I am could be the same world seems impossible. What word, what caress, would suffice to close the distance between us?

I try to reassure myself that the two of us aren't as distant as we seem. Separation is, at the heart of it, an illusion; nothing, nobody, in the world stands essentially apart from the rest. Still, the illusion of separation is convincing, sad, sometimes almost unbearable. It's love that helps me withstand the strain of it.

Headline from the Employment News, a curbside weekly: "Why Can't We All Just Get Along?"

ritual

The sidewalk gods smile on me: a small tube of Crest not quite empty, a clean rag to use as a washcloth. I throw away a sheet of plastic I've been toting around for protection in case of rain. Don't accumulate stuff that's not absolutely essential. It fast becomes a burden.

James, off on his own, is hitching along toward the Broad Street bridge, feeling downright elderly, when some dead plants next to the sidewalk catch his eye. Milkweed, waist-high. Fluffs of seed rise from open pods, migrate on the breeze. Inspired, he pockets a couple of pods, then hurries off to find me, wearing a silly grin.

When we connect, his face is much brighter than its early morning gray. "What's happened?" I ask, and he tells me to follow him. He has a surprise.

My imagination prospects for gold as James leads me west on Broad: a stash of blankets, maybe, or some out-of-the-way place he's stumbled upon, secure and warm enough to spend the night. . . .

Halfway across the Broad Street bridge, James stops suddenly, leans against the rail. For a few minutes the two of us watch the river swirling muddy brown below. Then James yanks off a glove and reaches into his coat pocket.

"Hold out your hand."

He lays a milkweed pod in my palm. Dead-brown, brittle, barely open. I look at him, puzzled. In his hand, another pod.

"I thought we could release the seeds over the river. Kind of a ritual: for each clump of seeds, we can name somethin' we gotta let go of, in order to keep goin' out here."

"Wonderful," I exclaim, knowing exactly what he means. There are so many things he and I wish we had out here, things we're used to having, that we may never have. (How intensely we humans crave a perfect life, in which we have everything we want and nothing we don't. How bitterly we resent the inevitable disappointment.)

36

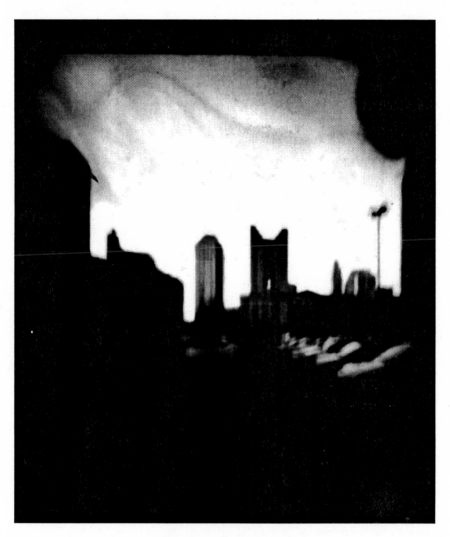

alley view of downtown

We dare not cling to our desires. They're too heavy, too burdensome to carry. They get too much in the way. *Empty your hands.*

I tug off my gloves, better to grasp the tufted seeds.

"You first," James says.

"I let go of my need for a good night's sleep," I say, casting a cottony fluff.

"I let go of my need for three meals a day."

"My need to be warm."

"To feel safe."

"To have more money."

"To be clean."

"To know what's comin' next. . . ."

More and more white wisps of down, tiny parachutes, float gently over the churning water. A few of the seeds will make it to land. Maybe one seed will survive to become a milkweed plant. And maybe one day a monarch butterfly will lay her eggs on the underside of its leaves—

"I let go of my need to feel loved—"

The necessity of the lowly milkweed: a monarch butterfly will lay her eggs nowhere else—

"I let go of my need to be me."

join

(**j.o.i.n., mid-morning.**) Joint Operation for Inner-city Needs, the sign reads—a relief agency run by the Catholic Diocese of Columbus, open for a couple of hours each weekday morning and afternoon. Waiting in a slow line behind a dozen people, I finally make it to the receptionist's window. She takes my name, checks my ID and asks what I want.

"A bus pass, please," I say.

"You'll have to wait," she says crisply. "*Next!*"

Off to one side, clothing racks and cardboard boxes full of hand-me-downs. I'm pawing through, looking for anything that might serve as a blanket, when my name's eventually called. I'm led at once through a locked door into a small cubicle, where sits Ethel, a smartly-dressed seventy-something volunteer.

"So," she says flatly, from behind her neat desk. "You want a bus pass."

"Yes, ma'am, it'd be a big help."

She's not convinced I need a bus pass, and says so. She starts shooting questions, pinning me down. Who am I—why am I on the streets—don't I have any family to help—where am I currently living—

She scowls at my last reply. "How could you possibly be staying *there?*"

38

she says accusingly. "That shelter is only for long-term residents."

"I'm what they call an 'overflow girl'," I say. Then, to prove I'm telling her the truth, I describe the shelter and the entrance interview; I even identify the shelter's confidential location. She still doesn't believe me. Beginning to feel irritated, I take a deep breath and calmly suggest that she call the shelter staff and confirm I stayed the night. She refuses.

Baffled, I don't know what more to say. What makes this woman so skeptical, so unyielding? Maybe she's been too often lied to, or too much taken for granted, or too long exposed to people in trouble. Maybe she's frazzled from working so hard to help while nothing ever seems to change. . . .

Ethel leans back in her chair, stares me down. "What made you decide to do this?" she asks. "Or did you just say to yourself, 'This is what I'm going to do,' and then you just did it?"

I'm stunned. *It's as if she knows.*

When I don't respond, she says, "Well, this will be *quite* an experience. Maybe you can write a book about it someday." She laughs suddenly, loudly, then quickly administers a bus pass. "Good for one day," she says, dismissively. "By rule, that's the only pass you're allowed this month."

table talk

(men's shelter in the downtown, lunchtime.) All around James the crowded lunch tables are buzzing with the news of Wilford Berry's execution by lethal injection, the first execution in Ohio since '63. Nicknamed the Volunteer, Berry had objected to all appeals on his behalf, preferring death to spending his life in prison for murdering a baker.

"It's just not right," a guy across from James says. "He shoulda repented."

"He had some balls, I tell ya," says another.

"God have mercy on him and his family."

"Didn't say a single word to his own relatives before he died—how *could* he?"

"Ah, he was a bastard."

The older man sitting beside James goes by the name of Colonel. Rumor has it that he has plenty of money, but prefers to live here, in the shelter. "A lifer," the men call him, as if doing hard time behind bars.

buffet

(downtown, lunchtime.) A whole loaf of white bread, dumped on the ground under a bush; stale, stiff to my touch, probably meant for squirrels. . . . A generous serving of spaghetti and meatballs, spilled from a styrofoam container onto the sidewalk. I bend over and sniff. . . . A street vendor peddling hot sausage sandwiches, greasy, topped with sautéed onions, red and green peppers. "Honey mustard," he cries to the air, "special sauce, if ya want it. . . ."

eyes

(ohio statehouse, noon.) Near where I sit, waiting for James at the Statue of Peace, busloads of elementary schoolchildren are arriving for a tour of the capitol complex. My tired eyes luxuriate in the children's bright red boots, pink hats, turquoise mittens, yellow coats; somebody has loved these little ones enough to bundle them up. Their energy's a delight, even as their teachers scold and cajole them into straight lines. They won't look at me, though. Not till they think I'm not looking at them—then they study me like a brand-new picture book. Already they're learning well.

Rarely am I able to make eye contact with men and women I pass on the streets. Pedestrians almost always lower their eyes when we meet, or stare deliberately ahead, or turn sharply to glance back over their shoulder, as if somebody behind them has just called their name. Anything to avoid.

It's been said that an infant first gains some sense of her existence, and some sense that she's loved, from the gaze of her parents. But what happens when a grown woman loses her way—when she no longer perceives (if she ever did) that her life has substance, and matters? In whose eyes might she still see reflected her fundamental worth? Who will deign to look?

his first

(twelve-step meeting in "the bottoms," early afternoon.) The smoke-filled room, the stale donuts and bad coffee, the round-robin discussion—all of these are a comfort to James. He's dirty and disheveled but not judged. Not that he's aware, anyway.

Scattered around the room are large coffee cans serving as ash trays. The nearest holds a couple hundred cigarette butts. When the meeting ends, James picks it up, asks the chairperson if he can have it. "Yeah, sure," the man says, giving him a strange look.

His first pinhole camera, maybe.

Anxious to work, he hikes to Deaf School Park, behind Main Library, and settles at a lonely picnic table. Before hitting the streets, he had made several pinholes, poking needles of various widths through thin pieces of brass one-inch square. Now, to make a camera, he has to mount one of these brass pinholes over a hole in his coffee can to serve as a lens. First, he drives a nail through the can, using a light metal mallet we found yesterday. Then, removing the nail, he lightproofs the can, spraying the inside with black paint and masking its plastic lid with black electrical tape.

Once the paint is completely dry, he'll select a brass pinhole and securely tape it over the larger nail hole. Finally, he'll cover the pinhole with a piece of electrical tape, which will act as the camera's shutter. To shoot a photograph, he'll simply peel back the tape, allowing light to pass through the pinhole lens, exposing a 5"x7" sheet of photo paper previously positioned inside the can.

After every photo he shoots, James will have to conceal the camera in his lightproof film-changing bag, then blindly transfer the exposed photo paper to a black storage bag. Every few days, one of his darkroom assistants will pick up a package of exposures and take them home to develop into negatives. James will want to see those negatives as soon as possible in order to judge the camera's performance. Pinhole photography is mostly trial and error. You can't easily judge exposure time, appropriate distance from the subject, or lens angle. Some shots, if you don't get them right the first time, you simply miss. Others you can shoot over and over, trying to get images that satisfy.

weed

(men's overflow shelter, bexley, late afternoon.) A major snowstorm is headed toward Columbus. Many homeless men who ordinarily sleep on the streets will take refuge tonight in city shelters. The Bexley shelter, responsible for the overflow from other facilities, is likely to be overcrowded. Latecomers may not get a bed. James signs in early, wanting not to sleep on concrete.

"Wanna go outside, smoke some weed with me?" asks the guy lying in the next cot. Last night: the same man, the same question, and a simple "no" sufficed. Now, to discourage the overtures, James says that he's allergic.

"Really?" the guy says.

"Yeah."

"D'ya getta rash?"

James nods, another lie to put the man off. The fellow leans toward him, his expression serious, and says, "Oh—y'know, I think *I* getta rash, too." Then, standing up to go, he laughs, says, "I smoke it anyway."

James tries to imagine being high, all five senses hyped to the max, in this place, so crowded and noisy and rank and tense. The thought sickens him. But hey, he says to himself, if getting high would help a guy laugh in this hole, maybe it would help him survive.

41

pack

(**downtown, early evening.**) Boarding the bus to return to the women's shelter, I ask the driver to please tell me when we're approaching the stop nearest my street. He frowns, stares straight ahead. "Don't wanna," he says curtly.

I don't want to ask him again and possibly provoke a scene. Uneasily I take a seat. How will I ever get off the bus at the right stop? Last night, on my way to the shelter for the first time, I was too exhausted to read street signs. Fortunately there was Sweetness, guiding my way like a mother hen.

Tonight, though, I'm alone, and anxious. I have to get off at the right stop. Wandering these streets after dark wouldn't be wise. It's a tough part of town.

Staring out my window, I see an elderly man hobbling down the sidewalk through a stinging snow, wrapped in a thin blanket. I shiver, deep and hard.

An older black lady sitting beside me leans into my shoulder, says in a low voice, "You goin' to the shelter?"

I nod.

"Me too," she says, obviously relieved.

No longer alone.

In all, five of us women get off the bus, hurry in a pack the few blocks to the shelter, as fast as we can go.

laundry

(**women's shelter.**) Tonight's intake worker, contradicting last night's, says that yes, even though I'm an o-girl, I may take a shower. She even rummages in a messy closet and brings out a clean bath towel and a variety of toiletries, as well as a sheet and a tattered orange afghan for use on my mattress. I'm overwhelmed.

Upstairs, at the bathroom door, I'm intercepted by Cindy, a long-term resident in the suite. She hands me a red sweater and white bib overalls, two pair of socks, a brown nightshirt to sleep in; all of them her own clothes, freshly laundered. "Take these," she says, over my protests, "and gimme your dirty ones. I'll do `em up for ya."

"Why're you helpin' me like this?" I ask her, close to tears.

"Why not?" she says, voice matter-of-fact. "People helped *me* when *I* was down. . . ."

I stand under the shower, water steaming hot, till my skin is smarting red.

conspiracy

(**women's shelter, late evening.**) I'm startled awake by a resident's screams—she's hysterical, just across the room—the door into our suite won't open, from either side—won't even budge—she's claustrophobic, totally panicked—two other women are trying to console her—a third's furious, late for a date—staffers outside the door can't agree on what to do next—loudly they curse the repairman who supposedly just fixed the knob—"Maybe he wasn't really no handyman!"—"Maybe he planned the whole thing! Y'know, like, *sabotage!*"—"Yeah, he prob'ly hates women"—

day 4: saturday, february 20

bottom line

(**downtown, late morning.**) Approaching noon. Feeling woozy. I've eaten barely a bite since yesterday's lunch of tuna and beans, the last of our canned goods from born-again Pete. Energy's spent. So cold. So much walking. James is holding up, having eaten breakfast at a men's shelter, here in the downtown. "Why don'tcha buy a cheeseburger at McDonald's?" he suggests.

89¢. Nearly a dollar. My belly wants to spend the money. My mind wants to save it for bus fare.

I withdraw from the counter without placing an order.

Out the window, a homeless man is moving a mountain of aluminum cans, bulging black trash-bags piled high in a shopping cart. Every bump and crack in the sidewalk threatens his load. Pennies, they'll pay him. He vanishes behind a curbside bus.

Suddenly I remember: Last night at the women's shelter, one of my suite-mates finagled a rare bus pass from a staffer, slipped it to me on the sly. She's already saved me $2.20.

I return to the counter, order the burger. It's barely warm, but I savor every bite, $1.31 to the good.

just sam

(**mid-afternoon.**) Digging in a dumpster across the rear parking lot of St. Joseph Cathedral. I toss James a Reese's Peanut Butter Cup, still in the wrapper. "Yum," he grins.

A plain wooden angel, country craft style, lies buried under a heap of

43

garbage bags. On a whim, James sets it on top of the bin, in plain view, just as a man in black walks up. A priest, maybe. He asks what we're doing.

"Just lookin' around," we say.

"Are you hungry?"

"Yeah!"

"Come with me," he says, with a friendly motion of his hand, and we don't even hesitate, following the stranger across the lot to the rectory's back door. Leaving us on the stoop, he goes inside and soon returns with a bologna sandwich, an apple and two cookies for each of us. "You can come here for food any day of the week," he says. "Nine o'clock in the morning, four in the afternoon. Got that?"

We thank him.

He says, "What's goin' on with you guys? Why're you on the street?"

"Just gotta sort some things out," we say.

His eyes brighten with tears. "Well," he says, collecting himself, "you take care, okay?"

We ask his name.

"Oh," he says, "I'm just Sam."

landscape

A sacred landscape has begun to emerge over our first few days on the streets: McDonald's on Broad, where James and I meet each morning to debrief after our nights in the city shelters; the Statue of Peace, where we meditate each noon, and where dear friends, at a discreet distance, often bless us with precious eye contact; the third floor of Main Library, where we relax, and read, out of the elements; Deaf School Park, where we write and construct pinhole cameras or simply laze when the sun's warm enough; the rear door of St. Joseph rectory, next to the cathedral, where (we've just learned) we can beg a sandwich twice a day. In these places we feel safe. Sometimes we even feel a sense of belonging, or at least of having the right to be on the premises, if only for a little while. But nothing is absolute. As we've discovered today, some of these places restrict their hours on the quiet downtown weekends, become less accessible. We adapt, but with sadness, a melancholy out of all proportion.

How quickly a place can become a haven. How little is required.

chicken

(salesian boys and girls club, late afternoon.) The back door opens. A man tosses a couple of large foil roasting pans into the trash. James elbows me in the ribs.

"the quiet downtown weekends": James and Phyllis on the streets
(Photo credit: Jihong Cole-Dai)

The lukewarm remains of chicken casserole. We draw fast-food forks from our coat pockets, and the banquet begins. Shriveling orange halves round out our meal; we nip the clean, fleshy parts like vultures picking at a carcass.

After a few minutes, we notice a cop car just down the block. Hastily we pocket our forks, jump a chainlink fence and slip down the nearest alley.

visibility

(**high street bus stop, late afternoon.**) End of our day. Taking leave of each other, headed to our respective shelters, James hesitates, looks at me oddly. "What is it?" I say.

"You're all eyes."

"All eyes?"

He nods. "That's mostly what I see of you, all day long. You're always bundled up against the cold, face-warmer pulled up over your nose, hat pulled down to your eyebrows. Your eyes are the only part of you that's visible. They're all I need to see, though, to know how you're doin'."

"So how'm I doin' now?" I ask him.

My eyes are full of tears.

kindergarten

(**men's shelter in the downtown, early evening.**) As the men wait for dinner, an anglo preaches about Jesus. In the very back pew, James drifts off, exhausted, till one of the preacher's friends starts playing a guitar, leading a hymn. James rouses himself to join in. The lyrics leave him unmoved, but he feels a power, all the male voices in unison.

Once the singing ends, the guys in the first two pews queue up to enter the cafeteria, each man signing his name on a tablet before going in to eat. Slowly the line trickles through the door.

Just as the next two rows are called, trouble erupts. A staffer starts yelling, accusing a homeless guy named Marvin of butting into line. "I was up here the whole time," Marvin says defiantly, and the men around him confirm he's telling the truth, but he doesn't stand a chance. This place is like kindergarten, James observes from his pew: once you've been labeled a troublemaker, you can't do anything right. Incensed, the staffer strides across the room, gets in Marvin's face, shouts, "Go sit down in the back of the room! You'll eat last, after everybody else!"

Marvin's too angry to sit. He paces back and forth behind James's pew like a hungry lion in a cage stupidly left unlocked; one brush of the big cat's body, and the door will swing wide open.

At long last, pew #17 is called. As James hurries to get in line, Marvin, still fuming, curses him, says, "Get the fuck outa my way!" Then, glaring at the staffer seated at the desk, he screams, "What gives, man? What gives?"

seconds

(women's shelter, early evening.)   Fried chicken, mashed potatoes and gravy, succotash, chocolate cake—the residents feasted tonight. Their leftovers are still on the table, getting cold, but if you're an o-girl, you can't touch. A lesson learned last night: residents eat dinner, o-girls eat snacks.

I hover near the food, feeling desperate. Pat, the staffer in charge tonight, finally relents under my hungry gaze. "Look," she says, "eat whatever ya want. I'll get in dutch for it—somebody'll tell for sure—but I think it's a stupid rule that the overflow can't eat and everybody else can."

I dish up a plate, in heaven for her trouble.

Over by the intake desk, a new woman, just beaten up by her man. As Pat tends to the woman's pulpy face, one of the residents keeps interrupting, like a child jealous of her mother's affection. "I wanna soda, I wanna towel, I wanna use your phone. . . ." With each interruption the new woman's eyes seem a little more dead. Tears slide down her cheeks, mixing with blood, and trickle into the corners of her swollen mouth.

I spoon up seconds.

When Pat finishes her first-aid, the new woman takes up a position just inside the door of the main room, leaning wearily against the jamb. Residents and o-girls brush past her, saying nothing, eyes averted. Sometimes the woman murmurs hello as they pass, then gestures weakly toward her bandaged face, mewling like a kitten.

For Godsake, do something. Uncertainly, I set down my plate, my fork. *Anything.* The crowded room seems full of obstacles. *Just get up (what to do?), try—*

Suddenly Sweetness is there. She wraps an arm around the new woman's shoulders, walks her over to a sofa, shoos away a couple of residents, settles in with the woman, holds her hand, lets her cry. . . .

So simple, if you'll let it. . . .

special delivery

Two black women set up ironing boards to press their jeans for work. I've never ironed a pair of jeans in my life, let alone starched a crease down the legs, but Toots and Billie could do it in their sleep. Over hot irons the two of them jive about their jobs, their men, their looks, their cooking. Other women gather around, egging them on. Toots is obviously the crowd favorite. Her delivery is priceless. She taunts, brags, razzes, rhymes, mocks. Sometimes her voice is music, sometimes sass, sometimes prophecy or preaching. Then, sometimes, it's just plain meanness.

"Ain't I free?" somebody shouts.

Toots laughs, says, "Honey, if ya know you is, you *is*. Since ya don't know you is, you *ain't*."

An hour or so later, the ironing done and jiving past, there's suddenly a sharp rapping at the front door. All around me women shriek and yell, rush as one body into the back room where they huddle in a tight hush of fear, all eyes fixed on a staffer as she calmly, warily, goes to answer the door—

Somebody's abusive lover, maybe, or a husband drunk with rage—

"Special delivery," the man says. "Sign here."

snake eyes

(**men's overflow shelter, bexley, middle of the night.**) James jerks awake. Some guy's yelling in the dark, not far away. "Get the fuck away from my shit, man!" Instinctively James gropes, checks his gear.

Seeing what you see when you're awake is hard enough. But like a snake you've got to sleep with your eyes open, too.

day 5: sunday, february 21

indulgence

(**st. joseph cathedral.**) 8:00 a.m. mass. We've come here not because we're practicing Catholics, though James was raised as one, but because we have nowhere else to go. This being Sunday morning, public buildings in the downtown are generally closed, at least till noon, and the weather's too nasty to remain outside.

Then, too, we've come here because this elegant cathedral, the seat of the Columbus diocese, is filling with people—people wishing not only to worship, but also to *be together*, acknowledging the higher, the truer, the loving, the just. Like them, James and I want to commune. We want not to be alone.

We've come here as well to indulge our senses. There will be light— dim in the nave, bright over the altar, gold metalwork gleaming, candles glimmering in hidden drafts of air; there will be color—liturgical cloths and garments appropriate to the season; there will be music—pipe organ and choir, hymns and chants soaring to the vaulted ceiling, then drifting as echoes into silence; quite possibly, there will be incense burning, and if not that, then the mingling of perfumes and colognes; there will be prayers while kneeling on soft cushions; there will be the barest taste of bread and wine. . . .

At the Passing of the Peace, congregants stand to greet those sitting around them, blessing them, wishing them well. The older white man directly in front of me, wearing an expensive suit, casually turns around to shake hands. When he sees me, shock registers on his face. I smile and grip his hand hard.

James and I would both like to be more presentable, this first Sunday of Lent. Back when we were kids, the dress code for church services was strict: for James, a collared shirt and dress pants; for me, my best dress and shoes. Proper attire was a way of showing respect, though to whom, God or neighbor, was never clear. It was simply a necessary part of the ritual: Good clothes, like good music, made for good worship. Those memories of religion in childhood remain strong, even after all these years.

Today our clothes are dumpy, dirty, sweaty, infested with fuzz balls. Both of us, upon arriving, peeled off a few layers, hoping for a less nappy look, but with each garment we removed, our body odor intensified. Fuzz and dirt, we decided, was better.

The priest's homily is based on Jesus' testing by Satan in the wilderness. He describes Lent as a time when we must face and overcome our temptations, especially through the practice of fasting. In his view, fasting is a temporary sacrifice of excess. For a period of forty days, we give up something we possess too much of, or do too often. After the forty days are up—well— what happens then, the priest doesn't say.

This interpretation of fasting, depending as it does on excess, strikes me as privileged. It tends to exclude those who have little while easing the conscience of those who have much. What if fasting, instead of being a temporary modification of lifestyle for the relatively well to do, were a deliberate change of heart undertaken by us all? What if it were less about giving up red meat or cigarettes or clothes shopping for a few weeks, and more about giving up, bit by bit, our rigid expectations of what the future should hold, our fixed assumptions about how the world should operate, our categorical judgments of how people should act, who they should be? Considered this way, fasting isn't a privileged practice—all of us can do it. Nor is it restricted to Lent, but a daily challenge.

The point in fasting isn't for us to become perfect, beyond reproach, but simply to exercise faith, opening our minds and hearts as best we're able, and learning from our mistakes. Over a lifetime of practice, something may rise up in place of the fear or greed or ignorance we've fasted away—something we've helped bring about but can't take credit for. Maybe our joy's more full, our compassion wiser, our kindness quicker, our patience longer, our suffering more humble, our determination to respond to the suffering of others deeper, more enduring. . . .

James, welcome as a Catholic, goes forward for bread and wine. When he returns, he opens his hand to reveal a communion wafer. Breaking it in two, he passes half to me, and together we consume the host. A sense of belonging, born from a simple gesture.

The man who earlier passed me the peace returns from the front of the nave still chewing his wafer. Spurning his original seat, he takes another, several pews further up the aisle.

gospel

(**central presbyterian church, mid-morning.**) James and I arrive in Fellowship Hall just as they're closing the breakfast line, run every Sunday morning for poor and homeless people. On today's menu: sausage gravy over biscuits, sliced peaches, cold milk, Little Debbies. Though famished, I save the sweets for later. Who knows if there'll be dinner.

Nine of us stragglers remain at the tables, trying to eat while the minister and a pianist lead us in worship. It's hard to sing hymns with your mouth full, hard to concentrate on a sermon when your mind's set on the hope of a second helping of biscuits. I wrestle my attention back to the minister, preaching now about how we poor folks will only find God in two places, the Bible and the church. "That's where God is," he says. "His *only* address. Folks like you oughta know—if you don't have the right address, you'll never find who you're lookin' for."

Those of us who stay through worship are rewarded afterward with sack lunches. Too bad that God, so confined within sacred pages and hallowed walls, won't be with us on the streets when we eat them.

a place of our own

In gentle flurries outside the church we chat with Jeff and Maddy, an anglo couple we just met over breakfast. They tell us that they've been camping in a woods, south of downtown, though they're careful not to say where, exactly; with a tent, tarps, sleeping bags and blankets, they're managing to stay warm enough, and dry. Even though the weather is wretched, they'd rather camp than sleep in city shelters, which don't allow unmarried couples or the use of alcohol. Jeff pokes fun at Maddy. "She's been a bad girl, got herself kicked outa two shelters for drinkin', can't never go back. Don't matter, though," he says, more serious now. "They treatcha like shit in them places."

Taken by the idea of camping, we ply Jeff and Maddy with questions. James, especially, can hardly contain himself. He's excited just thinking about a place of our own. He'd do almost anything to live in a place where he could get some decent sleep at night, nobody rolling over in sleep and slapping him, nobody moaning, nobody picking a fight, nobody maybe looking to steal his stuff—

A place where he could breathe deeply and not wish he hadn't; where he could take his clothes off and not feel the dirtier for it; where he could relax and not be assaulted by the hungry, angry, lonely, tired energy roiling in the room—

A place where at the end of the day he wouldn't have to see any more brittle and broken men, or listen to their stories, or witness how shabbily they can be treated, and how shabbily treat each other; where he could just close his eyes a while and not be bothered, and could be quiet if he wanted to, or talk, and cry when he needed to, instead of holding back—

A place where he could just—*be.* . . .

He'd do almost anything.

end of a roll

(**mid-afternoon.**) Downtown slows to a crawl on weekends, nearly empty of pedestrians, traffic flow light. After only a few days, weekday life on the streets has a familiar feel, a rhythm almost, and this carries a comfort, but now this weekend strangeness, and James and I are a little lost, like boats adrift.

Sweets, though, from the sidewalks: a Baby Butterfinger, a small bag of Reese's Pieces, two Certs from the end of a roll. Sharing the Certs, James and I improvise a tv commercial for breath fresheners—two mangy, stinky street people sucking on cool, clean peppermint. We're laughing hysterically when suddenly there's a furious flapping of wings up from the sidewalk near our feet, and a gray mourning dove settles onto an overhanging branch. A string of gold Mardi Gras beads dangles from its perch.

The dove stares.[11]

pieces

(**women's shelter, evening.**) Cindy, the resident whose clothes I wear, is putting together a 1500-piece puzzle, for the second time.

She misses Texas, where she grew up. She's been living at the shelter for two months, trying to put her life back together so she can go south again. "It's okay, bein' here," she says, "but I don't like minglin' with the others. 'Specially, y'know, the *niggers.*"

Before settling down to sleep, I read a while from Cry, the Beloved Country, the South African novel by Alan Paton. I borrowed it the other day from a bookshelf at the Agora. Stephen Kumalo, a Zulu minister, despairs of saving his son Absalom, arrested for murdering a white man. Each page cries out with the pain of apartheid, the crimes made possible by prejudice, poverty, and fear.

"The tragedy is not that the world is broken," Paton writes. "The tragedy is that it's not being mended."

rent

(men's overflow shelter, bexley, evening.) Lying on his cot, James glances around at his fellows, thinks, We don't pay any money to sleep here, but staying isn't free. We pay psychological rent. Every face shows it. Nobody brightens, entering this room. Might as well be a sign hanging out front: CHECK JOY AT DOOR.

He smiles to a new friend across the room. The man smiles back.

If only, James says to himself, nobody had to be here. . . .

day 6: monday, february 22

prayers

Now and then, especially when we're outside, I hear James and me offering spontaneous prayers of gratitude to inanimate objects: Thank you, bench. Thank you, boots. Thank you, ground. Thank you, sun. Everything is so immediate, and so graciously there, blessing it seems the natural thing to do.

Some scholars of religion say that primitive worship arose from overwhelming fear.

I wonder.

But then, perhaps profound fear and deep gratitude aren't so easily separated. . . .

beggary

(downtown, mid-morning.) Brilliant sun today, the kind that makes you think it cares, but I'm running low on money, and sunshine won't pay tonight's bus fare back to the women's shelter. I stand on a street corner near

St. Joseph Cathedral, eyes homed in on a smartly dressed businessman just down the block. As he comes my way, I rehearse my line, drawing a deep breath at the last—

My jaw clenches as he passes. I don't say a word. I don't even look at him. The scent of his cologne lingers before a breeze snatches it away.

At the same time, outside a thirty-story building along High Street, James is begging on my behalf, soliciting passersby for money as if he's done it all his life. "Sir—ma'am—can ya spare some change for the bus?" Nobody responds. Most won't even look at him.

I'd like to be more like James, but I'm loath to panhandle from strangers on the street. Needing the money simply isn't enough. Desperate as I am, still I've got to earn it. Deserve it. I don't want to feel this way, but I do. It's in the marrow of my grown-up-Protestant bones: money's the measure of your industriousness, and therefore also of your virtue. The more you work, the more money you have, the better person you are, the better life you lead: a myth without mercy, reducing the value of your life to your ability to make and spend (or save) a buck. It's a myth I've tried not to live by, but here on this corner it's my Mister Hyde, and I feel powerless as Jekyll.

I go to the back door of St. Joseph Cathedral and beg for an hour's work, without success. Then, on to The Place to Be, the café at Trinity Episcopal. Baseball Cap isn't around, fortunately. He's done enough for me already.

"D'ya have some odd job I could do for pay?" I ask the balding man behind the register. "I need $1.10 in bus fare to get to a shelter tonight, and another $1.10 to come back downtown tomorrow."

The man surprises me by opening the register. He counts out $2.25, then exchanges the quarter for two dimes and a nickel. He smiles, says kindly, "Dimes are better for bus fare, aren't they?"

Back on High Street, James, my grown-up-Catholic friend, closes his eyes in the flurrying snow, centers his thoughts and briefly prays a blessing on all the pedestrians on the block. When he opens his eyes again, he notices a tall, strapping businessman sporting a blond ponytail. As the man passes, James gives his spiel. "I'll see what I have," the man says, burrowing into his pockets. James hears the jingle of change. His heart lifts.

"There ya go," the man says, laying some coins in James's hand, the exact amount needed for fare.

"Thank you, sir. *Bless* you."

James bounds across four lanes of traffic, off to find me, excited as a little kid who just sold his first glass of lemonade.

My grandparents and other members of their generation have told me stories about the Great Depression, when begging was common and, as they put it, you practically had an obligation to respond. Whether that's truly how it was or just how they remember it, I don't know, but they tell me they would give the beggar whatever they could—a dime, a meal, a drink of water, a place to sleep. . . . "We didn't think twice about helpin'," they say. "It was just whatcha did, back then, because everybody was in the same boat. But things are different now."

Exactly how things are different now seems difficult for them to say, but beggary's no longer acceptable. Perhaps there was always some degree of shame in the asking, but now there's more resentment in the being asked. Those who beg must have some weakness in character that has reduced them to the indignity. Whether the beggars are unfortunates or miscreants, most of us "upstanding folks" think we're nothing like them; a distance has opened, with blame as the wedge. Now we don't have to look the poor in the eye. We don't have to listen to their stories. We don't have to give them a dime, a meal, a drink, a place to sleep. If we're careful, we may not even have to acknowledge their existence, despite the fact they're everywhere.

While street beggary has fallen into disrepute, institutionalized beggary has become commonplace, and tax-deductible charitable giving has emerged as a middle-class virtue. Beggar, if you want our money, don't stand on the sidewalk and try to panhandle our pocket change. Hold a fundraiser. Solicit us through the mail. Call us during a phone-a-thon. Deduct a designated contribution from our pay. . . .

In large measure charity has become depersonalized, reduced more or less to a financial transaction. Certainly there are reasons, however good or bad, for the change, but I wonder: has it helped to spawn the shadow side of street beggary which today so intimidates and offends us? To the degree that we regard those who beg from us as less than ourselves, we regard them, and often treat them, as less than human. Then we're surprised when some of them respond in kind, hassling us, lying to us, and worse. The shadow form of beggary has no honor, and no heart, but I suspect it has taken all of us to create it.

Begging is increasingly restricted and now illegal in some cities. By law in Columbus I can't approach a car stopped at a traffic light to ask for help. I can't panhandle near an ATM machine, or near the entrance to certain business establishments. I can't block the path of a pedestrian in order to beg—

As if I would. I can't even get up the nerve to ask a businessman for a quarter.

trifles

Any color, in whatever form, to relieve sidewalk gray: Plastic red poinsettias in a windowbox. A building by the river, painted olive green. A purple mail box. Yellow school buses. A sapphire blue convertible. A copper sunset, dancing on skyscraper glass and metal. . . .

Small courtesies: A stranger taking the time to search his pockets for loose change instead of rushing past you, pretending not to hear your pleas. A man giving you dimes instead of quarters for bus fare. A motorist waving you across a pedestrian crosswalk instead of making you wait. A woman bumping into you, then saying "I'm sorry" instead of "Get outa my way."

Nothing's inconsequential.

slaves

(j.o.i.n., mid-morning.) Waiting in line for the doors to open, we hear a middle-aged black man describe Columbus as a "come-up city." "You can getta leg up here, if ya hang tough," he says to the queue. "The jobs don't pay much and the bosses treatcha like slaves, but you can make it here. Maybe."

grubb

(holy family soup kitchen, lunchtime.) Aptly located on a street named Grubb, operating out of what was once a Catholic parochial school, is Holy Family Soup Kitchen. "The best soup kitchen in the city," in the opinion of our new friends Jeff and Maddy. On a cinderblock wall flanking its parking lot is the fading artwork of children long since grown: painted trees, stick-figures, hand prints, and in the middle of it all, a single question, brushed on in red, surrounded by empty gray space—

Why?

Inside the building, James and I become numbers 116 and 117, according to our index cards, and are instructed by a hallway monitor to join the food line when we're called.

Entering the basement cafeteria, we shed our coats and sink onto folding chairs, studying our surroundings. Stacked to our left are boxes of grapefruit, apparently free for the taking; straight ahead are four rows of tables, set end to end the length of the room. The main serving line runs across the very front; beverages, bread and desserts are being distributed at tables here in the back.

The place is a swarm of people, every age, from stooped white-beards and wizened women to skittish preschoolers. Some of the adults are dressed as impeccably as executives, others are casual; most look rough, like we do. Eyes: glazed, sharp, bleary, crazed, darting, twinkling, soft. A mayhem of clattering trays and cups, shouts and table talk, scraping chairs, laughter, mad

**question posed by the old schoolyard wall
outside Holy Family Soup Kitchen**

rushes up to the food line, banging pots and pans.

On the far wall is the portrait of a priest. Up front, hung above the serving line, da Vinci's Last Supper.

Waiting for our numbers to come up, I read an article about the soup kitchen in a stray copy of the Franklinton News, the thin newspaper of the Bottoms. Established nearly twenty years ago by the Holy Family Parish and its revered monsignor, Francis Schweitzer (the portrait on the wall), the place now serves 300-500 people a day, Monday through Friday, with only one paid staffperson, the rest of the labor supplied by volunteers. Much of its food comes from Second Servings, a program that redistributes surplus food from restaurants, hospitals and other facilities that would otherwise go to waste—

"111 to 120, 111 to 120!" booms a voice through a megaphone, and James and I leap with the others to queue up. Before us, a cornucopia of food: fried chicken, mashed potatoes, spaghetti, mixed vegetables, baked beans, chicken noodle soup, tossed salad. . . . Our mouths hang open in disbelief, and gratitude. The servers ask James, ahead of me in line, what he wants and how much. Soon every inch of his tray is covered.

My turn, now, but I'm speechless. So much to choose from. . . .

A memory rises up: Jihong's mother, visiting us from China, on her first trip to an American supermarket. In the produce section she wanders wide-eyed among enormous piles of green peppers and onions, potatoes and cabbage, fresh gingerroot. She has cooked with these ingredients her entire life, but now, stunned by the sheer abundance of food, she's incapable of choosing, seems almost afraid to touch anything, till finally she reaches out, closes tentative fingers around a single head of garlic. . . .

Today, Mama, I understand.

"Yes, please," I say, to a chicken breast.

My first selection made, the rest is easy.

Once everybody in the cafeteria has been served, many people return to the food line for seconds, or to fill small containers with leftovers. James and I rummage in our pockets, come up with two small baggies. We stuff them with spaghetti for our dinner.

This place being open for lunch five days a week is the best news we've had. From now on, hunger won't be so much of a problem.

wide-angle

(deaf school park, mid-afternoon.) Lying in sunshine on the frozen ground. Suddenly a panic sits me bolt upright. "We never had lunch today!" I exclaim to James, who bursts out in laughter. Then, realizing I'm not joking,

57

he sobers up, quietly reminds me that only a few hours ago we gorged down a huge meal at the Grubb Street soup kitchen.

Dismayed, I sink back to the ground. *How could you not remember?*

James is excited about a gift box he found this morning in a garbage can. "Measures 5"x6"x3"—the perfect dimensions!" he explains. "Pinhole cameras of different sizes and shapes create different photographic effects. The coffee can's images will be curved. Pictures from this box, wide-angle."

romp

Across the way a majestic white dog is on a romp. I can't take my eyes off him. "Here, boy!" I yell after some minutes of watching, and I'm overjoyed when he doesn't hesitate to come. *You don't care what I look like.* He lets me rub him down, whimpering and licking my face as though we've been too long apart. My body thrills at the affection. *Go ahead, touch me. Touch me all over. You don't care.*

His companions, a young anglo couple, keep their distance, but they don't order him back. "What's his name?" I call to them, laughing.

"Gord."

"Thank you, Gord," I whisper in his ear, and instantly he bounds away, one mighty lord of a dog.

routine

(ohio statehouse, late afternoon.) In a courtesy kiosk I drop change in a public phone and dial the women's shelter. Every night, around 6:00 p.m., the same routine: make the call, ask if they're taking overflow, and hold my breath, just a little. Tonight I'm told that I'm lucky, I'll be getting the last bed. My heart leaps, then sinks.

The last bed. What about the next woman who calls?

With security cameras all over the capitol grounds, state troopers are quick to roust anybody who looks suspicious. A trooper materializes now just outside the kiosk, on the High Street side, presumably intent on chasing me off. It's happened before. I slam down the phone and flee through the Broad Street door.

slippery

(women's shelter, evening.) A different suite, tonight; this one occupied, among others, by a chic but obviously mentally ill woman I call the Lazarus Lady. Nobody seems to know her name. A couple of nights ago, she and I got off the bus together at the poorly-lit shelter stop. Dressed to the nines, carrying a large Lazarus shopping bag, she hurried up the dark street. My clodhopper boots couldn't keep up with the quick click of her stiletto heels.

"How's it goin'?" I called over her shoulder, hoping she would slow down. We'd both be safer, walking together.

"They don't know what they're talkin' about," she exclaimed.

"'Scuze me?"

"Can't cross that street, y'know. Like, business is bad. Everythin's rumblin'. I can't wait to go. And then there's tomorrow. Believe it. Maybe I can work it out, if the century goes on. The store's still open. *So slippery.* Dim those lights!"

Lazarus Lady's mad monologue continued all the way to the shelter. Anything I said merely dropped into the breaths between her dismembered thoughts, and was swallowed whole.

Now, anxious to take a shower, I strip off my many layers of clothes in the tiny bathroom. I'm down to my undies when suddenly the Lazarus Lady throws open the door. Unleashing a hysterical tirade, she gestures wildly for me to get out. Her words are totally unintelligible, but one thing is clear: This is her territory, and she wants me gone. No negotiations. Hastily I gather up my clothes. There'll be no hot shower for me tonight.

(**men's overflow shelter, bexley, evening.**) James has spent five nights here, but up till now, rank and dirty as he was, he just didn't have the energy to shower. Tonight, finally, his desire to be clean is greater than his need to rest.

The showers, cordoned off by three moldy shower curtains, are located in the small staff room. At the moment, nobody's in line. James grabs a thin towel from a pile, slings it over the shower rod, then peels off his umpteen layers of clothes.

The concrete beneath his bare feet is slippery with suds and slime. He stoops his tall frame under one of the two showerheads, turns on the tap, picks up a sorry cake of soap.

inches

(**men's overflow shelter, bexley, late evening.**) A guy's griping about having to sleep only inches from the men on either side of him. He wants to move his cot. A staffer tells him, sternly, to leave it where it is. "Look," the staffer says, "our numbers are high due to the weather. We need to accommodate as many guys as possible. Space is gonna be tight."

Both men have a point, and neither is about to back down. They square off with strong language. Tension mounts till finally another staffer, a brawny black man with a calm voice and presence, steps in and manages to resolve the dispute.

James appreciates this staffer's manner. He treats the men like human beings. This morning, for instance, when the lights had blinked on at 5:30, the staffer had wandered the room, gently nudging James and the other lazies who had automatically rolled over in bed and covered their heads. "Hey guys, c'mon now, ya gotta get up," he'd coaxed, rather than hollering obscenities and kicking the men's cots like other staffers did.

Many members of the staff act like roosters strutting and crowing in a barnyard; they're always telling the men exactly what to do and how to do it "or else." One guy scolds incessantly. Earlier this evening, when one of only two available toilets in the shelter got clogged, he construed it as a sign of disrespect. He gave a stern lecture on toilet etiquette. Then, once he'd cleaned up the mess, he marched all the men into the bathroom to view the toilet, said, "I wantcha to see whatta fine job I done."

Now, finally, it's lights out. Exhausted men toss and turn on their flimsy cots, settling in, trying to get comfortable. The room begins to fill with an odd music of coughs, wheezes, belches and moans. Snores too, finally, though nobody sleeps soundly for long.

The men are constantly rousted. Guys who work night shifts need to be woken at various hours. Time after time, the staffers flip on all the fluorescent lights, bellowing for this man or that to "haul his ass outa bed." The entire room stirs with a tired growl. James, coming to, can't remember at first where he is. Then suddenly he does, and there's a rush of fear *(maybe somebody's stolen your boots, maybe somebody's searched your duffel, found your supplies, is wonderin' who the devil you are. . .)*. Gradually the panic subsides, till he's calm enough to feel the itch from the wool blanket, to smell again the hundreds of down and out men who've used it since it was last washed. Now he starts willing himself back to sleep, and he's only inches away when the lights flicker on again and somebody shouts, "So and so, move your sorry ass—"

day 7: tuesday, february 23

human enough

(downtown, morning.) Horn blast—James and I yank each other back to the curb—catch our breath—

Crossing the streets of downtown has become hazardous. Strangely unaware of traffic, both of us regularly step into the path of oncoming cars and trucks. We're not real enough to be struck down: this isn't what we think but how we act. The body comports itself according to what it senses, and after only a week on the streets, the message has gotten through, loud and clear: we're not here enough, not substantial enough, not human enough, to matter.

Blessings on that driver for laying on his horn. . . .

squatting

(early afternoon.) Inspired by Jeff and Maddy, we've decided to establish a camp, possibly in the woods along the Scioto River. Staying in the city shelters, James is getting precious little sleep, and I'm struggling every day to conjure up bus fare; then, of course, there's our old ambivalence about taking up the beds. Though camping will pose its own difficulties, we believe it's the better long-term option. Quieter, cheaper and in some ways safer than the city shelters, it'll also provide the solace of something our own. We hope to be camping by Saturday night.

This afternoon, having hiked south out of the downtown, we've been scouting the east bank of the Scioto for signs of human habitation. We'd prefer to pitch camp near some neighbors, possibly even Jeff and Maddy. But hours have trudged by, not a soul in sight.

Bone-tired and hungry, we're about to end the day's search when suddenly we spot a tent in the trees; then, an old refrigerator tipped on its side, with a pair of shoes neatly signaling its occupation; next, a couple of shanties, and a truck camper without the truck. So many camps, all apparently deserted for the moment.

Full of energy now, James and I explore the area for a suitable campsite of our own. Soon we find one in a strip of dead and immature trees between some railroad tracks and a water treatment plant. The site is well above the river, flat and somewhat concealed. We choose the precise spot to build a shelter, then clear away stones, sticks, bricks, bottles and broken glass, leaving duff to cushion the ground.

It's a start.

Done for the day, we set off again for the downtown, following the railroad tracks. As a southbound train approaches, we wave our arms gleefully at the engineer, and he responds with an earsplitting blast on his horn. It feels like a friendly acknowledgment, welcoming us to the neighborhood.

My face breaks into a grin. In a punch-happy burst over the screech and rumble of the cars, I holler at James, "*They* don't care!", and he whoops, gives me a spirited high-five. Nobody will roust us out here.

prospects

(**downtown, late afternoon.**) Aching for rest, ornery burrs stuck to our clothes, we slog along the potholed city streets. Whiffs of country-fried chicken, greasy kung pao and fresh donuts coax growls from our empty bellies. A hard hour after leaving our campsite, we finally collapse on a bench outside Main Library and jerk off our boots. They sit, steaming, on the sidewalk. Our feet, through three thick pair of socks, sweat perfect footprints onto the pavement. If we can, we'll have to replace our heavy boots; otherwise our feet will take a beating, hiking the roughly two miles between camp and the downtown twice each day.

We're inspired to have prospects. To have an idea that holds promise. To have something tangible to work on, to make with our hands, even from junk and rubbish. My notes are fragments. James's cameras are trash. Now our home will be fashioned from household refuse and workplace scraps.

We have no idea what kind of shelter we'll build, but this morning, before our hike to the riverbank, we stashed our first supplies: a large plastic banner, plus a length of purple burlap, bigger than a blanket, scavenged from a museum dumpster. This is the exact opposite of what people usually do when constructing their own home: first they brainstorm a design, then they create a blueprint, then they order the materials. Out here, the materials have to come first. Once we find them, they'll tell us what to do. We trust the process. It's a lesson we've learned from dumpster diving: you don't know what you need till you find it; once you find it, you know precisely how to use it.

Whatever form it takes, this new home of ours won't mean an easy life, if only because of the frigid weather. All this week the nighttime temperatures have been in the low twenties, even the middle teens, before the chill factor. At least the city shelters were heated; no such luxury in camp. I try not to dwell on this. Somehow we'll manage. Somehow we'll build a shelter that can keep us warm and dry, that can withstand wind, sleet, snow, rain. Once we've moved in, it'll probably take a blizzard to make us leave.

miracle

(**salvation army thrift store, late afternoon.**) Fed up with his uncomfortable boots, James tries on a pair of used white sneakers, moans a little in relief. "Like heaven," he says, but they're priced at $6. He offers the clerk 75¢, all the money he has. By some miracle, her manager approves the deal.

chances of winning

(**women's shelter, evening.**)   In the crowded tv room, over a romance turned up loud, the women talk: The pros and cons of letting a man give you money. The dangers of letting him dominate you. How to get your kids back in court. Today's lottery numbers and the chances of winning. Classic tv shows. Sickness—lots of sickness, body ailments. Sex. Weed. Folks you'd love to see again. The shelter staff. Caseworkers. Bosses. Horoscopes. . . .

(**men's overflow shelter, bexley, evening.**)   A pudgy black guy is talking smack to Winfield, a tall, dignified black man, fortyish, powerfully built, mentally ill. Something the pudgy guy says prompts Winfield to cock his sturdy cane, as if to strike. "Yeah, c'mon, ol' man, *I'll* take ya," says the troublemaker, raising his fists, punching air.

James, watching anxiously from his cot, is no more than ten feet away. The tip of Winfield's cane waggles like a baseball bat in the hands of a dangerous hitter. A staffer rushes over, tries to stop the fight before it escalates. After hot dispute, the cane is confiscated. Peace is made. Tentative, uneasy peace.

day 8: wednesday, february 24

the way

(**early morning.**) So many men stayed at the overflow shelter last night, this morning there aren't enough bus passes to go around. James misses out.

A two-mile hike into center city on an ailing foot.

Wet snow falls. Every step splashes slush.

James's new white sneakers, his Salvation Army miracles, are torture. The way they feel, their last owner must have been extremely flat-footed. They cramp James's arches, dig into his ankles, lock up his knees. He tries walking bull-legged. It doesn't help. He cuts slits in the leather with his knife, hoping for a little give. That doesn't help either, and now the shoes leak. He can't switch back to his old boots: they're miles away, wrapped in plastic, stashed under a bush near St. Joseph Cathedral, too heavy to lug around. All he can do is accept the inevitable: today his feet will be cold, and soggy, and sore.

A vanity plate on a hotrod parked on the street: UR WHAT UR.

He stops at a small park, rests in a gazebo. A large, metallic sculpture on the grounds catches his attention, somehow familiar. Eventually he realizes that its creator was one of his old art profs. The strength and grace of its abstract lines touch him deeply. While this morning he feels neither strong nor gracious, just to be reminded of his teacher—the man's lighthearted encouragement, the way he would accept almost anything from his students except lack of effort—is an inspiration.

red

(**downtown, grant hospital, mid-morning.**) James consults with a nurse about his right heel, festering and ugly red with all the walking. "Do you have any money?" she asks.

"No, ma'am."

"Here, take this," she says, handing him a dollar bill from her pocket. "Go buy yourself some hydrogen peroxide. That's what we'd treat you with here, along with lotsa red tape."

On a street corner near the hospital, a UPS express mailbox. All packages, it reads, are GUARANTEED OVERNIGHT.

I wish *I* were, James says to himself. I wish we *all* were.

revolution

(**early afternoon.**) Somehow James needs to secure a bus pass for tonight; otherwise, come sundown, he might be limping all the way back to the Bexley shelter. After noon meditation he hobbles over to a men's shelter in the Bottoms to beg a pass. A bearded, long-haired staffer who might have been a hippy in the seventies invites him to sit next to his desk. "Hey," the man says, introducing himself, "what's goin' on?"

James tells the staffer his situation.

"You on the streets over a girl or what?" the staffer says.

"Separated from my girlfriend," James says.

"Well," the man says, "let's see what we can do," and he starts asking the usual questions, filling out the usual forms.

After a while the staffer leans back in his chair and says, out of the blue, "Where's the spark in your generation? There's wars goin' on all over the world, and nobody protests. I'm worried 'bout you guys."

James likes this staffer. He seems interested in more than just giving a handout. A rare thing, out here, when somebody seems sincerely to care about how you're feeling, what you're thinking. James looks squarely at the man and says, "Well, I'm not that worried about us. I see an inner revolution goin' on in my generation. Its focus is on spirituality."

"I hope so," the staffer says skeptically, "but I don't see much of it." He

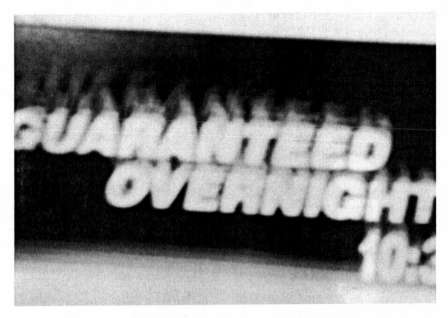

GUARANTEED OVERNIGHT: UPS express mailbox, downtown

reaches into his wallet for a bus pass. "Here ya go," he says. "Take care of yourself. If ya ever needa shower or a meal, you can come here."

distance

(**main library, mid-morning.**) "Excuse me, do you work here?"

I'm standing on the third floor of the library, where James and I have come to get out of a driving snow. I'm smelly, dirty, clomping around in clumsy boots and too many layers of bulky clothes, the top half of my coveralls hanging down loose around my waist—is this woman *seeing* me? Can she truly believe that I'm an employee of one of the best public libraries in the country?

The two of us are close enough to touch. "No, ma'am," I say, "I don't work here, but I'd be glad to help you—"

Suddenly she realizes. Her eyes widen, and she backs away, hands raised, as if afraid I might hurt her. "No—no, that's okay," she stammers, and hurries off.

Meanwhile, a white boy, maybe ten years old, just walked past the table where James is reading. James smiled and tried to make eye contact, but the boy lifted his chin and snubbed him. Earlier, the same boy had been observing James curiously from the stacks.

James understands the youngster's ambivalence. As a boy growing up in Manhattan, he, too, had learned to studiously ignore "the bums" who fascinated him. One homeless guy had routinely perched outside a church on uptown Madison Avenue. Instead of asking passersby for spare change, he'd say, "Can anybody spare a couple hundred dollars?" His humor (or gall) amused people, enticed people to give who normally wouldn't. As a friend of James liked to say, "If you can get 'em to laugh, you can get 'em to cry."

As a boy James had seen this same beggar several times. The man aroused James's interest, even got him to drop some change once. But mostly James exercised his curiosity about homeless people from a distance. Like the boy who just snubbed him, perhaps, he'd been too scared of their unpredictability to let them know he cared.

long distance

(**main library, late morning.**) James dials Phoebe's number in Connecticut, then leans back against the wall, slides wearily down to the thinly carpeted floor. Other patrons are in and out of the modest courtesy room, making phone calls, photocopies, change for dollar bills.

Finally, on the line, a far-away "Hello?" At her voice, James sighs, full-body.

66

As he and Phoebe take turns telling the goings-on of their lives, James wishes for privacy. He wishes for right words. Everything he says is flat, cool, thin, while just beneath that surface ice is a river, currents so powerful they'd sweep him away in an instant if he ever broke through.

At the end, "I love you." What he means to say is "Help me," but she, so distant, has no way to hear.

longhouse

(**riverbank, afternoon.**) Pitching camp, after the morning's snow. In a weed patch adjacent to the woods, James and I discover a half dozen rusty lengths of steel reinforcement mesh, the kind used when pouring a concrete floor to increase its strength. Three of the sections are bent into crude crescents. Instantly we know what to do. Dragging them to the campsite, we arrange them side by side, then lash them together with wire and pieces of extension cord, forming the framework of a miniature longhouse. Once finished, its entrance will face south, away from fierce north and westerly winds.

The frame of the shelter now rigged, we anchor it solidly to the ground with rocks and bricks. Then we step back to examine our work. The structure is maybe 5' x 9'—wide enough that when we're sacked out side by side, each of us will be able to roll over once; long enough for James's lanky body, plus some storage space. The ceiling is quite low, sloping from four feet at the front door to three feet or less at the back. A little cramped, but the smaller the shelter, the warmer.

We're actually ahead of schedule. Another good day's work, and we should be able to move in. The energy we have for our homemaking is remarkable.

solace

(**men's overflow shelter, bexley, evening.**) Settling onto his cot (last row, in the corner), James leans back against the wall. Peeling paint flakes off on his clothes. He doesn't bother to brush it off. The shelter is actually mellower tonight—or maybe the change is in him, now that he knows he'll soon be leaving, giving up his cot for a campsite on the east bank of the Scioto River.

John, the anglo on the next cot, volunteers to get James a job on his paint crew.

"Maybe," James says. "Thanks for the offer. I've got some things to work out first."

The man nods.

"Hey John, if ya don't mind my askin', why're ya here?"

"My girlfriend was too clingy. Needed some space, y'know. I let 'er have the old apartment. I'm just here till I can scrape some money together for my own place."

John seems the reflective sort. James asks if he has a faith of any kind.

"Was raised Pentecostal, down in Tennessee," John says, "but I don't go to church very often anymore."

"Ya doin' anything for Lent?"

John laughs, says, "Well, I gave up my dog and my house. That's enough. I don't feel compelled spiritually to give up anything else. I mean, *look* at us." The man gazes thoughtfully around the room. "We've all got our cross to bear."

So many men: the aging Vietnam vets, and the panhandlers you see every day working the same spots on the streets, and the men who day and night hide their eyes behind shades, and the loners who stare at the ceiling, or pace. Then there are the partyers. Every night they ask James the same question— "What'dya get into today?" "Not much," James says, "how 'bout you?" "Got blasted," they say, and sometimes brag their tales. The same proportion of men ask, with genuine interest, "Didya find work?"

Near James's cot stands a young anglo, head shaved smooth as a melon. He's swilling coffee, going for a buzz, showboating all the way. Time and again, he refills his two styrofoam cups from the brewer in the staff room, chugs the coffee down with firecracker eyes, then goes back for more. "Aaah, this stuff is hot," he exclaims now, shaking out his tongue to attract attention. The other men ignore him.

All at once, the guy sets his coffee down. Removing a wad of paper from his pocket, he unravels it, says to James under his breath, "Pssst! Take a look—"

A single white pill. "Morphine," the guy says, and pops it down with his ninth cup of java in fifteen minutes.

James has had enough. The shelter hasn't changed so much after all. The air is still crazy. Desperate for quiet, he sneaks out of the crowded sleeping room through a fire door, into a restroom that's off-limits. Sometimes, for the sake of his sanity, he ignores the rules, retreats here. He handwashes his filthy socks at the sink. He always feels a peace in doing this; the only real solace he's ever felt in this place.

How ironic, he thinks. I used to believe that "solace" was implicit in the meaning of the word "shelter." Not anymore.

west bank

(**women's shelter, evening.**) "Are you college-educated?" a white woman named Linda asks me.

"Yeah," I say. "Why?"

"The way you talk," she says. "The way you carry yourself."

"Yeah," says Faye, the white woman sitting beside her. "Almost like, what're ya doin' here?"

I smile faintly. "We all have our reasons."

"I went to college, too," says Linda. "Gotta great job, but I messed up. Too much booze. I'm on my way back, though. I'm workin' the Steps, gettin' back on my feet."

Linda and Faye tell me briefly of their struggles. Lost jobs, lost kids, lost loves, lost dreams, lost, lost, lost. They don't indulge in self-pity, though; self-blame either. "We made our share of mistakes," they say, "but the tide is changin' now."

"Y'know," Linda says after a while, "there's not enough housing for homeless women."

"Why's that, d'ya think?" I ask.

"Not enough funding," she says, with conviction. "The people with money—they don't wanna believe women get beat up. They don't wanna believe we can be alcoholics and junkies, or that we're lazy, some of us. They don't wanna believe *any* of it, so they just make like we're not here."

The conversation sags, burdened down. I smile a little, tell the women I wish them well. "This is prob'ly the last time I'll be seein' ya."

"How's come?"

"My friend James and I, we're gonna camp."

"God, girl!" they exclaim, "You gonna *freeze.* Where ya gonna camp?"

"By the river," I say.

"The *river!* You be careful—there's some rough people over there. Bad scene."

"Yeah, I'd take me an *uzi,*" says Linda.

The women are right: the riverbanks do have a reputation. The west bank, in particular. To ease their minds, I tell them that it's quieter on the east, where we're pitching camp. Cindy, who has been listening without comment from a nearby chair, abruptly leaves the room, then returns with some of my clothes that she has laundered and neatly folded, plus two more pair of heavy socks. "You'll be needin' these," she says quietly.

(**women's shelter.**) Deep in the night—hot argument downstairs—many voices—

A plumbing break—the main floor floods—

Little sleep for anybody—

Soon you'll be outa here—

You're lucky to have the choice—

69

on the

riverbank

day 9: thursday, february 25

iris

(**mcdonald's on broad street, early morning.**) Debriefing here, these early mornings after our nights in the city shelters, James and I have become acquainted with a worker named Iris. She started her job wiping tables and restocking condiments about the same time we hit the streets. Developmentally impaired, her vision poor, she has eyes for more than appearances, and a heart that knows no impediment. Whenever she spots James or me, she breaks into a huge smile and hurries over to give us a hug. We've come to expect her pep talks. "Don't worry, things'll turn around—Have ya found a job yet? D'ya want to apply here? I'm sure they'd hire ya—Have ya thought 'bout goin' back to school?—Isn't it a beautiful day?"

Now I ask Iris if she might be able to spare any trash-bags. "We could really use 'em," I say, "to move supplies to our new camp."

"How many d'ya need, honey?" she says.

"As many as won't getcha into trouble."

She returns with a fistful, and kisses.

stoop

(**men's shelter in the downtown, mid-morning.**) Needing more bedding for camp, James begs a staffer at the front desk for a blanket. Old, stinky, thin, holey—any blanket will do. The staffer refers him to the shelter director, just descending the stairs from the second floor.

"Can ya spare a blanket?" James asks.

"Why don't you stay here instead of on the streets?" the director says, ignoring his question.

"I'd rather be out."

"Well, I won't give you a blanket. I'm not gonna support you bein' out."

"Please," James pleads, "it's so cold out there—"

"No!" the director says, exiting the building. "You're not gettin' a blanket from me!"

James pleads his case to several other staffers, without success. Finally, a security guard across the room winks at him, says in a low voice, "Hey man, I'll getcha a blanket." The young latino escorts him to the door, says, "Go 'round back in two minutes. I'll leave a blanket on the stoop."

James and I have been shown remarkable generosity by folks who

73

themselves seem to have few re-sources, little status—folks like this security guard; the café worker who slipped me a ten; Iris at McDonald's; David, the man of God who emptied his wallet. . . .

game

(**downtown, mid-morning.**) On Broad Street, waiting for a traffic light to change, I'm staring absently at the sidewalk when an insistent tap-tap-tapping interrupts: the metal tip of an umbrella on cement. I glance up at the umbrella's owner, amused at the show of energy, or impatience, and recognize the man's face from the news. He's William Kirwan, president of The Ohio State University (one of my alma maters), a long way from campus.

I lean in, almost touch his shoulder. "What about that game last night?" I say. Kirwan, startled, looks down at me. The expression on his face is priceless—an initial boyish enthusiasm almost instantly overtaken by total bewilderment. For a swallow, he's speechless, perhaps stunned by the mere sight (or smell) of me, or by my having presumed to speak to him, or by the thought that a street person could possibly know, or *already* know, that last night his beloved Buckeyes had upset the Wisconsin Badgers. He's quick to collect himself, though. His eyes find their focus, and he breaks a wide grin that seems thoroughly ingenuous. Together we swap a few hoop dreams till the light changes and he disappears in a crush of pedestrians, umbrella tapping mid-stride.

moving day

(**early afternoon.**) Shoulders ache, legs burn, every step is an effort. James and I are loaded down with almost more bags and bundles than we can carry, some of them even lashed to our bodies. Throughout the morning, after successfully begging two brand-new polyester blankets at JOIN, we scavenged provisions for camp, going our separate ways to cover more ground. James hit paydirt: huge amounts of discarded packaging plastic, perfect for weatherproofing, and piles of insulation, four inches thick. Carrying it all, we count our blessings, but camp seems a county away.

something like home

(**riverbank.**) Around 3:00 p.m. we finally reach the woods. We wilt, dropping our bundles with deep groans.

No time to rest, though. The shelter must be habitable by nightfall. Only a few hours of daylight remain. We work quickly. We cover the shelter frame with plastic, then with insulation, and finally with tarps, securely tying each layer to the reinforcement mesh.

In late afternoon, I reluctantly take leave of James to rendezvous with a homeless woman I've promised to drive to Illinois. Once I'm gone, James continues our homebuilding, focusing now on the shelter's interior. He creates a floor by layering plastic and thick cardboard over the frozen ground. Then he fashions a nest from the few blankets and extra coats we've managed to gather. Lying on his back atop this bed, he carefully inspects the ceiling and walls, his fingers reaching through the reinforcement mesh to probe the plastic lining. If he's lucky, there won't be many leaks.

Finally, just before dark, James covers the open ends of the shelter with a meager hodgepodge of packaging plastic and trash-bags, the best he can do for now, since he's out of supplies, and out of time. Tomorrow he'll make improvements.

James breathes a prayer of thanks to Jeff and Maddy for inspiring us to camp. This time yesterday he was on the bus to Bexley, dreading another tough night. What a relief, now, to be here.

He feels a sense of accomplishment, too. Our shelter isn't exactly tidy, its skin of plastic and tarps held together by wire, electrical tape, bricks, rocks, and dead tree limbs; it isn't so well-proportioned either, fat with insulation in some places, thin where we ran out. Still, the shelter looks sturdy enough, and somewhat snug. Soon, maybe, it'll feel something like home.

James walks to the edge of the woods and surveys our new neighborhood: bridges to the north and south. To the east, a high bluff, on top of which looms the last row of houses this side of the river—old two- and three-story houses, which, from the rear, illumined by security lights, appear rundown. Dogs are barking in the backyards. Maybe they've spotted him.

At the bottom of the steep bluff are maybe a half dozen sets of railroad tracks, then the weedy field sloping gently to his feet. Then, not far beyond camp, there's the water treatment plant, and finally the river, with the Bottoms picking up on the other side.

What do you think goes on around here, James asks himself, after the sun's gone down?

community

(**early evening.**) Out by the railroad tracks James meets two middle-aged anglos, headed "up top," as they say, to a convenience store for beer. They already know about our camp. The more slightly built of the two, eyeing James, says, "I don't wanna know your story, and I don't wantcha to know mine." "Hey man, no problem," James says, holding up his hands as if looking down the barrel of a gun.

The other, stouter guy is circling like a caged cat, blowing into his hands for warmth. "I'm Rooster," he says, in a not unfriendly tone, "and this here's Jake."

James introduces himself. The three men shake hands all around.

Jake says, "Who's your woman?"

"Her name's Phyllis," James says, amazed at how much the men already know. His mind flashes to me, tooling up the highway to Illinois. Were he in my place, gone from the streets, he doubts he'd have the strength to come back.

"Hey," he says to the guys, "we gonna be alright down here? The cops gonna bother us?"

"Naw," Jake says, suddenly all smiles, "don't worry 'bout the cops. But we gotta look after each other. We're all in this together. We gotta little community here. There's Benny, who sleeps under the bridge—he's a security guard, works nights—and there's ol' man Calvin, next to you. Then there's me and my buddy Sarge, and there's Rooster here, and Enid, his ol' lady— hell, there's people all up and down this river."

The men light up smokes, offer James one, as they watch a slow train coming down the tracks; only three cars. As it rolls to a stop, Rooster says, "If ya need anything, these railroad guys'll help ya." He and Jake step up closer to the train, and a crewman reaches down, hands each of them a courtesy kit, standard issue to railroad workers: toilet paper, bottled water, first aid supplies, earplugs. Both guys give their kits to James, along with a half dozen signal flares—"good," they say, "for startin' campfires."

"Hey," Jake says now, "we may getta visit from Harold and Ada later. They bring food and stuff down here to help us out—"

"Ah, fuck 'em," says Rooster. "They should keep to themselves—"

"'Scuze me, Rooster," Jake interrupts, "but I'm *tryin'* to talk to our new neighbor here." Rooster scowls. Jake grins. "*Anyway*, as I was sayin', Harold and Ada can help ya out, James, and you can let *me* know, too, if ya need anything. Alright?"

"Yeah, thanks guys," James says, starting to walk away. "Have a good night."

"Hey man, ya need another tarp for your camp?" Rooster calls after him.

"Yeah."

"Well, there's an old green one under the bridge, there. It's all yours. Yeah, and there's a carpet factory up on the corner, there. You might wanna look in their dumpster, see if ya can get some remnants to lay over the ground. That ground gets *cold.*"

76

"something like home":
rough sketch of the shelter built on the riverbank

sheltered

(**camp, evening.**) Outside our makeshift shelter James brushes his teeth, then yanks off his boots and crawls in. Lighting our only candle, a gift from the streets, he wedges it into the hole of an empty soda can, then sets the can down in a boot to keep it steady. Can't be too careful, he warns himself; this place is a firetrap.

He pulls out some scratch paper, starts jotting down notes about the day. Now and then he raises his eyes to scan the ceiling and walls, still praying they're watertight. The plastic sparkles with candlelight.

He's uneasy. Despite himself, his thoughts keep returning to our first night on the streets, bedded down under the bushes outside the ODB. Will tonight be any less an initiation?

The shelter sits on a slight slope, he notices now. He struggles to get comfortable, adjusting the layers of cardboard and plastic beneath him on the floor, but nothing helps. Finally he gives up, blows out the candle, buries himself under the blankets, pulls them over his head. In the darkness he imagines Phoebe's hand playing with a strand of his hair, nestling in the small of his back. . . .

Totally spent, he free-falls into sleep.

big mama

(**late evening.**) "James! Hey, James! Harold and Ada's here. Wouldya like to meet `em?"

It's Jake's voice, just outside the shelter. James rouses himself, groggily pulls on his boots, still half in a dream.

Headlights dissect the night woods. Jake leads James up to the field, where stand a dozen or so people, mostly teenagers—Carl, Jane, Brian, Tim, Brenda, Louis. . . . Nobody named Harold or Ada.

"Now," Jake says to the group, in a parental tone, "I shoulda checked with James before I called 'im out. He may've wanted some privacy. It's not proper etiquette to impose—"

"It's quite alright, Jake," James reassures him, but Jake's a gracious go-between, and he's wearing a big grin, now, watching all these people so eager to help the new guy on the block. The group presents James with candles, a flashlight, a blanket, a meal in a styrofoam box. Overwhelmed, James is speechless. The kids ask him if he needs anything else. "I could really use a sleepin' bag," he says, dreaming big, and immediately an adult retrieves one from a truck. James can't believe the kindness. His first night on the riverbank feels like a poor man's Christmas.

The kids direct James's attention to a black Blazer parked nearby, urging him to go say hello to Ada Martin, the woman they affectionately call Big Mama. She organized this volunteer effort, they tell him, along with her husband Harold, who was unable to come tonight.

Ada rolls down her window as James walks up. Chronically ill, she can't be out in the cold. She's big-boned, black, with a pretty, round face and gorgeous eyes. She asks for a hug. James leans in as far as he can, and she gives him a tight squeeze, says, "We love ya, baby. We'll see ya again soon."

day 10: friday, february 26

neighbor

(camp, early morning.) James meets our closest neighbor for the first time. He lives almost directly beneath our shelter—a rolypoly groundhog. He always looks both ways before making a move. Rarely does he stare straight ahead.

carpetbagger

(mid-morning.) Behind a carpet factory James tugs and wrestles large remnants out of the trash bin, enough to thickly cover the cardboard-plastic floor of our shelter. He's stuffing them into two long, durable plastic bags when a cream-colored Acura pulls up. A white man steps out, glaring.

"Can I have these scraps?" James asks.

"Yeah, okay," the man says, after a moment's thought, "but if my boss comes out, I said nothin' of the kind."

James hurries.

Behind the dumpster is a steep sixty-foot slope dotted with briar bushes, strewn with trash. He flips the clumsy bags end over end down the hill, dodging broken-legged chairs, upended shopping carts and soggy mattresses, dislodging them from sticky briars with swift kicks.

At the bottom of the hill, he heaves the first bag over his shoulder like a wounded comrade-in-arms and lumbers off toward camp, maybe a half mile away. By the time he drops it in front of our shelter, his shoulders and back are stiff and sore, but he's excited, and returns at once for the second bag.

(camp, late morning.) The slamming of car doors. The squelch and static of walky-talkies. James peers out the shelter door, heart racing. Two squad cars, up in the field. His gut turns. Are the cops here to roust him? He sinks back on the blankets. Please don't put me out, he thinks—*please*—

The cops head into the woods further down. James waits. After a tense twenty minutes or so, they're back at their cars, and soon on their way. Who, or what, he wonders, brought them down?

bums

(ohio statehouse, early afternoon.) After meditating at the Statue of Peace, James walks into the capitol to use the restroom. Noticing a neat stack of toilet paper rolls, he grabs one for camp. Somehow it seems fitting, not at all stealing, to let the State of Ohio care for our bums.

bed-in-a-sack

(downtown, afternoon.) In a dumpster on the Franklin University campus, giant bags of shredded paper. Grabbing two of them, James sets out on the long hike back to camp, knowing just what to do. This morning he scavenged two garment bags from the boxes at JOIN. Once he stuffs them with shredded paper, they'll serve as mattresses.

On Front Street, James passes by an ivy leaguer putting a squash racket into the trunk of his car, a forest-green Infinity buffed to a high shine. A few hours ago, James had encountered this same man just as he was climbing out from behind the wheel, his teeth clenching a fat cigar, a Harvard v-neck sweater under his suit-coat. The man had thrown James a sneer before turning turned up the sidewalk toward a law office.

Now, though, James chuckles. The man has changed into a jock's clothes. Pale, hairy legs show under his tan trench coat: the very image of a mad flasher. The eyes of the two men meet. No sneer this time. The ivy leaguer seems embarrassed to have been seen in public wearing duds other than suit and tie.

corpse

(riverbank, evening.) James meets up with Jake and Rooster along the tracks. Rooster tells him the cops crashed his camp this morning after receiving a report that somebody had carried a dead body into the woods. "Them cops," Rooster says, "they come right into my tent, pulled me outa bed! Grilled me good."

Good God, James says to himself, did somebody on the hilltop spot me lugging one of those bags of carpet, and think it was a corpse?

80

day 11: saturday, february 27

urges

(camp, early morning.) With the subtlety of a drill sergeant, James's bowels roust him out of bed. Every inch of his body is sore, reluctant to move, but he's got to hurry. The nearest bathroom, at White Castle, is a brisk ten minutes' walk from camp: south along the tracks; then, at the bridge, up a steep embankment to street level, where traffic is already picking up, early birds on their way to work, night owls on their way home. Headlights blitz James's swollen morning eyes.

Since hitting the streets, James and I have both been at the mercy of our bowels. Some days constipation, other days diarrhea; always, it seems, the urge, especially when we're farthest from a toilet. We regularly volunteer status reports and trade tips for promoting healthier bowel movements; bad jokes, too, but they're only jokes by half.

please seat yourself

(mid-morning.) In the dumpster behind Einstein Bros. Bagels, James thrills to see a clear garbage bag, tightly tied, full of day-old bagels still soft to the touch. He pockets two wheat bagels for me, suspecting that I'll soon return from Illinois, and chooses two garlic and onion for himself. Then, strolling around to the front door of the deli, he walks right in, past ogling customers, and casually seats himself at a small table. The shop is warm, yeasty.

Thumbing through a Dispatch, he chews, savoring the crusty flavors. He totally belongs.

in the presence of grace

(mcdonald's on broad street, late morning.) Serendipitous reunion. James waves at me from behind the rain-beaded window, grinning but looking a fright. When I join him inside, he tells me his nights in camp have been tough. Thankfully dry, but terribly cold, and deafening with trains. "Looks like you haven't slept much yourself," he says then.

I sigh.

"Tell me everything," he says. "Start with Grace. Who was she, exactly?"

I smile, a little. The irony of the name. *Yes, who were you, Grace, exactly?*

"She was an o-girl at the shelter," I say wearily, then add, in understatement, "but I didn't really know her."

You and I had never spoken at the shelter—you seemed wary of everybody, and proud—but twice we'd met. One night, overhearing you ask a staffer for a toothbrush, I'd given you a brand-new Oral-B, still in the box, found just that day on the sidewalk. Another night you'd arrived at the shelter after all the bedding was taken, and I gave you my tattered orange afghan. You never said a word during these exchanges, never made eye contact. Your back was ramrod straight, your bearing dignified, your eyes cast down. Sensing your humiliation, I'd wondered who you were.

Early Thursday morning, as I was leaving the women's shelter for the last time, I saw you again. I was cutting through an empty lot to the bus stop, and there you were, an attractive young black woman in a tailored red coat, clutched against the cold behind a donut shop. Although I didn't know your name and would presumably never see you again, moving as I was to the riverbank, something compelled me to shout into the icy wind, wish you a good day. You didn't respond. Maybe you didn't hear.

"Later that same morning," I tell James, "I bumped into her at JOIN. I didn't recognize her at first. Not till I noticed her red coat, and the way she avoided my gaze, even as she greeted me, drew me aside."

"May I speak with you?" you said, very politely. Precise diction, and an accent; African, I thought.

"You are the one who gave me the toothbrush?" you asked, finally meeting my eyes, and I nodded. You said, "Do you have a driver's license?"

"Yes."

"Are you a good driver?"

"Yes."

"Do you have insurance?"

At this I hesitated (which world am I living in?), *then told you I wasn't* sure.

Your name, you said, was Grace.

"She wanted to move to Rockford, Illinois," I explain to James, "northwest of Chicago. She wanted to make a fresh start." My voice is thin, raspy, from exhaustion. I swallow hard, summoning more energy for words. "Problem was, her belongings, which were in storage, needed to be trucked out, and she didn't know how to drive. She asked me if I'd do it."

"Just like that?" James's eyebrows shoot up, and I nod.

Your boldness startled me. "There's nobody else to take you?" I said. "A friend? A relative?"

"No, I have asked everyone I know. Please," you said, the begging obviously a disgrace, "I am desperate."

82

I believed you. "When ya wantin' to leave?" I asked.

"Late this afternoon—maybe five o'clock."

"That soon. . . ." I thought of James, of our shelter on the riverbank not yet complete. So much to do, so little time, the cold dark only hours away. "Do you already have a truck?"

"Yes, I have rented a truck," you said.

"Standard or automatic?"

"When she said the truck was an automatic," I say to James, "that pretty much cinched it. I couldn't 've driven a stick. I asked 'er how I'd get back to Columbus, and she promised to buy me a bus ticket."

"Risky," James says.

I shift uncomfortably in my seat. It offers no give. "Yeah, well. . . . Anyway, after I left you at camp that afternoon, I met up with 'er, and she got us on a bus out to the east side. Wound up at a U-Haul rental, where we needed to get her boxes loaded into a ten-foot truck. Mosta the boxes, in a storage unit out back, were too big for us to move."

You wanted to pick up some guys off the street to do the labor. You insisted. So, despite serious misgivings, I cruised the neighborhood, daylight fading fast, while beside me in the cab you prayed fervently for a few good, strong men. Prayed to no avail. After half an hour, I managed to convince you that we should return to U-Haul, offer a tip to one of the employees for his help. I knew that you could afford it. At the bus stop I'd noticed the thick roll of cash in your purse.

"It was all of seven o'clock before Grace and I finally drove away from U-Haul. But I have to tell ya, James, once we got goin' on the highway, it felt great, havin' my hands on the wheel of that truck. Movin' at more than pedestrian speed. Watchin' the lights of the city fadin' in my rearview mirror. I was feelin' pretty good, till all at once I remembered you—your first night in camp, and I had no idea what you were goin' through. After that, there was no leavin' the streets behind, no matter how many miles I drove."

You wanted me to drive the estimated 350 miles to Rockford straight through. I told you I'd try. You'd brought a few snacks; I was terribly hungry, had eaten nothing since late morning, but I carefully rationed the chips and crackers you offered, realizing my next real meal could be a long way off.

You told me a little about what you were leaving behind, what you hoped lay ahead. As I listened, the details of your story impressed me less than the ice in your voice. With each mile I grew more uneasy. My anxiety only deepened when you claimed that God had willed every action you'd ever taken in your life. You could do no wrong, you said, so long as you called upon the Lord—

For some reason your voice cut through me like a shard of glass.

My fingers tear at one of the bagels James has brought me, mindlessly reducing it to pieces. "A couple of hours up the highway," I tell him, "Grace and I stopped for a fill-up, and our truck died, right there at the pump. Not even a click when I turned the key. I called U-Haul, and they said a certified mechanic would have to check it out. There we were, parked at a service station, and we had to wait for 'em to dispatch a tow truck from forty-five minutes away!"

At long last, around 10:30, a jump. Back on the road. You dozed in fits. I pressed hard on the intractable gas pedal, trying to ignore the throbbing ache in my bum right knee, scarred by three surgeries. Testy ever since my fourteen-mile hike on Ash Wednesday, the knee was now swelling up stiff. Pain was shooting up through my thigh, burning into my hip. Keeping me awake, at least.

A long, groaning rumble from my stomach. "Why don'tcha eat?" James says, gesturing at the remains of my bagel. "Can't seem to eat," I say. "Maybe in awhile."

I reach for my cup of hot water, begged at the counter. "Sometime after midnight," I pick up the story, "we pulled over again for gas. Truck stop, this time. Grace wandered off toward the restrooms. I paced the tarmac, stretched, tried to limber up. Then, when I went to get back in the truck, I discovered that Grace had locked the keys in the cab."

Across the table, James groans.

"Somebody called the sheriff for help. He got there around one-thirty in the morning. Really had to work to getta door unlocked—almost gave up too soon—but finally he got in. Grace and I climbed into the cab, anxious to be gone. I turned the key—and there was nothin'. *Nothin'!*"

"What a nightmare," James says softly.

I negotiated with U-Haul for an hour before they agreed to allow the mechanics there at the truck stop to look under the hood. The chief mechanic had a hunch, painstakingly detailed, about what might be wrong. Daft with exhaustion, I couldn't comprehend what he was saying. Meanwhile, you stood across the room in a pout, clearly blaming me for all our misfortunes. When I spoke to you, asked you questions, you scarcely responded.

"The repair will take several hours," the mechanic said. "Why don'tcha both get some sleep?"

"By then," I say to James, "it was around three a.m. Eight hours since we'd left Columbus. We shoulda been in Rockford. Instead, we were spendin' the night in a truck stop lounge. Sleepin' in orange plastic chairs bolted to the floor."

"When'd ya finally get goin' again?"

"A little before sun-up. Chief mechanic told me as we were gettin' ready to go that the truck was 'a heapa junk'. Warned me not to shut the engine off before we got to where we were goin'. So we took off—" I drop my head into my hands for a moment— "and just a coupla hours down the road, we got lost."

I could feel it. So close to Rockford, and now we were going the wrong way, even though you insisted we weren't. You wouldn't allow me to consult your map. With your back against your door, you stared at me non-stop, as if I were a demon you didn't know how to exorcize. I tried not to look at you. Kept my eyes on the road. The pain in my leg was torture.

In the middle of nowhere, we approached a ramshackle service station. The fuel gauge was well above empty, but I lied, told you that we needed to stop for gas.

I fueled the truck with the engine running.

Inside the service station, I asked the kindly proprietor how to get to Rockford. "You'll have to turn around," he said. "Rockford's about an hour and a half back. Can't miss it."

I close my eyes, press them against the heels of my hands, trying to relieve the sting of bloodshot. Suddenly I feel like I'm dreaming. My sleep-deprived mind, playing tricks. Under the table I force my bad leg to stretch out straight. The pain makes my jaw clench. I regain my wits.

"So finally," I say to James, "we get to Rockford. Now, Grace had told me she'd arranged to store her belongings at a Baptist church while she found a place to live. But when we arrived at the church, around ten o'clock, the staff didn't know what arrangements she was talkin' about. We waited for three hours, till the minister showed up. He told us there'd been an 'unfortunate misunderstanding'. Grace would have to find storage space elsewhere."

As I drove away from the church, still reeling from the minister's words, you suddenly presented me with a crisp $20 bill from your wad of cash. Empty as my pockets were, the money in my hand scarcely made an impression. After nearly twenty hours on the road, and with scarcely any sleep in over thirty, I was in a numb fog. Beyond hungry. Beyond feeling the pain in my leg. I was just trying to drive. Every step on the brake, every flip of the turn signal, every press on the accelerator was an act of will.

At a facility across town you rented a storage unit. Then we cruised the streets till you spotted a skinny, shabbily dressed white man, maybe retirement age, collecting aluminum cans along the roadside. You ordered me to stop and ask him if he'd help us unload. I pulled over but refused to speak for you. I didn't want any part of it. I was only there to drive.

You made your pitch charmingly through the window. He fell for it. "I got emphysema," he said, climbing in, "but I'll do what I can." You didn't tell him what I already knew, that you wouldn't be paying him a tip for his trouble. Just like you didn't pay the U-Haul guy.

By the time the three of us got the truck unloaded, the man was breathing hard, coughing up thick phlegm. His insulated sweatshirt was soaked through. "That was a work-out," he gasped, wiping his wet forehead on his sleeve.

Back in the truck, you instructed me to drop the man off where we first found him. When he got out, he waited expectantly at the door. You shook his hand, thanked him for his time, and abruptly pulled the door shut.

Driving away, I watched the old man growing small in my rearview mirror. He bent over, hands on knees, and stood like that till I couldn't see him anymore. An instrument of the Lord's will.

The $20 you'd paid me was burning in my pocket.

Now I slide Grace's $20 bill across the table to James, a sad confirmation of events. James stares, doesn't touch the money.

"We dropped off the truck at U-Haul, then walked a coupla blocks through drizzle to the nearest bus stop, to catch a bus to the Greyhound terminal."

You stood far from me. The air was thick. I didn't understand what had happened between us, didn't have the energy to figure it out. C'mon, bus.

Suddenly you strode over to me, waved a $10 bill in my face. "Take it," you said, the command like the cold snap of a steel trap.

"No, you keep it. I wasn't expectin' to get paid for drivin'. Just a bus ticket home."

"Take it."

"You already gave me twenty dollars."

"So?"

"So I don't need any more money. Besides, you're gonna need all the money you got to start over."

"Don't take it then," you said. You stuffed the bill into your coat pocket. Then, with a voice dripping venom, you said, "Many people would be grateful if I tried to give them money."

I drew a deep breath. "Look, Grace, I'm sorry. If it means that much to you, I'll take the money. I was just tryin' to be helpful. I thought you might need the money more—"

"No! It is too late now. You did not want the money, so you are not getting it!"

The energy around us was crazy. I was spinning. "Grace," I said, "have I offended you somehow? Are you angry at me about somethin'?"

"Angry?" you hissed. "Why do you think I'm angry?"

"Your tone of voice. Your silences. Your starin' at me in the truck—"

"This is your evidence? It means nothing. Nothing! Don't you think I am grateful to you for bringing me here?"

Your question reeked with sarcasm. Irritated, losing my calm, I said, "No, Grace, I don't. You've paid me some money, but you don't seem at all grateful—"

"Stop it!" you shrieked. "Just stop it! I do not want to hear anymore. Just be quiet!"

Furious, you strutted off, then stood with your back turned to me, waiting for the bus, your red coat darkening in the pelting rain.

"At Greyhound," I tell James, "Grace bought two tickets. She kept one, threw the other at my feet, then took a seat across the lobby. I picked my ticket up, made sure I was bound for Columbus, turned it over and over in my hands. Such relief!"

"Where was *she* goin'?"

I shrug. "I wondered about that. I mean, it was almost dark. All her stuff was in storage. I don't know what she was doin'."

A few moments of silence, then James asks when I finally got back to Columbus.

"This morning, around four," I say. "Thirty-three hours after I drove out of Columbus." I lean back in my seat, flex the ankle in my bad leg.

"Where'd ya go, at that hour?"

"Nowhere. It was pourin' down rain, it was dark, it was cold, my knee was sore and swollen—no way I was goin' anywhere. I settled into a chair in the terminal, hopin' to nap till sunup. *That* was a mistake—"

Pain explodes—

Jolted from a restless sleep, I groan, clutch at my bad knee. Somebody's just kicked it, and hard.

"Got some proof ya gotta right to be here?" a man's voice growls.

Dazed, I can't comprehend what's happening. "I'm sorry," I say, squinting up at the voice, finally making out a security guard, "but what exactly d'ya want from me?"

"Why ya here?" he says, his eyes like a mean dog's.

"I got off the bus a little while ago. It's not safe to just go out wanderin' the streets at this hour."

"Got your ticket to prove it?"

"Yeah. Here—" I dig my crumpled ticket out of my coat pocket.

"Ain't nobody pickin' you up?" he says, studying it. "Ain't no place else ya can go?"

"No, sir. I'll be leavin' soon as it gets light."

"Make sure ya do."

"I watched him go. He strolled by other sleeping people with complete indifference. Understandable, I guess. They didn't look anything like me."

Tears are bright in James's eyes. Seeing them, a knot rises in my throat, won't budge.

"Of all that happened on that trip," I say finally, "the thing I don't understand is the drastic change in Grace. I can't stop thinkin' about it. We were gettin' along just fine, and then—well—*something* happened. Somehow I feel betrayed."

two cups

(**mcdonald's on s. high street, late afternoon.**) "Couldya spare two cupsa hot water?" James asks the lady behind the counter as I'm settling into a booth. She pours the water, is about to hand him the styrofoam cups, when her manager stops her, tells her to charge 30¢. James says, truthfully, "I've only got one penny in my pocket." The lady glances at her boss, lowers her eyes, says, "Sorry, I can't serve you," and tosses the cups of steaming water into the trash can.

calvin

(**late afternoon.**) Einstein Bros. closes for the day. Returning to the deli's dumpster, James retrieves the garbage bag of bagels he'd discovered this morning. Then, heading back to the riverbank, he plays Santa along the tracks, dropping off bagels at various camps, leaving a few in plain sight when nobody's home.

Approaching a tent camp, he calls out, "Hello, anybody in there?"

No answer.

"Hel-*lo*," he repeats.

After a couple seconds a gruff voice says flatly, "What."

"Hey man, d'ya want any bagels?"

A grizzled old man, in his seventies maybe, sticks his head out the tent, says, "Whaddya want?"

"I've got some bagels. D'ya want any?"

"Can't eat 'em. My teeth's bad."

James nods, lowers the heavy bag from his shoulder. "I'm James. What's your name?"

"Calvin."

"Nice to meetcha, Calvin."

"Yeah, yeah."

"I just built the camp down the way."

"Yeah," the man says, "I noticed. Ain't there a woman with ya?"

"Yeah, her name's Phyllis."

"Ya'll met Jake and Rooster?"

"Yep."

"Well, be careful. They use drugs and liquor, make lotsa noise at night. I don't go over there. I stay away from 'em, much as I can."

88

"Ok, Calvin, thanks for the warnin'. I'll be careful. See ya later."

"Ok, `bye," the man says, and the tent flap drops back.

etiquette

(rooster's camp, early evening.) Dinnertime. Rooster (minus Enid) and Jake (minus Sarge) have offered to cook us spaghetti. The two men build a fire in a deep-bellied charcoal grill, fill a dirty cookpot with water from a jug and set it over the flames to boil. A little tipsy, they disagree on everything—how much wood they should feed the fire, how much time they should boil the pasta, whether to put hot dogs in the sauce. . . .

Time groans by. The day's been too long. Silently James and I weigh our desire for food—*hot* food—against our need for sleep, while Jake lectures us on neighborhood etiquette. "We're all in this together," Jake says, stirring a pan of spaghetti sauce. "Everybody watches out for everybody's stuff. Just try to keep your place neat, and don't make a big fire or the people up on the hill will call the cops. Don't use water from the river—it's damn polluted. If ya scrape up enough money for a night at a motel, invite everybody to come and clean up, hang out, watch tv, that kinda thing—"

The water's still not boiling. At this rate, we'll be eating at midnight.

"Everybody out here's gotta story," Jake says. "You don't need to know ours, and we don't wanna know yours—"

This rule is immediately broken. Jake and Rooster start speculating, affably, on what might have brought James and me to the riverbank. James, they decide, is probably just down on his luck; me, they can't figure. With few women living along the river, they have few stock stories to choose from.

They tell us they'll soon be leaving town. Jake's wanting to avoid a jail sentence for a misdemeanor, and Rooster, in trouble with his old street gang as well as the cops, will tag along. "Got some money comin' in," they say, "that'll pay our way to Florida."

Now, though, they want to go up top for more beer and smokes. James and I are to stay behind, keep the fire going. Rooster leans over and whispers loudly in James's ear, "If there's any trouble while we're gone, there's a nine-millimeter in my tent, under my pillow." He pats James reassuringly on the shoulder, then disappears with Jake into the dark.

Uneasily James and I tend the fire, watch the pot that never boils.

not for profit

(rooster's camp, mid-evening.) Headlights sweep. Car doors slam. Anxious voices seep down into the woods. Rooster, afraid of cops, hightails

89

it toward the river. "It's just them people from Take It to the Streets," Jake hollers after him, but Rooster's already gone.

I've heard of Take It to the Streets, a nonprofit organization founded years ago by Harold and Ada Martin. Over the years the local news has regularly reported the group's ministries among homeless people, especially those living on the streets. Most of its volunteers are recruits from Columbus churches. As fate would have it, James encountered Ada Martin (*a k a* Big Mama) and a troupe of teenage volunteers his very first night on the riverbank. Now, only two evenings later, another visit.

These volunteers, led by Sabrina Martin, daughter of Harold and Ada, are mostly middle-aged adults. They've brought us lunch-meat sandwiches, hot soup, candles, prayers. Next time, they say, they'll try to bring more blankets.

Sabrina draws me aside, discreetly asks, "D'ya have everything ya need, y'know, as a woman?"

stalked

(camp, middle of the night.) Exhausted as I am, sleep is out of reach. We're constantly assaulted by noise. During one short stretch, a train rumbles past so loudly that our shelter shakes, a low-flying plane drones, a police helicopter chops over, hot rods burn rubber and sirens scream on streets up top, highway traffic buzzes along on the interstate. . . . The noise peels off in layers but never strips all the way down to silence.

Maybe you couldn't bear it, if it did.

The claustrophobia that attacked me our first night on the streets is back again, and stronger. Little more than twelve inches separate my face from the ceiling of the shelter. The air is close. Bundled in four layers of clothes, buried beneath blankets, I feel tangled up, caught in a net. Every so often I squirm out the shelter door into a cold rain, squat and urinate in the dead weeds, grateful to breathe.

day 12: sunday, february 28

welcome

(early morning.) On the way to breakfast at Central Presbyterian Church, James and I make a pit stop at the Greyhound Bus Terminal. I'm nervous, going in; the last time I was here, a security guard kicked me.

I clean up a little in the restroom. When I return to the lobby, a security guard—a whitehaired old black man, this time—is waiting for me.

"Ya don't have no business bein' here," he says. Part-statement, part-question.

"No, sir, just passin' through."

"There'll be no more *passin' through*, ya hear? Next time I catch ya I'll call the cops. Ya don't wanna be goin' to jail, now, do ya?"

"No, sir. I'm sorry. I won't do it again."

"Okay. Thanks for listenin'."

"You're welcome."

I turn to go.

"Wait—miss—"

The old black man sidles up to me, lowers his voice, says, "I'm gonna tell ya how to get 'round this here thing, but don't tell nobody I told ya."

"I won't," I say.

"See that fast-food joint just inside the terminal doors? Them restrooms in there is public. Can't nobody stop ya from goin' in there. Ya can get yourself some hot water and sit in there all day long if ya want. Don't tell nobody I told ya, now."

Meanwhile, in the men's room, James is in trouble. Some rowdies, up to no good, have kicked in the door of his stall, then the fellow's next to him, taunting and menacing the two men before moving on to hassle a third guy at the sink. Wild-eyed, they look to James like gang members who partied all night.

He hurries to leave. Their shouts follow him out the restroom door.

Out in the lobby the old security guard immediately accosts him, says, "You ain't allowed in this terminal. Leave now. Ya got no business bein' here."

As James is being rousted, the rowdies spill out of the restroom. Passing by the guard, one of them sticks out his tongue. The guard turns away, says nothing.

robbed

(central presbyterian church, mid-morning.) Hot, thick oatmeal with milk, butter and brown sugar. I've never noticed how real butter spoils the palate. Now I crave it. My tongue soaks it up. Across from me, James licks his lips, grinning like a cat.

Our friend Jeff, who inspired our move to the riverbank, pulls out a chair. His glasses are cracked, the frames taped together. Tiny red cuts score a purple bruise over his right cheekbone. "Maddy got robbed last night," he says. "She always holds the money I make, but she's not smart about it. I tried to fight 'em off.

"I just don't know what to do," he says in frustration. "We try to get our act together but this kinda stuff keeps happenin'. We prob'ly shouldna been where we was, but y'know how it is. We both like to party a little. We get stupid when we been drinkin'."

"Is Maddy okay?" we ask.

"Yeah, just sleepin' it off."

We ask Jeff if he got the bricklaying job for which he recently interviewed. When he'd told us about the interview, his eyes had been eager. "I like physical work," he said. "I like usin' my hands. It's been hard, waitin' to hear."

Now he shakes his head. "I lost out," he says. "The company didn't have no way to get in touch with me. What's a guy s'posed to do when he doesn't have a phone?"

preaching

(**st. joseph cathedral, late morning.**) In his homily the priest says how sometimes there's no logic, no reason to suffering; it's simply a mystery, nothing more can be said. I draw new comfort from this familiar idea. Self-pity, even a vague resentment, has been dogging me since I got back from Illinois. *Grace, why had our trip unfolded as it did? Why had you grown more hostile with each passing mile? Why can't I forget your red coat, darkening in the rain?*

Maybe "Why?" is a child's question. Give it up. Move on. Grace was there, you were there; what happened, happened. That's all.

Tired tears burn. The choir's gentle chant floats down from the balcony in a minor key. Finally, on the last chord, the song resolves, tenderly, to hard-won joy.

When you try to help somebody, you can't invest yourself in a particular outcome. You can't even hope for a grateful response. If you want to help, you just try to help—period. Without conditions. Without expectations, either of yourself or the other. Sometimes you'll make mistakes. Sometimes you won't be appreciated. You might even get hurt. That's life. Still, you do it. You offer yourself up, even to be broken, like bread upon some altar—

This is what I preach to myself, sitting up a little straighter in the pew.

browsing

(**main library, early afternoon.**) Drenching downpour. The granite frieze above the front entrance reads, OPEN TO ALL. James takes refuge.

Third floor, as usual. Nearby in the stacks a woman is browsing for a book. Lost in thought, she cups her hands around her breasts through her sweater. James's eyes swell with tears. "I miss Phoebe," he whispers, nobody to overhear.

Phyllis on the front steps of St. Joseph Cathedral
(*The swirls of light are parishioners passing by her
during the long exposure.*)

shadows

(**camp, evening.**) Heavy rain drips and splats on tarp and plastic. Inside our shelter, we're dry, but somber as a dark room when the fire's died out. James props up his injured left ankle, gingerly presses the swollen flesh. Tonight, crossing the tracks on his way to camp, he hopped a rail, and the ankle gave. "I've had worse sprains," he says, "but I sure didn't need this." Our one candle flickers, throws petty shadows.

day 13: monday, march 1

clean

(**early morning.**) Daybreak: Quickly up top to White Castle, where I use the toilet, then down a back alley to SuperAmerica to shampoo my hair and dry it briefly under the hand dryer, then back to White Castle to brush my teeth and clean up a little, maybe even wash out my underwear, if I'm lucky. Too much time spent in any one bathroom spells trouble, I've learned, especially if it's a single. You lock the door behind you, and soon a manager comes banging and hollering for you to get out.

I'm making do with spitbaths. ("Birdbaths," Jake calls them.) I could take a shower at one of the women's shelters downtown, but only if I put myself on a list and hang around the building till 9:00 p.m., hoping to get a turn before the bathrooms are closed to non-residents for the night. Afterwards, I'd have to hike all the way back to camp in the dark—not the smartest thing for a woman to do, especially on the riverbank.

James has a much easier time of it. The showers at the men's shelters aren't necessarily pleasant, but at least they're available to non-residents during daylight hours.

tramp

(**riverbank.**) The railroad tracks, we've decided, would be a quicker way to the Grubb Street soup kitchen than our usual street route. We set off for lunch in mid-morning. Getting anywhere out here takes time; you can't just get in your car or hop on a bus. Our legs are racking up seven or eight miles a day, especially now that we're camped on the riverbank. Ankles and knees, even the healthy ones, groan.

I tramp the uneven ties north. James hitches on his sprained ankle alongside the railroad bed, grateful for the crushed coal soft underfoot, fine as black sand. We both feel a consolation, being out here: nobody staring at us, or studiously ignoring us; no traffic to dodge; little noise but for the occasional train.. "If I closed my eyes," James says, "I could almost be walkin' a New England beach, deserted in winter."

good move

(holy family soup kitchen, lunchtime.) Across the table from me are a young black man, his six year-old daughter and four year-old son. They just arrived in Columbus a few months ago from Florida. "Things are startin' to come together for us now," the man tells me. "At least," he says, "I hope so."

The girl is combing her hair with her fingers. Her young face is beautiful. I pull from my coat pocket a big pink comb I got at the women's shelter, reach it across the table. "Wouldya like to have this?" I ask.

Her eyes light up. She stretches out her hand.

"Thanks," says her father, snatching the comb away. "I can really use that."

The girl stares at the tabletop; no pout, just a blank stare. She doesn't eat another bite.

"You have kids?" the father asks me.

"No," I say.

"Good move," he says.[12]

dealt

(riverbank, late afternoon.) In the silence under the bridge south of camp, a joker lost from a card deck lies atop a pile of broken and empty forties, some of the bottles still sheathed in brown paper bags. "For some reason," James says to me, "scenes like this don't make it into beer commercials."

A dirty piece of tablet paper slides down the nearby embankment, dealt by the wind's hand. "Journal Entry #2," by a schoolboy named Michael: "You should have the right to do what ever you want to do. like a whit person want to hang out with a black person. Other people shouldn't think about what you do they should think about what they do."

staying (2)

(camp, early evening.) Sundown, one to two inches of new snow on the ground. I dread this time of day. In another hour or so, James and I will say goodnight, and soon after snuffing out the candle I keep bedside,

95

pile of empty forties under the bridge south of camp

the claustrophobia will begin to stalk me down. Nothing keeps it at bay for long, once I'm in the dark—not even imagining Jihong's body against mine, though every night I feel him teaspooning me, more real than a memory. This is a peculiar suffering: the enemy is in my own mind. My last defense, at the point of panic, is to grope for a match, relight the candle. Like a pesky demon the phobia shrinks back a little from the candle's glimmer, and I huddle there, rocking, as James sleeps, my arms wrapped tightly around my knees, as if otherwise my body might fly apart—

I lay prayerful hands on James's puffy ankle. The day's been agonizing, for him.

Still, though we're both hobbled a bit, we're surviving. We have a roof over our heads; we're relatively warm enough at night, even if we wake each morning to a coating of frost on the ceiling and walls; each day we manage to get a little rest and some food. . . . We've figured out the fundamentals. Wryly, now, we notice that we've even raised the bar, allowing ourselves to desire more and better than we've got. Our shelter should be warmer, dryer; our food more tasty, not so stale.

In the days that remain, I suspect, our greatest adversity may not be physical. One way or another, we'll manage to maintain our bodies. But will our minds be able to cope; our hearts, to bear up; our spirits, to resist despair? *There, you finally said it. Even you are feeling despair.*

"D'ya ever think about leavin'?" James asks me, lighting a second candle for the heat.

"Of course I do. Every day. Just like you."

"How will ya know if it's time for you to go home?"

"Well, I always ask myself why I'm wantin' to go. Is it because I'd prefer not to be so tired and cold, so scared, so lonely—or is it because I feel compelled to leave, moved by Spirit, just like I did in comin' out? Asking that question always seems to put everything into perspective. Obviously I'd like to be more comfortable. But that's not enough reason to quit. Not for me."

day 14: tuesday, march 2

specimen

(**downtown.**) This morning my spirit is fragile, easily wounded. As I walk along Broad Street under a warm sun, resentment surges. One minute I feel like a specimen under a microscope—stared at, mostly from cars. The next minute, being shunned by pedestrians, I feel utterly invisible. Maybe they don't look at me because my appearance disgusts them, or maybe they're afraid I'll beg; maybe they don't want to enter my pain, and one look at me is all it would take. Whatever the reason, they do their best not to see me, while my warped reflection fills their sunglasses:

I'm just a lazy bum. I wanna handout, a free ride. I'm a stupid drunk, a strungout junkie. I'm violent, I'm schizo, I'm paranoid. I don't care about anybody but me. I'm on the streets 'cause I wanna be. I'm a lost soul. . . .

Maybe I'm many of these things, maybe none at all—what do you people know? But my worst flaws and frailties aren't so different from yours. Some of *you* are lazy. Some of *you* would like a free ride, buying your lottery tickets, going on game shows, leaping at frivolous lawsuits, obsessing over stocks. Some of *you* are addicts, grappling with hidden cravings, appetites out of control. Some of *you* are violent, especially at home, behind closed doors. Some of *you* are afraid, depressed, messed up in the head. Some of *you* are self-absorbed. Some of *you* have made tragic choices out of desperation, anger, overwhelming grief. Some of *you* feel lost, like me—

You probably don't like admitting these things. Maybe that's why I offend you: I'm a public reminder of your own imperfections; your own shame, even. If you ignore me, maybe you can go on pretending you've got no problems.

But I'll tell you something. Whatever problems you've got, whatever problems I've got, they're not who we are. Nobody's a caricature. You and me, we're human beings. It's just we forget sometimes, and need each other's help remembering.

flesh

(**men's shelter in "the bottoms", early afternoon.**) This city shelter is as big as a warehouse, choked with cigarette smoke. Homeless men sit around asking each other for smokes or quarters, staring at a beat-up tv, staring at the backs of those watching tv. To James, most of the men look like they're waiting around to die.

"Can I take a shower here?" he asks a staffer at the registration desk. "I wish ya would," the staffer jokes, and he loans James some shampoo, a towel and a used bar of soap.

The shower room is filthy. The tile walls are almost black with dirt and mildew stains, the tile floor brown with thick scum. There are eight showerheads, a single drain.

An anglo stands at a nearby sink, staring into the wall mirror. As James watches, the man reaches into his mouth, pulls out a diseased piece of gum— an actual piece of his flesh—and sloughs it off on the edge of the basin. Another anglo walks in, picks up a soiled towel and wipes off his crack pipe.

James hurries to lather up, using a stray pair of jeans as a shower mat. In the end, he says to himself, even getting clean feels dirty.

security

(**downtown, early afternoon.**) Seeking food for our dinner, I head south to Holy Cross Church. The food line hasn't opened yet, but seventy or eighty people are already queued up. (Before I hit the streets, a Columbus cop said to me, "Y'know, homeless people are just like birds. The only thing they care about is fillin' their bellies. They'll flock to wherever the food is, just like a buncha pigeons.")

Weary from the walk, I slink around the corner from the church and sink onto the ground, resting my back against a tenement stoop, grateful for the sunshine on my face. Mothers with infants, elderly men pass by and ask me if I know where the sandwiches are. "You're in the right place," I say. "Just go 'round back."

A short, thinly bearded black man saunters by me, hands buried in pockets. I remember him from Grubb Street. He always wears a Civil War-style cap, Union blue. Several big, shiny badges glint against his blue wool coat.

As he reaches the corner, the man abruptly turns around, comes partway back to me, says, "You okay?" In his get-up, he reminds me of a kindly neighborhood cop on patrol.

"Just restin'," I say with a smile.

"Okay then," he says somberly, moving on. "They'll be startin' the line soon."

The food line runs through an annex to the church. Its primitive foyer is unlit and unheated; a hundred or more of us crowd inside. At the head of the serpentine line, steps descend to a closed basement door. Impatience mounts as the crowd waits for that door to open. Voices rise, toughen; male, mostly. Laughter's shrill, and mean. Arguments break out. Bouts of pushing and shoving. Then, suddenly, shouts—"Security! Security!"

A fight's on, maybe—somebody needs help—

A burst of laughter, now. "Hey, Security!" somebody yells, "Ya gonna save the world? How ya gonna do that?"

They're yelling at Blue Coat. His Union cap is all I can see—he's surrounded by taunting, jostling men. "Hey, Security, where'dya get alla them badges? Lemme have one!"

I can hear his silence, can somehow feel the fierce battle he's waging with himself. It's a battle he can't win. Finally he lashes out, his voice fire and brimstone, his words a crazy babble. He isn't mentally stable, that's clear, and

99

the bullies, delighted to have broken him, egg him on, many in the crowd laughing hysterically, others shrinking back, lowering their eyes, covering their ears—

The man is saved by the basement door, opening at last. The head of the line surges down.

same direction

(riverbank, mid-afternoon.) Meeting Calvin near the railroad tracks, I introduce myself. James has told me about this neighbor of ours: his tent camp, his teeth too bad for bagels, his warning about Jake and Rooster.

"Where ya headed?" I ask casually, since we're walking the same direction.

"Don't like people askin' me where I'm goin'," he says. "'How're you?', or 'How's it goin'?'— that's okay. But when people ask me *where* I'm goin', I say, 'Straight to hell, if I don't straighten out!'"

treasure

(camp, late evening.) Before sleep, a comforting ritual as rain pelts the shelter. James and I each hold a votive candle, naming simple things that brighten our life out here: a treasure found in the trash, sunshine, the affection of an animal, the smell of spices or fresh bread, a lucky penny on the sidewalk, soap, a good bowel movement, a loved one's voice on the phone, the singing of birds at dawn, a cup of water when we're parched, hot water when we're cold. . . .

day 15: wednesday, march 3

the professor

(riverbank.) God, it was cold last night. Once I crawled out to pee in our bucket and found two or three inches of new snow on the ground. Wind whipped my bare bottom.

Fonder of warmer climes, Jake and Rooster left town this morning for Florida. Saying goodbye to them, James and I had mixed feelings. Selfishly, we'll miss them as neighbors—though we've only lived here a week, they've been kind to us—but certainly we wish them a better life down south. Jake told us that his roomie Sarge will continue to live at their shanty. Rooster, with no mention of "his ol' lady" Enid, urged us to move into his tent.

James and I have no interest in relocating, but this afternoon I do go over to claim Rooster's grill. On the path leading into Rooster's camp, I almost collide with the Professor. Bespectacled, a neighbor from further downstream, he has a reputation for being able to answer any question put to him, no matter how trivial. Apparently he's quite the reader. James and I often see him studying in the library.

The day James and I scouted the riverbank for a campsite, we passed by the Professor's place: a refrigerator tipped on its side in the woods, a pair of shoes marking it as a home.

Now the Professor tells me that he's taken up residence in Rooster's tent. His days of sleeping in a refrigerator are now past. "Good for you," I say, instantly abandoning all thoughts of the grill, in case he needs that, too.

day 16: thursday, march 4

war zone

(white castle.) 6:00 a.m. Shivering at the counter, James pulls an empty styrofoam cup out of his coat pocket and asks an employee if she might please fill it with hot water. He's half-afraid of her answer.

"I'm not allowed to accept cups over the counter," the woman says, "but I'll take care of you."

I'll take care of you: so comforting to hear those words from a stranger. He'll bundle them up, carry them with him all day.

"Last night," he says, joining me wearily at a table, "I dreamed I was a soldier in World War I. Got shot in the knees. Got to go home. I was so excited, I woke up—but I was still on the riverbank. My knees were throbbing *really* hard.

"This," he tells me, his eyes full of the streets, "is a war zone of a different sort."

enemy

(riverbank, mid-morning.) The railroad tracks are quiet, contemplative, under fresh feathering snow. James and I trudge into the stiff wind, heads bent, tripping now and then on the snow-covered ties. Left boot down, right boot down. Left, right, left. I watch my plodding feet as if they belong to somebody else.

The wind is just the wind.
The snow is just the snow.
The cold is just the cold.
Don't make them the enemy.

I almost step on it before I see it: a dead dog, glazed with snow, decapitated by a train.

back off

(**holy family soup kitchen, lunchtime.**) The crowd is thinner today, as it has been all week. Government checks are out. For the moment, there's less need. Some people without permanent addresses have their government benefits deposited directly in a bank account; others have them sent to a P.O. box, or to a shelter or social service agency.

James and I begin stockpiling food for the weekend, when this place will be closed. We fill empty eight-ounce yogurt containers with goulash, wrap bread and cookies in napkins and stuff them into our coat pockets. As we work, an anglo on crutches hobbles by our table, soup sloshing on the tray he's trying to carry. I leap up, offer to help.

"Will—do—it—myself," he growls through clenched teeth.

I back off. It's so easy to presume too much.

Ready to leave, James heads up a side aisle to return his tray, only to have his way blocked by a burly black man sprawling in a chair between the table and the wall. James has noticed him here at the soup kitchen before. He always wears an oversized army coat. He always looks mad.

"'Scuze me, buddy," James says.

The man pretends not to hear. Others at the same table tell him, "Scoot up, man! Let the guy pass!" He ignores them.

As gently as he can, James says again, "Hey, man, can I please get by?"

Teeth clenched, the man glares up at him. One good eye, one eye crossed, both of them so glazed they could be cubes in a bar drink. Tension mounts till it's almost unbearable. Finally, with a sneer, the man shifts, just enough, toward the table.

no joke

(**downtown, late afternoon.**) Homeward bound. The workday has ended. Thousands scatter. Our ears catch bits of stock talk, job blues, dinner plans. Outside the upscale City Center Mall, a smartly dressed black man of retirement age tells three black teenage boys in hip-hop jeans, "These streets ain't no joke." Overhearing, James thinks of the joker he saw lying atop the beer bottles under the bridge. Kids, listen to the man, he pleads silently. Take the old guy's words to heart.

jackpot

(**downtown, evening.**) Bathroom emergency on First Avenue. The three-mile walk to a Twelve-Step meeting has churned James up. Passing a church, he tries every front and side door. Locked up tight.

Around back, though, cars are pulling into a full lot. The rear door's busy. Inside the church, a buzzing, smoky auditorium: bingo night. Hundreds of people at the tables, waiting for lucky numbers, packs of smokes stacked beside their game cards.

James lunges for the men's room.

beloved

(**camp, evening.**) Despite the extreme cold and the merciless drafts in the shelter, I'm burning only one votive candle, rationing our supply. We have only one tapered candle and two stubs left.

Breath hangs in the air. I shiver beneath the blankets. The shelter's so much warmer when both of us are here.

I prop Cry, the Beloved Country against a stray shoe. Serious fiction is difficult to digest from the underside. These past nights I've been rummaging around in this book as if it were a trash bin, scrounging for whatever scraps of sustenance might be there, not thinking too much about the story at large. Too much to bear. "There's only one thing," I read now, "that has power completely, and this is love. Because when a man loves, he seeks no power, and therefore he has power—"

Love—

My eyes leave the page.

We're so quick to say that love is patient, and kind, not envious or boastful or rude. It never ends, we say; it bears everything, it believes and hopes and endures—*everything*. But mustn't we also say that love is sometimes impetuous and tough, desirous and brazen; that sometimes it does end, or is at least transmuted; that sometimes it buckles because not yet mature, doubts because there's good reason, despairs because it doesn't yet know how to do more, be more; that sometimes love does in fact give up? Let there be power in confessing: yes, we know love, and not only as children do. We know it in all its glory, but also in its weakness. It's as much heartache as ecstasy, never unsullied. It demands our life, and won't let us go. . . .

This afternoon, to escape the rain, James and I went to the Agora and

103

asked if we could volunteer at the day-center for homeless families. Soon we were washing down grubby plastic chairs. The place was full of children: infants, toddlers, grade schoolers. Among their parents, we recognized Appalachian hillbillies by their accent, Somalis by their dress. Most of the families were huddled around a huge tv screen, eyes glued to The Princess Bride, a fairy tale spoof—entertainment for some, English lesson for others. *Who knows about happy endings—*

Take It to the Streets pays me a call, outside, bringing dinner. Tonight's volunteers are a youth group and their adult leaders from First Community Church. Though nervous, the teenagers seem more open, less inclined to dictate the action, than many of the grownups who have visited our camp. "It's so *cold* out here," they say, "and the weather's been rotten, so why don'tcha stay in a shelter?" When I tell them why, they say it's a familiar story, heard in other camps around the city.

I tell the kids, too, about the significance of seemingly small things, like the simple kindnesses of the railroad crewmen who offer us supplies, and wave at us, and sometimes toot a greeting. "Everything ya do *matters*. Like your comin' out here, and takin' time to talk to me, to treat me with respect even though you don't know me and maybe are a little scared of me—these things *matter.*" Listening, the kids dig their gloved hands deeper in their coats, breathing clouds. They don't look away from me. I feel in their gaze a rich consolation, and tell them so.

They're gone, now. I pick up my book: "Cry the beloved country for the unborn child that is the inheritor of our fear. Let him not love the earth too deeply. Let him not laugh too gladly when the water runs through his fingers, nor stand too silent when the setting sun makes red the veld with fire. Let him not be too moved when the birds of his land are singing, nor give too much of his heart to a mountain or a valley. For fear will rob him of all if he gives too much."

day 17: friday, march 5

blue

(**riverbank, mid-morning.**) Along the railroad tracks north of camp, under a gunmetal gray sky, James and I meet up with a black man. "Name's Blue," he says, reaching out to shake hands. "I've gotta shack in the woods, over there. There's another shack, back of it, not bein' used. You guys can stay there if ya want."

"Thanks," James says, gratefully, speaking for us both, "but we've gotta place further down."

Together the three of us walk the tracks. Every so often Blue stoops down, picks up a stone from the gravel, examines it briefly, then either tosses it aside or pockets it in his jeans. As a boy, he tells us, he loved hunting for rocks. He'd take them home and carefully clean them with a toothbrush and baking soda before polishing them with varnish. Listening to him, I'm reminded of my own childhood, when I'd scour plowed fields for pieces of sandstone and quartz, fool's gold and flint. I'd carry my treasures home, coat them with clear nail polish and glue them into flat cardboard boxes for display. "I'm gonna be a geologist when I grow up," I announced to my parents, as certain as a schoolgirl could be, and for my next birthday they'd bought me The Illustrated Guide to Rocks and Minerals.

I wonder if anybody was there to encourage Blue, all those years ago—he looks about my age—but before I can ask him a locomotive horn blasts up ahead. We've just started across a trestle from the south side, and now a slow train's about to cross from the north. James and I, both hobbled, want to turn back, get off the tracks, let the train pass, but Blue shouts, "We can beat it!" and begins to run. Stupidly, or with a little faith, we hitch along behind him as fast as we can on our sore legs. The train brakes sharply. The trestle shakes. The air pulses with deafening sound—

You can't hear him, but Blue's laughing hard.

makin' it

(**"the bottoms," early afternoon.**) Leaving Holy Family Soup Kitchen, we slouch with a fellow named Morris toward downtown skyscrapers. James asks him how he makes it on the streets, day in and day out.

"The Man Upstairs," Morris says. "*He* keeps me goin'. Y'know, just one foot in fronta the other." A pause, then, "Lord, I wish spring'd hurry up and come."

gettin' out

(**riverbank, late afternoon.**) Passing by Rooster's old camp, James and I hear somebody holler, say, "Hey guys, c'mon back—"

It's not the Professor. Of all people, it's Jake. He should have been in Florida by now.

"We never got outa town," Jake tells us in a hangdog voice, feeding a big fire in the grill. "Rooster's money didn't come through. Actually it was his ol' lady's money—you guys ever meet Enid? Whatever. The money didn't come.

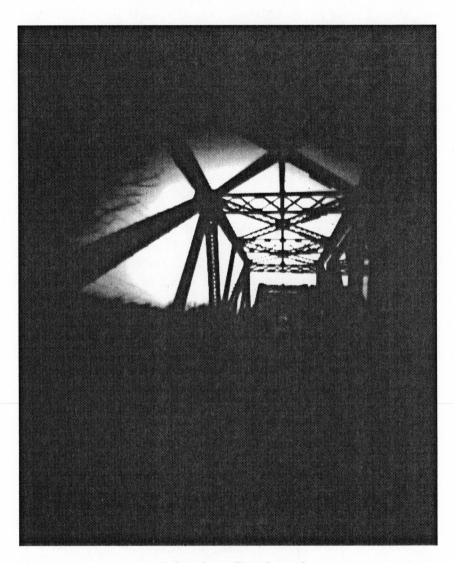

crossing the railroad trestle

We gotta coupla nights at a motel though. Got cleaned up a little."

Tonight the Professor's back in his refrigerator.

rounds

(camp, evening.) James and I dig a small firepit, then set in a small grill we've scavenged from the woods. Having already gathered a supply of kindling, we ignite a wet-wood fire with a railroad flare. Red flame hisses and smokes. Purgatory.

At last there's a strong blaze. "Smells like home," I say wistfully, laying on another piece of brushwood. We enjoy the fire's lively sizzle and pop till a light rain chases us inside.

Some time to write, then we put out the candle. We snuggle down beneath our blankets to the sound of rain on plastic.

Maybe ten minutes later, a car horn blares, not far away. Then, somebody running in the brush—a series of yells—

"Who d'ya think it is?" I whisper.

"Don't know. Whaddya think we should do?"

"Don't know."

We hear more yells.

"Cops?" I suggest.

"Maybe those gangbangers after Rooster. God, I hope not—"

Footsteps outside the shelter.

"Hey, you guys! You in there?"

Jake. We groan in relief. He tosses two brownbags of food through the door, says that Harold Martin's making rounds of the camps, delivering cold meals in the rain.

day 18: saturday, march 6

sense of style

(camp, mid-morning.) Dotting the tracks are little dunes of white sand, used to improve a train's traction on the rails. During a lull in the rain, James and I lug some of it home in a five-gallon bucket (our toilet) and scatter it around the campsite to help cut the mud. Then we lay a stray sheet of plywood over the sloppy ground directly in front of the shelter. Finally, we rig more plastic over the door to protect against the weather.

"So, Irishman," I say, stepping back, studying our little home, "what do we call this architectural style?"

"Evolved crude," he says.

property values

(**main library, early afternoon.**) The library, when it's open, continues to be our best refuge from the weather, and we're not the only ones who seek it out. In fact, even more homeless people pass time here than we originally thought. It's as if some of them exist in infrared, and you can't see them till you put on night-vision goggles.

James runs across an article in today's New York Times about St. Francis of Assisi. Born in the twelfth century to wealthy merchant parents, he lived a spoiled, carefree life till a stint in the army, followed by imprisonment and severe illness, transformed him into a mystic and mendicant. Thereafter regarded as a fool, he solidified his reputation when he stole the expensive cloth from his father's warehouse and sold it to fund the repair of a tumbledown church. Ordered by the local Catholic bishop to restore what he'd taken, Francis stripped off his own rich garments and handed them over. Walked away naked. For the rest of his life, he wore a tunic of rough brown cloth. Poor man's cloth.

"This change in dress," says the article, "was certainly a signal, made centuries earlier by the Buddha, that doing without had been elevated to an existential option. . . ."

In mid-afternoon James and I roust ourselves from poorly disguised naps at our reading table to attend a performance in the library auditorium by the African-American Youth Choir and Storytellers. The participants range in age from four to thirteen years. Some of them radiate immense energy. My aching feet, sweating in my clodhoppers, marvel at their stomping and leaping and stepping out to the rhythm of deepbellied drums. They throw their bodies with abandon, laying claim to the dances of their ancestors, while the drummers, an old woman and a young boy, let fly their hands. . . .

(**late afternoon.**) Stepping out the door of Main Library, James and I are greeted by huge snowflakes, so wet we can hear them dropping onto our coats. The air is turning colder by the minute, but for now, in the quiet of snow falling on snow, all the world feels gentle.

We take the German Village route home, wandering a maze of alleyways. German Village is a restored neighborhood south of downtown. In the mid-1800s its biergartens and narrow cobbled streets were crowded with German-speaking brewers and bakers, bricklayers and tanners, storekeepers and hausfrauen. Today its residents are no more German than Greek, and its

statue of the Buddha in a frozen meditation garden

property values, ever climbing, are considerably more than working class.

The architecture here is conservative, solid and plain. Clean red brick dominates: tiny brick cottages, larger brick Italianate and Queen Anne houses, brick rowhouses, brick carriage houses and sheds, brick privacy walls with black wrought iron fences, brick restaurants and giftshops and churches. Beneath our feet, designer-brick sidewalks.

In a cobbled alley behind a red-brick garage squats a snow-crusted couch, in good shape but out of style, apparently headed to the landfill. What luck! Its hefty foam-rubber cushions, joined together to form a mattress, will be both softer and thicker than our paper-stuffed garment bags, which in the space of one night had quickly flattened into bedrock.

James and I each set two cushions atop our head. Steadying them with our hands, we continue on down the street.

We pass a swanky German Village restaurant. The sight of us seems to amuse the diners at window seats. James manages a wave. A man and woman at a table for two exchange a smile. "I miss making people smile," James says.

splurge

(camp, evening.) In consumer culture, there's only one thing to do when you doubt your place in the scheme of things: Shop. Spend. Buy. In my heart I don't believe in the gospel of consumption, but hearing a weak jingle of change from my coat pocket, I'm suddenly a feel-good convert. We still have around $15 left from Grace's $20. I confess to James that I've been feeling stingy, carrying it around, reluctant to spend even a penny for fear we might need it later. I don't like playing the miser.

"What would help?" he asks.

"Well, what would you say to a splurge?"

He grins.

So tomorrow we're going to blow a couple of bucks. Probably we'll buy something outrageous to eat: two slices of Chicago-style pizza, or a pint of Homemade Brand ice cream, or a chocolate torte from a German Village pastry shop. Thoughts of the food inspire pleasure; thoughts of the purchase, a peculiar consolation.

gold

(evening.) On the corner of Kossuth and Front, a bottle of Cuervo Gold Tequila lies in a puddle, three shots left in the bottom. A good drunk, James says to himself, headed for a Twelve-Step meeting, would never leave a drop.

Back in the old days, tequila was one of his drinks of choice. At $16 a bottle, it would always give him a boost, then knock him out so cold he could have fallen face-down in a gutter of rainwater, stayed there till he drowned.

Since he's been on the streets, James hasn't drawn the usual inspiration or reassurance from Twelve-Step meetings. Maybe the reason, he admits to himself as he reaches the door of tonight's meeting, is that I don't go to be *real.* I go because I can walk in, no questions asked, and be warm for an hour, maybe hear a good joke, drink some coffee —beyond this, I have no expectations. To make real connections with the people, to experience the power in their stories, would require me to let my guard down, be vulnerable—I can't do that. Not out here. If I did, I'd totally collapse. Too much grief lurks under the composure. Too much. I need to be *strong—so* strong—

"I'm James," he says to the roomful of eyes, "and I'm an alcoholic."

muster

(**camp.**) Well into the evening, an army of volunteers arrives. Alone in camp, I yank on my boots, then crawl out of the shelter and stumble up the path to greet them, lighting my way with a guttering candle. For now, the snow has stopped.

A wave of troops surrounds me, all adults. They present me with a flashlight and loose batteries, as well as two bags of food, just as a breeze snuffs my candle.

An older black man steps up, introduces himself as Harold Martin; now I have a face to go with the name. When he asks, I lead him down to see our camp, followed by maybe a dozen volunteers.

"Somehow," Harold says, "I had the idea James and you was further down the river." He lifts the plastic over our shelter door and flashes his light inside, then circles the shelter, inspecting its construction. Apparently it doesn't pass muster. "We gotta tent ya can have," Harold says. "I'll bring it out, next time I come."

"We're doin' fine," I say. "Please give the tent to somebody who truly needs it."

Harold's insistent, but I'm stubborn. To accept the tent would be like taking up beds in a city shelter. It doesn't feel right. Finally I seem to convince him that James and I are staying warm enough, and dry.

Now the volunteers, after presenting me with yet another bag of food, join hands and start to pray. A rambling, if passionate, prayer. Not wearing a coat, I'm soon shivering uncontrollably. My grip on Harold's hand is a vise. Finally he breaks into the prayer and ends it. "You're cold," he says to me. "Get on back inside."

111

millennium

Harold and his troops head out, but before I can retreat into the shelter with my bags, two more women start down the path into camp. Worried lest they trip in the dark, I go to meet them. Dorothy and Maybelle, elderly, black. Dorothy invites me to her church, says, "You people could teach us a few things, y'know."

"Oh?" I say. "Like what?"

"We're all very concerned about the millennium," she says. "Y'know, like how we're gonna live without water and heat and all. You people could really tell us a few things."

I rest a hand on her arm, say, "There's only one thing ya need to know."

"What's that?"

"Don't be afraid," I say, very deliberately, leaning in close. "Don't *ever* be afraid."

Her eyes widen in the moonlight. Then, very quietly, Dorothy says, "That's right, isn't it?"

For a moment the three of us women stand together in silence, the cold and snow forgotten.

"Can I give you a hug?" Dorothy asks suddenly, and she pulls me and my bags into a long bear hug. She's a big woman, with a bulky camel-hair coat. Her perfume reminds me of fresh rosemary leaves. I wonder how ripe I smell.

"It's a good night for angels," I call after the women, as they begin making their way back up the path. Dorothy stops, glances back at me. "You're the angel," she says, and I laugh.

farce

Before the women are all the way up the path, yet another wave of volunteers starts down. I'm already juggling three bags of food, a flashlight, loose batteries and a candle—and now two full-size blankets, a New Testament, and a large trash-bag about to burst with assorted bedding, clothes and window treatments (*yeah, window treatments*) are deposited in my arms. As the volunteers clasp hands and plunge into yet another prayer, I fight like Lucille Ball in a comedy classic to hold up my clumsy load.

Once the prayer's over, a bearded man who has visited before steps up, says, "I've been thinkin' 'bout you guys every day. Is there anything ya need?"

His asking is kind, but my arms are weakening. I summon the patience to answer. "As a matter of fact," I say, pinning down the New Testament

112

with my chin, "we could use some more candles. The flashlight you brought tonight will be helpful, but candles give off heat."

He nods. "Yeah," he says, "and besides, it's a different kinda light."

I smile faintly. That much, he understands. I shore up my sagging load with a knee. My balance is precarious.

"Look," the man says, blind to my predicament, "I work at a food pantry. I'll try to get s'more canned goods and bring 'em out next week with the candles. All I could bring tonight was canned peaches and salmon. Government food."

He slips the handle of a bulging plastic grocery bag around three fingers of my left hand, the only place left to put it. "Hope ya can carry all that," he says with a grin, and leaves.

day 19: sunday, march 7

peace

(st. joseph cathedral, late morning.) During the opening hymn of mass, a powerful voice seizes my attention. Not quite on key, but impassioned, colored by a European accent. I locate the singer across the aisle, a few pews up: a wispily bearded, balding man, gaunt, sagging on metal crutches. He and the crutches look long acquainted.

The old man knows the hymn lyrics by heart. He sings them voraciously, with only loose regard for the pipe organ's tempo. Sometimes his head tilts back as he sings. As I follow his gaze up into the vaulted ceiling, my tiredness lifts.

At the Passing of the Peace, I leave my pew to shake the hand that belongs to the voice. "Peace to you," I say to the old man, and softly add, "You sing with a full heart." His bushy gray eyebrows shoot up quizzically. Then, a smile.

For James, as for me, the Passing of the Peace is one of the highlights of mass. The handshakes are telling. He gets some firm ones today. One man, in the next pew up, is clearly surprised by James's smile and hearty grip. The woman with him doesn't bother to turn around; her uneasiness was plain from the moment they sat down in front of us.

Another, older gentleman has been glancing repeatedly at James throughout the service, casting scowls. Now, during the Peace, at the last possible moment, he turns around to shake hands. As he and James touch, the man's face instantly brightens, and he breaks into a smile that seems full of relief, even joy.

113

currency

(**downtown, afternoon.**) On the sidewalk, a full pack of Newport Menthols. James picks it up, puts it in his coat pocket. Jake and Sarge, every day they search the ground, the streets, for half-smoked butts. Tomorrow they won't have to.

Out here, cigarettes are a currency of good will. In our other life we don't smoke, but out here we try to pass them on when we find them and accept them when they're given.

freedom

(**downtown, late afternoon.**) Time for our much-anticipated splurge. Yet, as James and I consider our epicurean options, the greatest pleasure for the cheapest price, we're totally, helplessly, stumped. Having granted ourselves the freedom to indulge, we seem unable to exercise it. Weighing the possibilities demands too much energy. The appeal goes flat as a slashed car tire. Finally we decide to go home.

On our way back to camp, we browse in trash. Tomorrow must be collection day: full garbage cans line the street, many labeled RESIDENT USE ONLY—VIOLATORS WILL BE PROSECUTED. Lifting their lids to browse, James and I joke that we surely qualify as residents, given the amount of time we spend digging in such receptacles.

German Village trash rarely disappoints. Today is no different. From an industrial-sized dumpster outside Thurn's Bakery and Deli, James pulls two liverwursts, Gold Medal Brand, still sealed. He holds them up with a triumphant grin, like a mountain man who's bagged a critter for supper.

Now, from Einstein Bros., yet another trash-bag full of day-old bagels. Laughing at our luck, we sniff one bagel after another—garlic herb, sundried tomato, blueberry, apple cinnamon, whole wheat, cracked pepper. . . . Tonight we'll feast on bagels spread with liverwurst and grilled over a smoky fire. For dessert, government peaches. Splurge for free.

removed

(**camp, early evening.**) In the glimmering of a candle I pick up The Crucible, by Arthur Miller, a paperback I salvaged from a cold rain. I read it once, long ago: a tale of testing, and tragedy; of outrageous suspicions, false accusations, rigged trials, punishments without mercy. Neighbor is set against neighbor, husband against wife, parent against child—even the heart itself is riven.

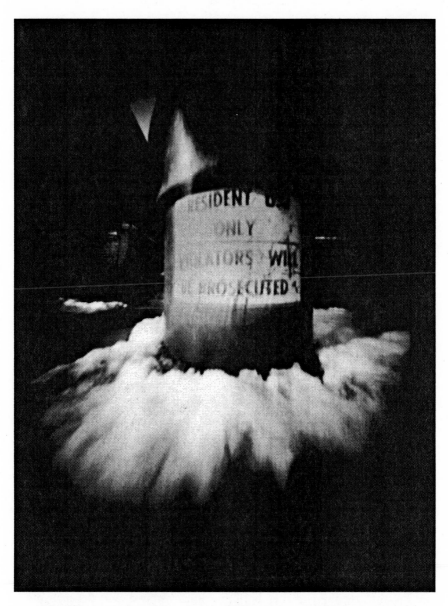

RESIDENT USE ONLY—VIOLATORS WILL BE PROSECUTED

The pious seventeenth-century folks in Miller's play, whose fear of witchcraft swiftly becomes hate masquerading as faith, consider the woods outside Salem the Devil's last preserve. I smile sadly at this. We're not so far removed.

mercy

(**camp, late evening.**) James and I go up top, just before bedtime, to use the restroom and payphone at Wendy's. By the time we return, a half hour later, some angel of mercy has deposited two brownbags of munchies and sandwiches, even some fruit, on the roof of our shelter, plus some slightly used candles, and two more blankets. We laugh till we hurt.

From a pamphlet left with the food: "Jesus was homeless. Rejected by his family, accused of being a drunkard and thought to be crazy, Jesus walked from town to town, spending most of his time with people out on the streets. He was criticized for associating with poor and dirty people, and often was in trouble with the authorities; he occasionally got run out of town. He knew what it was to be hungry, thirsty, and tired. . . ."

day 20: monday, march 8

spree

(**j.o.i.n., mid-morning.**) Anxious to replace my cumbersome boots, I ransack through a foul-smelling box of used shoes. Most are children's sneakers or women's high heels, but finally, an ugly pair of canvas and leather hiking shoes, size nine, with reinforced ankles and deep tread. They're three sizes too big, but probably manageable if I stuff wadded paper in the toes and continue to wear three or four pair of socks. They're not waterproof like my boots, but I can tie plastic bags around my stockinged feet to serve as a lining.

Inspired by my luck, James scrounges a pair of construction boots, one size too big but much better, he believes, than his white Salvation Army sneakers. Those, slashed by his knife, he throws away.

Up at the service window a young latino is trying desperately to make himself understood. He speaks only a smattering of English; the volunteer, no Spanish. In the end they both give up, frustrated, and the man moves slowly toward the door, head hanging.

"Buenas días," I say, as he passes by.

His head jerks up. "Buenas días! Habla español?"[13]

"Un poco,"[14] I say apologetically.

116

The man erupts in a torrent of Spanish. I drown in an instant. Waving my hand back and forth, shaking my head, I tell him I'm so very sorry—"Lo siento, lo siento!"—wishing I'd taken high school Spanish more seriously, all those years ago. "No comprendo," I tell him, "no comprendo."

The man hands me a piece of paper. A legal document, in English. Skimming, I learn he's just been released from jail on his own recognizance; for what crime, I don't need to know. I hand the paper back to him with a helpless shrug.

The man's calmer now. Somehow he makes me understand he has nowhere to go. I want to help him, but how?

He's wearing only a windbreaker. Today's temperature probably won't rise above freezing, even if the sun manages to shine. If the guy has nowhere to go, at least he could go nowhere in warmer clothes. I tug on his sleeve. "Muy frijole!" I say, pulling the Spanish out of the air, hoping it means "very cold" but half afraid it's nonsense, or an insult.

I grab a shirt from a clothing rack, hold it up. "Free!" I shout, as if the man were deaf. Maybe this English word can cross the divide.

"Uno?" he asks, raising an index finger.

"Mucho!" I say, handing him a grocery bag. "Mucho, mucho!"

He stares at me in disbelief, then takes the bag, walks over to the racks and begins to shop.

kgb

Standing near me is a striking older woman. Her silver hair is beautifully styled, her cosmetics skillfully applied. If not for her clothes, clean but worse for the wear, you'd expect to see her strolling through City Center Mall with a designer shopping bag slung over her wrist. "Olga," she says her name is, after I introduce myself. Her accent betrays European roots. When I inquire, she tells me that she was born in Czechoslovakia but has lived in the U.S. for decades. "You know, my dear," she says, her term of endearment a caress to my ear, "I speak seven languages."

Now that Olga's started talking, there's no end. With rolled *r*s and staccato *t*s, she launches into a very articulate but mostly unintelligible conspiracy story about KGB death threats, U.S. government plots, the disappearance of her millions, a life spent on the run from secret agents. The deeper she goes into the story, the lower her voice drops. "The KGB came for me in the middle of the night," she murmurs, tears pooling in her eyes. "They strung up my woman friend in the basement, but I got away—I broke my ribs jumping through a window, but I got away. I was still wearing my nightgown. They will never take me. *Never!*"

Beside her on the floor rests a worn leather valise and a battered suitcase; close against her body she clutches a large handbag. From this she draws a worn heirloom Bible. Tucked inside its gilt pages are scrawled notes and crumpled documents from lawyers, banks, government agencies. These papers are her life. She displays them to me one by one, tries to explain.

"They say I am *dead*," she says. "They say my money is *gone*. They say I cannot *prove* that I am alive. They do not *want* me to be alive. They would rather have my millions."

Tears spill down her powdered cheeks. She dabs them away with a lacy kerchief. "Thank you for listening, my dear," she whispers. "I have to let this out sometimes. Otherwise I explode."

Olga's story is either tragic or mad, maybe a little of both. I want to listen, I want to give her the space she needs to vent, but her energy has become so intense, every word a suppressed burst, I feel my spirit draining away. She's like a black hole sucking up light.

"The KGB is closing in," she says under her breath. "I must leave right away. That is why I am here, to get a bus ticket. To Detroit. I will be safe in Detroit."

Suddenly Olga becomes calm. She glances around, checking to see nobody's listening, then says, "You know, dear, I am writing a book about all of this—"

The space between us collapses.

"My dear," she asks, "do you need a pencil?"

I disappear in her. "I can always use a pencil," I struggle to say.

From her handbag she digs out a long, black pencil with a red pen-cap over the lead. "Here," she says. "I do not need this. The woman who gave it to me thought it was an eyebrow pencil, but it is not."

I notice now: Olga's eyebrows are expertly drawn. No hair there to entangle with the brows of the ancestors. That old Zen saying, my Ash Wednesday prayer, turns to sad lament.

"The KGB," she says, "tried to kill me by setting a fire, and my face was badly burned. You would never know it now, except for my eyebrows. My eyebrows have never grown back."

shoe swap

(**camp, evening.**) Around dinnertime Jake stops by to chat. He happens to mention that Enid, Rooster's companion, has no boots. Take It to the Streets brought her a pair to try once, but they were so big she couldn't wear them.

"What size is she?" I say.

"Don't know," he says. "Real small."

118

"Here," I say, "give `er my ol' boots to try. Size six. Maybe they'll fit."

An hour or so later, Jake returns, carrying a pair of men's leather workshoes, size ten, almost new. "Enid," he says, "thanks ya for the boots. These are the shoes they brought `er awhile back. Prob'ly won't fitcha, but they'd sure keep your feet dryer than the ones ya got on."

Once Jake leaves, James and I build a fire in our firepit. When the flames are burning easy, James rests the toes of his "new" construction boots on the grill's edge, letting the heat warm through. "Y'know, I could swear," he says pensively, "that I've seen these boots before."

"How's that?"

"A construction worker stayin' at the overflow shelter had `em on one morning when he asked me if I could spare a pair of socks. My first reaction was, `Sorry man, I need `em.' Then I glanced down at his boots—*these* boots. Bare black ankles were stickin' out the tops. Obviously the guy needed some socks. I gave `im one of the three pair I had on.

"Now I've got his shoes. I wonder what *he's* wearin'."

craziness

(**camp, late night.**) Jerk myself awake—nightmare—can't remember—
Slow down—breathe—
"James—"
Shake his foot—
"James!"
"Wha—whassup?"
"Need your help—"
"Wha's goin' on?" James props himself on an elbow, head low, eyes shielded from my flashlight beam.

"Sorry to wake you—needed to hear a familiar voice."

He stares at me. I'm crouched low on my knees, totally panicked, like a muskrat caught in a steel trap, ready to gnaw its leg off.

"What happened?"

"Nightmare. Can't get calmed down. I wanna get outa here bad, but Jake and Rooster's goin' at it out there."

We listen to the commotion outside, our neighbors arguing ugly. Minutes pass. Finally I can't stand it anymore. "James," I say, "I've gotta move, burn somma this adrenaline. I'm goin' up to White Castle. Maybe I can steer clear of the guys."

"I'll go with you."

Into our coats, our shoes. Out the shelter, up the path. We're just to the field, thinking we're clear, when we bump into Rooster. "Don't be alarmed," he

119

says, "if ya'll hear a ruckus later. It'll just be Jake gettin' what he deserves—"

Craziness. James and I stumble toward the tracks.

It's after midnight when we sink into chairs at White Castle. The brisk walk and nippy air have calmed me down some. James and I small-talk. We stare out the windows. We wait. For what, exactly, I'm not sure; some sort of resolution.

James is sagging in his chair, almost asleep, when all at once the nightmare rushes back into my mind, swift as a flash flood: Olga, standing directly behind me, insane as a prophet. She leans in over my right shoulder and whispers a dreadful truth, her breath hot in my ear, hot on my skin—

What she said I can't remember—such things in dreams you can never remember, they're far beyond your grasp—but the monstrous thing is still there, angry and sick, pounding away in my chest.

I begin to weep. There's a sad relief in the veil having lifted, if only this much. Ever since leaving JOIN, I've been haunted by Olga; all day long I carried her through the streets, carried her like a worn leather Bible stuffed full of terrible secrets. Time now to lay her down.

day 21: tuesday, march 9

sinking

(riverbank, early morning.) You waken before dawn, by some miracle having managed several hours of deep sleep, and emerge from the shelter into steadily falling snow. A bank of white, muffling all sound. The wind's down, at least for now, the air moist and warm. Anxious to use a bathroom, and to get warm, you slog through five or six inches of wet powder toward White Castle, following the railroad tracks. The rails, glistening steely black against unbroken white, disappear not far ahead into snowy haze. For all the world it looks like the sky has fallen.

To get up top, here at the bridge, you have to leave the tracks, take a footpath up the steep embankment. You're the first person up, or down, since the snow started. Sinking into snow up to your ankles, you climb up a few steps, slip on buried forties, land on your belly, slide down till you stop. Grabbing hold of dead weeds, you pull yourself to your feet, dig in a toe, take a step up, ease forward, take another step, slip on more bottles, land hard on your bad knee, go sliding down again with a groan. You're completely covered with snowdust, now, and sweating, but this is your only way up: to crawl over the waste of other people's lives. You feel like you're stepping on bodies.

120

enid

(**riverbank, mid-morning.**) Here where the riverbank is most populous, homeless feet have packed a narrow trail through the deep snow along the tracks. Tramping the line back toward camp, I meet Enid, and step aside into several inches of fresh powder to let her by. Her tiny feet, I notice, are swimming in my old sixes.

torment

(**riverbank, mid-morning.**) Headed up the railroad tracks to Grubb Street. I swing my right leg from the hip, bad knee refusing to flex. James walks ahead of me, leaning into a northerly wind, his feet chugging like steam engines, breaking the deep snow to make my going a little easier.

James says that his "new" construction boots are pure torment. "An old story, I know," he complains, "but they absorb water like sponges, they chafe my bad ankle, there's no padding left in the soles. . . . I can't bear to wear them much longer.

"What's that old proverb—" he says, "'Don't judge a man till you've walked a mile in his shoes'?"

Beneath an overpass we pause to catch our breath. On one of the walls are two graffiti in close juxtaposition, the first spraypainted in bold block letters, the second in a trembling scrawl:

SAGE

Evil Never Dies

From my pocket I take the pencil Olga gave me yesterday; the pencil that could never redraw her missing eyebrows. Kneeling, ignoring the pain, I gently press it down into a low drift of fresh snow that's blown under the bridge.

May you walk hand in hand with the ancestors.

citizens

(**downtown, early afternoon.**) Snow has fallen throughout the morning like flour sifting from heaven. Schools are canceled, civic events postponed, but thankfully the federal district courthouse is still doing business. That's all that matters, to me. This afternoon, almost twenty years after he left China, the land of his birth, Jihong will be sworn in as an American citizen.

Approaching the courthouse, I spot Ron, a dear old friend, clumping up

graffiti beneath a dark overpass

the sidewalk in his rubbers, shoulders hunched against the wind. Braving the weather and hazardous roads, he and his wife will be among those attending the naturalization ceremony. Overjoyed to see a familiar face, I wait at the courthouse steps, scarcely able to contain myself.

Ron walks right by me, as if I weren't there, starts to climb the steps.

"Sir, d'ya have a quarter you can spare?" I ask.

He turns back, peers at me, exclaims, "Is that *you*?"

Once through the doors and metal detectors, Ron and I hurry to join other friends in the hall outside the courtroom. I imbibe their good will. Everybody's excited for Jihong, already seated inside. Loved ones of other citizens-to-be are clustered around us, laughing and chattering in a babble of languages.

Finally a court official ushers all the spectators into the courtroom. My eyes scan the crowded seats—Jihong's up front, in the second row of immigrants, looking dapper in the black double-breasted wool suit he wore at our wedding, five years ago. Seated with him are forty people from twenty-one nations, each of them a story, each of them making a new home.

How far this federal courtroom seems from that Ohio State classroom where Jihong and I first met. Though he already held a doctorate in chemistry, Jihong had enrolled in a composition course I'd been assigned to teach, wanting, he said, to improve his writing skills. During the term, I'd gradually, unwittingly, fallen in love with him, seduced by his essays about his childhood, sometimes funny, sometimes sweet, always thoughtful and fluent. Now the boy who celebrated the Chinese new year by engaging in firecracker battles with his friends, lighting the wick of each pao-zhang with the glowing tip of a cigarette—that boy stands here a man, on what was once the alien side of the world, raising his right hand. . . .

No firecrackers in my pocket today, sweetie, but a small American flag found in a dumpster. Welcome to freedom.

bosom

(late afternoon.) Everywhere, ponds of street slush. Dirty snowdrifts have clogged the sewer drains; the salty runoff has nowhere to go. Careful as I am, watching my every step, my socks are wringing wet. So much for plastic-bag liners.

Coming to the red-brick Catholic church in German Village, James and I slip inside to rest, reflect, and lay prayerful hands on our ailing bodies. The sanctuary is empty. We sidle into pews halfway up the aisle, remove our hats, our gloves, our coats.

Silence.

Yank off our shoes.

Silence.

This isn't like the silence of a library—you feel the difference profoundly. Silence in a library has to do with absence: the absence of noise, of outward distractions. It's built on rules, on submission to custom and its custodians, those kindly librarians who *shhhhh!* at you over their reading glasses like serpents licking dust. If you were somehow to find yourself alone in a library after closing hours, everybody else gone home, you'd break this silence without much thought, muttering to yourself as you searched the stacks, reading a poem aloud with verve, exclaiming at an insipid editorial, even grinding your new pencil down to a stub in the sharpener, just for the grating sound of it.

In an empty church, like this one, on this late Tuesday afternoon, the silence is different. It's all about presence. Presence you can't name, not for what it truly is; presence you can't see, but you can feel, if you bring your heart across the threshold from the world outside the door. This church could just as easily be a synagogue, or a mosque, or a temple—it isn't a religion that you meet here, necessarily, but yourself, and that inexpressible mystery which lies beyond you, of which you're the merest of parts. This presence requires reverence, not obedience. There's no need for rules, no need for enforcement. You're alone, nobody's around to hear—still you don't talk, except in the barest of whispers. You don't walk around, except to go and kneel at the shrine, and light two small candles, though you've no donation to make but your prayers. Prayers for things beyond words and even thought. Prayers of the open heart.

This silence is alive. It creates itself, one moment to the next, and makes possible a change.

Silence—

Two people meet for the first time. Maybe for the only time. What fills the fragile space between them? What do they offer each other in the silence—absence, or presence? Reverence?

Afternoon light is dying. Above us rises Mother Mary, in stained glass, hands crossed over her bosom.

domesticity

(**evening.**) Tonight is laundry night; our first in three weeks. Pinching our pennies, we should be able to afford one load of laundry a week from now on.

In a dingy laundromat on S. High, we play avoid the roach while stuffing our gamy clothes into a washing machine. Obviously the small tub won't hold all of our clothes; we could easily fill three or four loads. Time for hard choices.

The machines eat our quarters like slot machines, but finally our clothes are clean and dry, sparking with static. Domestic joy bubbles up as I sort and fold.

day 22: wednesday, march 10

no need

Yesterday afternoon, with eight inches of new snow on the ground, my spirits were as low as they've been since my first night on the streets. I asked James if the weather was affecting his mood. He said no, and for the rest of the day I leaned on his strength, as he sometimes leans on mine. Rarely are both of us depressed at the same time.

This morning I'm much better. All things pass.

Living in the outdoors has made me more attentive to things from which I'm insulated, or distracted, in my other life: a few degrees' drop in temperature; a slight shift in the wind, or its lying down a little; the one cardinal trilling amidst a squabble of crows; the way a gray sky modulates from slate to smoky to mottled to pale; how the sun doesn't rise all at once, but slivers over the horizon, just when the cold is coldest; how cold in your body can begin to burn like heat; how when your fingers slip from tingly to numb, suddenly you can't distinguish cold from wet—

In any one day are many days, in any one hour many hours. No need to be patient, waiting for change to come. It's already here.

legal tender

(j.o.i.n., mid-morning.) According to our sometimes unreliable Street Card, obtained from the library, three medical facilities in the city provide health care, at no charge, to homeless persons. Maybe one of them will supply an elastic wrap or brace for my ailing right knee.

Here at JOIN local calls of three minutes are permitted, free, Arriving before the doors open, I sit down wearily on the floor of the crowded foyer. Before long an argument breaks out between a homeless guy named Winfield and a sequined male transvestite who obviously delights in provoking him. I haven't seen the transvestite before, but Winfield shows up nearly every morning at McDonald's on Broad, toting a leather satchel full of photocopied documents and handwritten notes. Pages and pages. I've heard him say that he's on the run from the feds and the tobacco companies; he believes they've put out a contract on his life. He spends his afternoons in the law library at

Ohio State, researching his rights.

With a linebacker's body, an attorney's intellect and a black preacher's tongue, Winfield's not somebody you soon forget. You're just not sure he's sane.

In their battle of words, the two black men notice me listening (in the cramped foyer you can't *not* listen, but everybody else is pretending not to hear), and they begin to play up to me. I haven't a clue what they're arguing about; it's the intensity in their eyes, their voices, that has me hooked. Sometimes, though, a whole sentence, or even a cluster of thoughts, sneaks through the crazy bombast, making complete, even elegant, sense.

Now the transvestite says to me, "Life's all 'bout money, don'tcha agree?"

I gesture helplessly.

Winfield pulls out a dollar bill, snaps it smooth in front of my eyes, says, "What does this say? Do you *see*, miss? 'Legal Tender.' *Legal. Tender.*" He laughs scornfully, says, "As if anything we're asked to do for money is tender. Sometimes it isn't legal, either. Just ask the tobacco companies. All for this—"

Winfield waves the bill dramatically, then stuffs it deep in his pocket. "But here's the thing, miss," he says, pointing the silver grip of his cane right at my nose. "Human life is far more valuable than money. *Far* more. Money can always be retrieved if you lose it. Life—it's just plain *gone*."

At about this same time, James is circling a puddle of slush several streets away. He notices a $20 bill floating in the gutter. Picking it up by a corner, shaking it off, he glances around for a pedestrian who might have dropped it. Nobody. Helplessly he stares at the wet bill. For four weeks he hasn't had more than a couple of bucks on him at any one time. Now he doesn't know what to do.

Finally he puts the money in his pocket. Walking up the street, he imagines the look on my face when he shows it to me. He pictures us in a High Street drugstore buying elastic wraps for his ankle, my knee. He fantasizes about buying tickets to a movie, one night when it's whipping cold; maybe even getting a big tub of hot buttered popcorn, maybe even hopping a city bus to the theater and back. . . .

doctoring

I dial the first number on my list, a hospital. A recording tells me to call back between certain hours to arrange a rendezvous with a mobile medical unit. Too much bother, I decide, for them and for me.

The second number is a free clinic at the Columbus Health Department. "The clinic's only open," says the person who answers, "on Monday nights."

Almost a week's wait.

I dial the last number on my list. A nurse informs me that no elastic wrap or brace can be dispensed without my first seeing a doctor. Would I care to make an appointment?

I thank the nurse for her time and hang up. I don't want to answer a doctor's inevitable questions about who I am, why I'm on the streets, what happened to my knee.

Guess I'll have to follow James's lead and doctor from a dumpster. Every morning he wraps his sore ankle in a length of blue plastic discovered in somebody's trash.

meat

(holy family soup kitchen, lunchtime.) Over full food trays we chat with Morris. My acquaintance with him dates back to McDonald's on Broad, that morning after my first night on the streets. I didn't know his name then; he was just a graybeard with glasses who thought it wise to take life one day at a time. Soon after, James met him at the Bexley shelter. These past weeks, we've eaten with him several times here at the soup kitchen, but we haven't seen him in a while, and today he's full of stories, not all of them easy on the ears. James and I struggle to listen without passing judgment.

"I'm sorry, what's your name again?" Morris asks James now, for the dozenth time since they've met. James reminds him, and Morris smiles through his beard, says casually, "Oh, that's right."

My name he always remembers.

Morris says, "This beard, y'know, sometimes I get tired of it, but I just don't look like me without it. I shaved it off once and my family didn't know me. Besides, my granddaughter likes to play with it."

"D'ya see your family often?" James asks.

"No," he says. "Not really."

James pushes back his chair, leaves the table to use the restroom. Morris watches him wend his way through the crowded cafeteria and finally disappear into the hallway.

Now he fixes his gaze on me. For a long minute neither of us speaks. Somehow I sense what's coming. I work harder at buttering my dinner roll.

"There's somethin' I want very much," Morris says finally, his voice like putty, "but I don't have the money right now."

I bite into my bread. He waits. Finally, tired of the feel of his eyes, I say, "What's that, Morris?"

"A nice young woman like you."

I chew, refusing to say a word, or even to look at him. He begins to

127

fidget. The silence thickens till at last he seems to realize he's overstepped. "But—I want—I wantcha to know," he stammers, "that I appreciate you and James's company very much."

"Thank you, Morris," I say, now looking him straight in the eye, just as James returns to the table.

This isn't the first time I've rebuffed a man since hitting the streets. Here at the soup kitchen, where there's maybe one woman to every nine men, I often feel like a side of beef hanging from a meat hook, prepared for inspection by wolves. James and I are assumed to be a couple, and this obviously affords me a measure of security. When he isn't with me, the stares become more brazen, the comments more suggestive, the brushes against my body more frequent, less accidental. Still, James isn't with me to be my bodyguard. Coolly, deliberately, I try to keep my distance from every man I meet. This is probably the best course, but I can't help feeling ambivalent, knowing how easily prudence can turn into hardness of heart.

lightproof

(afternoon.) James sits under a busy overpass, changing the photo paper in his pinhole camera. On the walls all around him, Fuck Yous and garish demon faces. Fear lurks here, waiting to pounce on shaky confidence, bland hope. His fingers fumble in the lightproof bag.

pain and wonder

(main library, afternoon.) Thumbing through a back issue of the Dispatch, I run across a comment attributed to a director of one of the city's homeless shelters. She maintains that if you aren't mentally ill when you hit the streets, you soon will be. At first her statement offends me. Then I think of how I've been beset by claustrophobia and panic attacks, and how bouts of depression sometimes drag James and me down—

An anglo struts across the room. The back of his jacket reads "PAIN and WONDER—Athens, Georgia." Pain and Wonder. The name of a business, probably, but also an apt description of our experience, living in the between.

modesty

(camp, evening.) I meet Ada Martin for the first time. Sitting in her Blazer, she looks younger than her forty-nine years, and fairly robust, considering how ill she's been. According to the Columbus Dispatch, this well-known angel to the homeless needs a heart-lung transplant.

"Ya doin' okay?" she asks sweetly. "Is there anything ya need?"
We talk tampons. I have little modesty left.

drought

My body is in drought. I've never felt such an intense longing to be
touched. To be comforted by even just an arm around my shoulders, or a
hand to hold, or fingers stroking my mussed hair. . . .

day 23: thursday, march 11

crave zone

(white castle.) 6:30 a.m. Hardly slept last night. The Dispatch had predicted
the overnight temperature would drop to fifteen degrees; might have gone even
lower. My bladder complained, sent me five times out to the bucket.

Homeless folks are traipsing into the joint to get warm. Posted all around
us are bright ads, reminding us, as if we need reminding, that we're in "The
Crave Zone." I open the morning paper.

In my other life I rarely read a newspaper; no need, the important news
still seems to reach me. But out here I want the paper. Reading its pages
seems a basic necessity, a tenuous connection to a larger world from which I
feel terribly removed. Every morning I hang around White Castle, hoping
some customer will leave a copy behind. Today somebody did. Actually
this same customer, a distinguished older black man who keeps the sections
in order and refolds them precisely when he's finished, has let me have his
Dispatch the last two days. This morning he even walked across the room to
hand it to me. Smiled, didn't say a word.

I twist in my seat, trying to get comfortable. On my way here I took a bad
fall on glare ice, landed squarely on my tailbone. My body is taking a beating.

Two articles in today's Dispatch warrant more than casual attention. In
the first, concerning Operation Feed, an annual food drive benefiting local
pantries and soup kitchens, I learn that while the Columbus metropolitan
area has a booming economy and a record-low 3% unemployment rate, it
also has a 17% poverty rate. Lots of jobs, in other words, but too low-paying
to meet the bills. Most of the higher-paying jobs are concentrated in the
suburbs, far from the people who need them most; so far, in fact, that the city
bus lines don't even run there.

The second article reports on a recent survey of homeless families. Asked

129

to identify the primary causes of their plight, they most often cited eviction, loss of income, relationship problems, and lack of affordable housing. The basic reason for homelessness, according to this study, is poverty—not, as commonly believed, mental illness or substance abuse, which affect homeless people only at about the same rate as the general population.

trash

(**downtown, mid-morning.**) Opening the lid of a dumpster at the corner of Naghten and Church, James finds it nearly empty of trash, so he crawls in, lowering the lid after him. He doesn't like to change photo paper out in the open. Too conspicuous.

A sliver of light penetrates the crack under the lid of the dumpster. Inspired, James and his wide-angle camera happily play with that little light as if they're best friends. He experiments with various exposures and angles, bracing the camera first between his knees, then against the side of the dumpster. Leg muscles cramp. Butt and hips fall asleep.

After each shot, a change of photo paper—a time-consuming process, but worth the effort. James likes the symbolism of light, especially since hitting the streets. If he's lucky, one of these shots will actually be usable, but using pinhole photography, the odds are against it. In a week's batch of twenty-five or thirty negatives, only two or three ever turn out.

Propping open the dumpster lid just a tad, James notices an American flag billowing in the wind across the alley. What a vantage point from which to shoot it! Holding his camera for an exposure of around twenty seconds, he doesn't dare move, or the image will blur. As he waits, stock-still, he reflects on how often he's been treated like trash since hitting the streets. Now, lounging atop the few trash-bags in this dumpster, he's surprisingly comfortable, and safe from eyes that skewer—

Suddenly the dumpster lid opens. A woman is ready to toss in her garbage. Clumsily James rises up to stop her, stammering an apology. She jumps back with a scream and runs, her bags spilling on the ground.

frames

(**downtown, early afternoon.**) James calls the workplace of one of his darkroom assistants to arrange a photo swap. The two of them rendezvous every ten to fourteen days; he exchanges new negatives for prints she has produced from his earlier shots. These prints he'll study carefully, evaluating the performance of his cameras.

At the moment, though, his darkroom assistant is away from her desk.

James asks the receptionist on the other end of the line for directions to their office building. "We're located in German Village," she says, "near Wasserstrom, near Banana Joe's—"

Given their general location, James figures that he must walk past these establishments almost every day, yet he can't place them. His frame of reference, his landmarks, are totally different from the receptionist's.

"Where's your office from the Salvation Army?" he says.

conspicuous

(**main library, mid-afternoon.**) A small, third-floor reading room with a window view. Outside, a white-out.

Alone in the room, James and I take off our shoes so our burning feet can breathe. I seat myself at the lone table in the room, pull The Crucible out of my pocket. James lies down on the floor with an anthology of Pablo Neruda's poetry, propping his sore legs on a chair. His bad ankle is throbbing and tight; the ball of his foot, tender. He reaches to probe it, ever so gently, and his right shoulder pops. It's been doing that a lot lately, with noticeable pain.

Suddenly a security guard appears, purposefully, as if he's been dispatched. "I'm gonna have to ask you to get off the floor," he says to James, his tone flat. As James wearily rouses himself, the guard, a stocky black man, looks from our stockinged feet to the book in my hand, then back to our feet. Obviously he's of divided mind. Our casual behavior has violated library custom; he should make us leave the building, but. . . .

I lower my eyes to my book, conspicuously turn a page—

The guard makes his decision. "Both of you put your shoes back on," he says firmly, then moves on, casting an uneasy glance at us over his shoulder.

spotlight

(**camp, late evening.**) James and I are about to blow out our candles for the night when we hear voices carrying down through the woods. Then, our names being called—

"Take It to the Streets. Has to be."

"Shouldn't visiting hours be over by now?"

Neither of us is anxious to get out of bed. Reluctantly, James pulls some clothes over his long johns, starts slipping on his boots.

Now, from right outside our door, Harold Martin's voice. Startled, James lifts the plastic flaps to crawl out of the shelter, only to be blinded by a cluster of dazzling lights. Shielding his eyes, he struggles to his feet, bewildered.

A chorus of voices says, "Hi, James!"

Long seconds pass. James senses expectations in the air, as if he might perform some sad song and dance. He waits, unmoving, in the glare of the lights. Finally Harold Martin clears his throat and begins reading a list of supplies the group has brought us tonight, including two gently used ski suits, of which he's obviously very proud.

"Where's Phyllis?" he asks then.

"Lyin' down," James says, still wondering about the lights.

Harold calls in to me, says he'd like me to come outside. Frustrated, James leans down, lowers one of the plastic flaps over our door. "She's tired," he says. "It's late."

Harold hesitates, then slips James a small paper bag. Tampons.

Suddenly James notices a small red light next to one of the big bright ones. Now he knows. Anger rises hot. He's being videotaped, "homeless man helped on the riverbank." Part of him would like to smash the camera he still can't see against a tree.

James swallows hard, holds out his hands, accepts the supplies and the ski suits. Then, mumbling some quick Thank yous and Good nights, he hastily retreats into our shelter.

day 24: friday, march 12

dreams

(**white castle, early morning.**) At a nearby table, Jake and Rooster are mulling over the classifieds. They hope to have enough money soon to rent a cheap apartment. Florida's a dead dream.

"I'm tireda this shit," Jake says. "A person just can't keep livin' like this. Hell, I've lived all over. Always on the move. But ya get tireda not havin' the simple conveniences—a phone, a shower, a stove, a fridge, some heat. Ya lose your self-respect after awhile. *You* know what I'm sayin'," he says, tipping his head in my direction.

Rooster says, "You and James, you move into my tent once I'm out. Then the Professor can move into *your* place. You guys need to be warm. Need to be able to stand up and move around."

"Let the Professor have your place," I say. "James and I are warm enough. Besides," I say, stretching the truth like a rubber band about to snap, "our shelter's *cozy.*"

Rooster and Jake exchange a glance, then laugh loudly. I blush.

They toss me the rest of their newspaper. An article on the effects of welfare reform explains how difficult it is for poor people to obtain health care coverage. No longer covered by Medicaid, they can't afford to self-insure, and they rarely receive benefits at work. Those who suffer most, as a result, are the children.

The children.

Fact: If you're a child in this country, you have a one in five chance of growing up poor. More than fourteen million American children live in poverty, and that number is rising.

Fact: If you're a child living in poverty in this country, you're four times more likely to die from disease than a child who isn't. You're also much more likely to suffer from malnutrition and other serious health problems. In short, you need medical attention more than most, and you're among the least likely to get it—

The children.

The other day, in the restroom at Grubb Street, two little girls were talking in the stall next to mine. One said to the other, "My family's gotta place now—it's gotta upstairs and *everything*! We're gonna have so much fun!"

aaron

(holy family soup kitchen, lunchtime.) Two guys next to James are rapping about their struggles with alcohol. The black guy says how he's staying away from the booze now; the white guy wants to quit, too, says he's been sober for three days and is feeling pretty good, but he's still afraid he won't make it.

The black man leaves the table. The anglo—short, finely bearded, maybe in his fifties—James offers him a pamphlet listing Twelve-Step meetings held all over the city.

"What is this?" the fellow says. "Some kinda book? I can hardly read, man."

"These are meetings for people who want to quit drinkin'," James says. "Meetings have helped me a lot. You ever gone to one?"

He says, unconvincingly, "Oh yeah, I been to some."

James briefly describes what it's like, working the Steps. Then, feeling inspired, he asks the man where he plans to go, now that he's finished lunch. The fellow says that he wants to get a bed for the night at a nearby shelter.

"I'm headed that direction, too," James says. "Let's go!"

Sensing James's excitement as he prepares to leave, I throw him a guarded look, as if to say, "Slow down, don't push it," but he's too wrapped up in the prospect of helping the man to catch himself.

Once they're out the door, he says, "I'm James, by the way."

"Aaron," the man replies, shaking hands.

trees

Aaron is limping badly. "Got hit by a car three weeks ago," he explains. "Least, that's what they told me when I come to. I gotta go see the doctor— the shelter's gettin' me in to see somebody in a coupla days. Shoulda been killed, the way that car hit me."

"Sounds like it wasn't your time."

"Yeah," he says, "I ain't ready to go yet. I wanna see my granddaughter. My son don't want me around her till I clean up my act."

"Y'know, Aaron, I used to drink—I was a mess. But I haven't hadda drink in over two years now. I just needed to believe there was somethin' greater than me that could help."

"Myself, I believe in Jesus," Aaron says. "But I ain't so right with 'im now." He thinks a minute, then says, "Coulda tree be somethin' greater?"

"As long as you can find strength in it."

He brightens. "A tree. Yeah, I know some big ol' trees that's been 'round longer 'n me."

James says, "Aaron, if ya go to those places in that pamphlet, they can help. I can help ya, too. But ya gotta wanna stay sober."

"Yeah, I want to."

"You don't have to go through this alone. There are lotsa people who've been where you are and made it through. They'll help ya out."

By now James and Aaron have reached the homeless shelter. "Think about it," James says. "If ya want, I'll come by sometime and talk to ya s'more. Take care, buddy."

"Yeah," Aaron says. "You too, James."

Walking away, James is so charged up that he scarcely notices the drug dealers working the corner.

brothers

(**riverbank, late afternoon.**) James's latest fashion: black Everlast sneakers, culled, once again, from a box at JOIN. Lightweight, an exact fit. "Walkin's a cinch now," he says, but he's keeping the construction boots, just till he's sure.

James strolls over to Jake and Sarge's shack to ask if we might borrow a pan. Their campsite is very neat and organized: one trash-bag for empty bottles, another for paper and garbage. A small grill sits between two plastic chairs puddled with rainwater.

James raps on the door of the shack. "Hey guys," he calls, "it's James—"

Jake invites him inside, and Sarge clears away some clutter so he can sit down. The place smells like an old station wagon—musty, lived-in, stale with cigarette smoke. Jake and Sarge each light a smoke on the flame of their gas stove, and soon they're bantering like brothers, needling each other, poking fun. James feels good, laughing with them and getting better acquainted, especially with Sarge. Up till now, he's struck James as not so friendly, but now he just seems rather shy, even oafish, with a droll sense of humor that catches you by surprise.

James asks how they built their place. Sarge rolls his eyes. "It was a bitch," Jake says, with a smoker's yellow smile.

sobering up

(camp, early evening.) "I've gotta slow down with Aaron," James tells me, warming some leftover noodles from Grubb Street for our dinner. "I was too excited today, too zealous, as if in an instant I might get 'im to turn his life around."

For James, getting sober hadn't taken very long; naturally he wanted the same for Aaron, so this afternoon he'd leapt in with both feet, trying to help. He'd even considered the possibility of becoming Aaron's sponsor and leading him through as many of the Steps as possible in the short time remaining before Easter. But getting sober, for most addicts, is a long and torturous process. Nobody can force the change, or speed it up. "Everything's up to Aaron," James says. "While we're together, I'll be as present to him as I can. Beyond that, well, I'll hope, and I'll pray, but I have to let go of the outcome."

Compassion requires dispassion—James and I talk about this at length. The deeper our compassion, the more our efforts to alleviate the sufferings of others are grounded in calm, impartial concern. We are neither excited by success nor disappointed by failure, being detached from the outcome of our own actions. We have no expectations. We don't interfere, or impose our will. We don't rush, don't grasp, don't force, don't pry. We give nourishment without trying to grow the plant; we give guidance without trying to take over the journey.

Being present to another person, having compassion for him, doesn't mean living his life. We have to set boundaries in the relationship; otherwise, our spirit bleed outs, and his seeps in, till neither of us has a center from which to choose or act. But what boundaries are appropriate? Where does the wisdom and energy come from to maintain them?

135

There are no ready-made answers. Even good intentions won't ensure we'll act for the best. So we must practice, practice. Day by day, we must try to cultivate more integrity, empathy, courage and smarts, gaining from our errors in judgment, our fumbles and muffs. Day by day, we must learn to walk with people instead of trying to carry them, disciplining our minds to recognize the difference, and our spirits to live it.

Compassion, in this deep sense, may seem more a spiritual ideal than a livable ethic, but James and I have known a few individuals who have grown to embody it. They're not perfect—they still make their share of mistakes—but they're utterly devoted to the well-being of the world. They enter the suffering of others with neither pity nor pride. Their caring is tireless, and humble: they have nothing to prove, no goal to reach, no time-table to follow. They have learned to listen when it seems time to listen, to speak when it's time to speak, to march when it seems time to march, to sit still when it's time to sit still. Everything in its season.

Such people are our spiritual elders. We follow their light through the dark dark wood, stumbling over what remains hidden.

day 25: saturday, march 13

home movie

Today, as it's turned out, is family day. James's father is flying in from New York City. My parents are driving in from Kentucky, five hours south, and my younger brother is coming from two hours north with his family. All of them, plus Jihong, will be at the Statehouse during noontime meditation; afterwards, a reunion behind closed doors at the Agora.

By happenstance, our relatives' visit will mark the halfway point, or thereabouts, of our sojourn on the streets. James and I both feel ambivalent about seeing them; the inevitable questions, the impossible answers, all mingled with terrible longings for which we have no words. We'll still be the loved ones our families remember, yet in many ways strangers, too, just as they'll be to us.

Scenes of the impending reunion play like a jiggly home movie across the screen of my mind, all in black and white: the touches, the hugs, the hand-holding, the eyes searching—and then somebody says, "Haven'tcha had enough? Isn't it time to come home?", and I have to tell them, if only I can muster the strength to tell them, "No, the Thing isn't done with me. . . ."

136

upscale

(**mcdonald's on s. high, mid-morning.**) James is waiting for his father, whom he's arranged to meet over breakfast. He's leafing through some stray sections of the Dispatch when, to his dismay, our neighbor Calvin settles down with his own paper at the very next table. Calvin looks intently at the pages, but his eyes don't move. He doesn't seem to be reading; more like he's acting a part, wanting to fit in. Every so often he glances nervously around the room. Obviously he isn't in a hurry.

James's father arrives promptly at 9:30. "Hey Turks," he grins, leaning down for a hug, but James jumps up and quickly leads him past Calvin's table, out the door. "Sorry, Dad," James says, "but we need to get outa this neighborhood. I know too many people."

Once in the rental car they exchange a quick hug. "Your nose is red," his father says. "You've got that 'homeless boozer' look."

"It's from bein' out in the sun and wind," James says.

They drive to Katzinger's, a faddish deli in German Village. Nobody will recognize James here. Too upscale. The place is warm with the aromas of baked goods just out of the oven and specialty coffees, freshly brewed. Standing in line at the counter, James's father wants to buy him breakfast, as well as food for later. Though grateful, James declines his offer and purchases a cup of coffee with street change.[15]

"What do you *do* with yourself all day?" his father asks, once they're settled at a table. "You must have alot of time to *think*?"

James smiles a little. How familiar, he thinks, your tone of voice, your pattern of speech. I've missed our talks—missed *you*—more than I realized. Out here, I've tried not to think much about you. Thinking about anybody I love just makes the distance between us more painful.

But now, James wonders, how to tell you what you want to know? How to tell you that most of my time and energy, every day, goes just to walking—to a gas station to clean up, to the soup kitchen to eat, to the library to get warm? How to tell you that I don't spend too much time reflecting, because I'm just too tired, too hungry, too raw? How to tell you that I'm gradually losing myself—that I see ghosts of me hanging around the Statehouse, the alleyways, the churches, the tracks—I can't call them back home, and I can't scare them off—I don't know who I am—

scorched

(**camp, late afternoon.**) For me, the reunion is over. All the touching, all the tears, all the catching up on family news, all the questions—over. I'm

137

dried up. Scorched like a tea kettle left too long on the stove.

I replenish our pile of kindling, build a slow fire. Then, using a jagged piece of brick, I work at scraping the charred remains of last night's noodles out of our cookpot. The labor is simple, requiring attention but not thought. Just what I need. I'm nearly finished when Jake shows up, obviously drunk, with an armload of firewood. Clumsily he deposits the pieces on our modest woodpile. They're just the right size for our grill.

Jake waves off my thanks, makes a move to go, then turns back. "Y'know," he says, in a sweet tipsy slur, "anytime ya wanna get warm or anything, just c'mon over. Me and Sarge, we gotta little propane heater. Gets real toasty. Besides, I don't wanna scare ya or nothin', but I worry 'boutcha bein' alone over here. If ya ever get scared, just c'mon over and sit with us."

"I appreciate that, Jake."

"I *mean* it. It's rough out here. You know that, well as anybody. It's good, you stickin' by your man through thick and thin. I know it's a little thin right now, but if ya hang in there, it'll get better."

"Thanks, Jake." *You're a brother.*

"So if anybody ever bothers ya over here, you just holler, and me and Sarge'll be right over to chase 'em off. You remember that."

solidarity

(camp, evening.) Well after dark. Four carloads of volunteers have begun to make their rounds of the camps. Hungry, waiting alone by the fire, I realize, grudgingly, that I've begun to depend on these food drops, made on Thursday and Saturday nights. Usually the volunteers are under the supervision of Sabrina Martin, daughter of Harold and Ada. Sometimes her parents show up, too, but they can't be everywhere at once. Their organization delivers food all over the city.

Tonight the first people into camp are anglos from an evangelical church. People from this same church come every Saturday, always with the same bag of rations for each of us: Christian literature, a pair of socks, two Nutri-Grain bars, a large bottle of vitamin C tablets, several four-ounce cartons of both fruit drink and expired milk. For the most part, these are things that James and I don't need. Tomorrow, as usual, we'll throw out the milk, then consolidate the remaining contents of our two bags of goodies and tote them to a soup kitchen, quietly leaving them on a hallway table for others to claim.

"Is James lookin' for work?" one of the men inquires now, offering me a pack of cigarettes, which I refuse.

"Yeah," I say. "I am, too."

138

"So what kinda work's he lookin' for?"

"Honest," I say, and the group erupts in laughter. When they calm down, they pray briefly for James's quick success in finding a job.

"Will you guys be at next Saturday's camp-out?" somebody asks after the Amen.

Stifling a laugh *(isn't every day a camp-out?)*, I say, "What camp-out d'ya mean?"

"Harold and Ada's sponsorin' an overnighter. All the street people and volunteers are gonna spend the night together at Mad Dog's place, on up the tracks. There'll be food, and a bonfire, and a big-screen tv—everybody's invited. Even some tv people."

"Is that so?" I say, wondering if anybody had consulted Mad Dog before planning this shindig.

"Yeah," they say. "It's s'posed to give us volunteers a taste of what it's like to be homeless, and also allow us to express our solidarity with people like you."

"Uh-huh," I say, glancing around the group. "So, you all gonna be there?"

Nobody says a word. Not right away. Then the confessions start rolling out, all the reasons they won't be able to make it. Scheduling conflicts. "Such short notice, y'know." Some in the group seem genuinely regretful, others appear relieved.

"Well," I say, "James and I prob'ly won't make it either. We're not much into crowds."

this is home

A stout white woman traipses down the path, introduces herself as Kate. Quite the cook, she has baked some homemade lasagna, served up now with dinner rolls in foam containers. She has also prepared a box of supplies for James and me: peanut butter, pork and beans, baby sausages, tapered and votive candles, two glass candle holders, four rolls of toilet paper, a tube of Colgate, tampons, several disposable razors, shaving cream, feminine body wash. . . .

"I've been thinking of you two all week," she says tearfully, "wondering what I could bring you."

Her thoughtfulness moves me deeply. Many of these supplies James and I will actually be able to use. "Are you with the same church as the others?" I ask, making conversation.

She bristles. "*No,* I'm *not!*" she says. "I don't even like being *associated* with them. They just *barge in* on folks, not knowing what kinda mood you're in or anything, and then they're upset when one of you gets *mad*."

She stares at our shelter, says, "I mean, *this* is your *home*. . . ."

day 26: sunday, march 14

come-as-you-are

(central presbyterian church, mid-morning.)   Five minutes late for breakfast. The serving line for poor and homeless people runs on strict middle-class church time, not come-as-you-are street time, but the scowling door monitor lets us in anyway. James and I hurry to the kitchen windows, faces bright red, trying to catch our breath. White ladies with silver-gray hair spoon up sausage gravy over hot biscuits, adding extra when they hear how far we walked in the bitter morning's cold to get here.

At least we weren't plodding through snow. The weatherman had predicted a big storm overnight. Counties just south of the city are socked in under eighteen inches of snow. Here it's nippy, but not a flake.

Over breakfast we sit with our neighbor Blue and his new friend Elena. She's been staying with him in his shack up the tracks since being beaten and robbed four days ago. If I don't look at the bruises on her tanned face, she closely resembles an old friend of mine—her eyes are soft but bright, her middle-aged body earthy and lithe, her presence full, even now, under the influence of alcohol—but of course I can't look at her face and not see the bruises. Blue's tender with her, and protective. She touches him with affection. The sight makes my heart ache. You don't see many people touching each other with tenderness out here. You don't see many people touching.

Elena says, with great calm, that she's used to roughing it; that not so long ago she was living in the mountains of New Mexico with no running water, no indoor plumbing, no heat. Her voice is gentle, like an old love song.

A youth group is visiting from a Presbyterian church out in the suburbs. While we eat breakfast, one of them wanders among the crowded tables like a minstrel, strumming a mellow guitar. Then, to begin worship, the group leader reads the gospel story of the rich young man who goes to Jesus, says he's been keeping all the commandments, asks what else he must do to have eternal life. Jesus tells him to sell his possessions, give the proceeds to the poor, and follow. Not exactly what the guy wanted to hear.

Ordinarily at this point the minister would tell us all what the scripture passage means. But this morning he isn't here. The visiting youth group invites a discussion. Several homeless people venture opinions about the text, arguing its implications with the vigor of seminarians. The exchange is refreshing. For a change, nobody seems in a rush to leave.

"God isn't opposed to people havin' possessions," says a passionate young black man named Michael, getting in the last word. "God's opposed to people *losin'* themselves *to* their possessions. It isn't materials but *materialism* that gets in the way of our faithfulness."

Prayers, now. Today, no minister speaking on our behalf; the young people encourage us to pray aloud the prayers we want to pray. The petitions are few, brief, simple, poignant. Elena's voice is so soft, it seems hardly meant for hearing. "Our loving Father," she pleads, each word measured and grave, "I ask you for guidance. Show me which direction I should go."

The tables empty. James and I stand up, don our coats, then shake hands with Blue, with Elena. For Elena, this isn't enough. She hugs me, hangs on, sags. I struggle to hold her up. One of her tears moistens my lower cheek. Blue reaches out, gathers her in. I struggle to let her go. "Gotta take care of each other," she mumbles as Blue shores her up, leads her slowly toward the door.

So many of the folks we meet out here say the most tender things; some, even as they're killing themselves, slow as gin.

On a car parked outside the church, a vanity plate: HUMAN FRM.

traces

(**camp, early evening.**) I've thrown some lumps of coal into the fire tonight; another gift from the railroad tracks. It's taken a while, but finally they've begun to glow. You smell the sooty burn before you see the smoke.

I'm writing on photocopies of old birth certificates. My dirty fingers leave traces on the paper, black smudges, tiny lines that swirl; ephemeral prints of a body, a person, a life.

Today I felt very emotional, very raw, like a wound when its scab has been torn away. At mass, where the priests were wearing rose-colored chasubles instead of the usual purple (a reminder, they said, that we've now entered the second half of Lent), it didn't take much to prompt tears: the wafting frankincense; a word, any word, in the first hymn; a fleeting thought of my father, now probably back home in Kentucky, planting his new rose bushes; a priest who, shaking my hand, said, "How're you doin' today?", as if he genuinely wanted to know—

It doesn't take much.

James and I now have more days behind us on the streets than lie ahead. Till lately I haven't let myself think much about the end of this ordeal, but here by the fire my thoughts drift to our last day like smoke to heaven. I do so look forward to not having to struggle for everything I need; to not being deep down in the bones tired; to not being filthy; to not feeling invisible, or despised. This scant dose of anticipation I permit myself, an indulgence made possible by my life of privilege. After all, leaving home on Ash Wednesday was entirely my choice; going home will be, too. What of those people who have no real home to return to? To what do they look forward tonight?

Is anybody missing *them?*

Fire crackles. Overhead, a honking gaggle of geese, flying in elegant silhouette across the orange-streaked lavender sky. Now a blue heron too lifts in flight, and suddenly I'm back in childhood, behind my family's house on the east bank of the Blanchard River, where long-legged herons, wading in the shallows, would wing away if you got too close. The sight, or the memory, makes me lay down my pen. I'm so happy, out here, for the company of birds. . . .

bon apetit

James enters camp, kneels beside the fire in the grill. Like rabbits from a hat he pulls from a sack two rounds of focaccia bread topped with cheese, tomato sauce and spices, courtesy of the Einstein Bros. dumpster. Laughing at our luck, I plop them on the grill to warm.

James and I are terribly grateful for any food that we can forage, or that we're given, out here. Like the biblical loaves and fishes, no matter how little we possess, somehow we always seem to have enough. Still, we feel a poverty around food that has nothing to do with quantities. It has to do with intimacy. We want more affinity with what we eat—

You want to decide what food you'll fix, and how you'll prepare it. You want to scrub and mince and dice and chop, almost slice your finger. You want to overcook the pasta and overbake the bread. You want to set the table, sit down with somebody you love, and eat slowly by candlelight, savoring each bite. Then, at meal's end, you want to clear the plates and let your hands wrinkle up red in hot, soapy dishwater. . . .

Out here, our connection to food is almost entirely animal. We consume it to stay alive. Gratitude, yes—we feel it profoundly, and this may set us a little apart from vultures and wolves—but without apology we confess: we still desire pleasure.

This too, I believe, may make us less the beast.

robin hood

(**camp, middle of the night.**) "Jeremy! *Jeremy!*"

"Does that sound like Rooster?" James says, with a dozy groan.

"I think so," I say, propping myself on an elbow, "but who's Jeremy?"

142

The yelling draws closer. Somebody's crashing through the woods.

"James," I say, "he's calling *you*—he's just mixed up the names. Prob'ly been drinkin'."

"Jeremy! Hey, *wake up!*"

Rooster's just outside our shelter now, stomping around, hollering nonsense at the top of his lungs. Closer than James to the door, I stick my head out. "Whassup?"

"Where's Jeremy?"

"If you mean *James,* he's sleepin'—"

"Well *hell,* tell 'im to get outa bed and c'mon out here, see this shit I brought!"

Shoving my feet into the nearest pair of shoes, I crawl out, making excuses for James. As I stand up, Rooster proudly dumps a garbage bag full of packaged meat onto the frozen ground—hot dogs, sausage links, processed hams. He dances around the pile, snorting and whooping in the moonlight. Apparently he's robbed a convenience store. "Yessirree," he squeals, "I'm a goddamned Robin Hood! I steal from the rich, give to the poor! Gonna feed every motherfucking homeless person out here!"

I don't say a word.

"I tell ya, that bag was *heavy,*" Rooster says, flexing a bicep. "Proved to myself I'm still a young man! Hey, I'm goin' back for more—you guys want steaks? Ol' Robin Hood'll get some for ya—"

"Rooster," I say, "we don't want any steaks. I appreciate you thinkin' of us, but—" I stop in mid-sentence, not knowing how to finish.

"I'll come by later and pick up the meat I want," Rooster says. "How much should I leave for you guys? What'll ya eat?"

"To tell ya the truth, we don't need any of it," I say. "Besides, the critters—"

"*Hell,*" he says, "if the critters get into it, they need it worse than you do. Look, I'll just leave ya'll some steaks, and some hot dogs, and one o' these here ten-pound hams—"

day 27: monday, march 15

loot

(**early morning.**) James and I want it to have been a dream, but no, at first light, Rooster's loot is still lying in a heap outside our door. Thankfully, though, no steaks.

143

Presumably Rooster came back last night for the meat he wanted. James and I stare at the remaining forty pounds, wondering what to do. Finally we bag up as many packages as we can carry and set off on the long march to the nearest soup kitchen, hoping no one will see.

jabberwockied

(**downtown, late morning.**) I'm a scarecrow in the wind. My steps seem almost to miss the ground. I don't know how to use my feet. Deliberately I pick one up, stamp it down, pick up the other, stamp. Carrying myself used to be so easy.

Vanity plate on a hot red sports car: ABOUT ME.

My spirits, James's too, have been low ever since Saturday. To reunite with our families, we had to pass like Alice back through the looking-glass; everything that used to be so easy and familiar there was now jabberwockied, but we stayed as long as we could, happy at least to feel loved—

Then, all at once, it was over.

The emptiness that remains is crushing.

Across the way, a shaggy mutt lies chained and dispirited in muddy snow, while in the same yard two guys shoot hoops, no net on the rim. A threesome deals drugs on the corner, while a woman stares wistfully out the first-floor window of her ramshackle house, watching for a parade that will never come.

Outside police headquarters a cruiser lurches back and forth, back and forth, the cop trying to parallel park.

I walk to St. Joe's Cathedral for some uninterrupted quiet; its lofty nave, especially when empty, never fails to soothe, lifting my spirits above the cold streets. In the vestibule, I'm dipping my fingertips into the holy water (I don't know what it means, exactly, to touch this water to my forehead, but it's customary here, and somehow a comfort) when I notice a flimsy cardboard box resting on the floor, wrapped in plastic. The box contains a few muffins and dinner rolls, and a deli bun thickly spread with chicken salad: the kind of food somebody might carry away from a generous soup kitchen. Whoever it belongs to must be in the nave.

I go inside, seat myself in a back pew, glance around. Nobody.

My stomach growls.

The ceiling soars.

Over the next hour or so, several parishioners come and go. I meditate a while, then simply rest, drawing consolation from the cavernous silence and the solitude, the streets so near, so far.

Footsteps approach from the chancel. I open my eyes to see "just Sam," who, weeks ago, gave James and me sandwiches at the rectory's back door. He looks taller than I remembered.

"How are you?" he asks.

"Okay. You?"

He grimaces, moves on as he says, "Oh, you just can't *trust* some people. . . ."

After a few minutes, he's back. "Y'know," he says, "there's a box of food in the entry."

"I saw that. I thought it prob'ly belonged to somebody who'd come in here, but nobody was around."

"Tell ya what," he says, "if you go out and get that food right now, it's yours."

"Really?" I say.

"Really."

"Well, okay," I say, "but only if you remember one thing."

"What's that?"

"You can trust *me*."

He smiles a little. "I'm countin' on that."

Now Sam tells me that "something valuable" has just been stolen from the sanctuary—"again." "You try to keep the place *open*," he says, sounding dejected, his words trailing behind him as he walks off. Watching him go, I can't help suspecting that the food James and I will eat for our dinner was left behind by a thief.

our georgie

(**afternoon.**) James and I hike to Greenlawn Cemetery, hoping to visit a grave recently featured in the Dispatch. We're not prepared for the cemetery's size—400 acres, according to the man at the cemetery office, producing a map; more than 160,000 graves and crypts, the earliest dating back to 1848. Buried among the magnificent old trees and gently curving lanes are such notables as the preacher Washington Gladden, the aviator Eddie Rickenbacker, the humorist James Thurber, and of course, George Blount. To the boy's grave the cemetery man quickly marks the route, a practiced routine.

George Blount, 1867-1873. Died from a fall at the age of six. Perched up high on a granite chair, facing west, even from a distance the boy wrecks your heart. Tiny Tim in stone.

For years now, according to the newspaper, some lady has been dressing George Blount against the cold of winter. This year she has decked him out in a blue knit cap and matching scarf. Around him lie various offerings: pacifier, doll baby, teddy bear, box of crayons and coloring book, sun-bleached

Georgie

Christmas stocking. One of his hands is full of pennies, some of them shiny, others copper-green.

Way over in German Village, the bells of St. Mary's are tolling, faintly. I hear but neglect to count the hour.

A foot marker reads "Our Georgie," yet the boy seems to be alone; no parents, no siblings buried in adjacent plots. I go up to him and remove his blue cap. The elements have worn him into an old man, bald and blind. The left side of his face is dark and pitted; the right side, light and smooth.

James kisses George's cheek. I replace his cap, making sure his ears are covered. Whatever brought us here remains. God bless us, every one.

world beautiful

(**riverbank, late afternoon.**) James and I are resting by the river when Rooster happens by, clean shaven, dressed up and smelling of cheap cologne. He swigs a brownbagged bottle, tells us he's going to church. Somebody from the congregation will soon be picking him up.

Earlier, I'd run into Rooster along the tracks. "I'll be stoppin' by your place to pick up the resta my meat," he'd said, still high from his misadventure.

"Gosh, Rooster, I'm sorry, but James and I thought you'd already taken whatcha wanted. The meat that was still there this mornin', we gave away."

"Ya didn't keep *none*?" Rooster had tugged his knit hat low over his eyebrows. "Well," he said, finally, "I guess that's okay, if somebody really needed it. By the way, I'm sorry I didn't getcha no steaks, but when I went back to the store, the cops showed up. I had to sneak outa window and climb up on the roof to get away."

The river invites contemplation. I perch on a boulder a little ways off from the guys, gaze on the water. Rooster, meanwhile, has James's ear. "Dead bodies been found all 'round these parts," he says in a low, guarded voice. "They found a black guy on the other side o' the river, decapitated, wearin' his boxers. A coupla weeks ago, a woman's body washed ashore after she jumped off the south bridge. Some fucked up shit 'round here."

Rooster's been in jail twice. "The first time," he says, "was down in Kentucky. I killed this teacher—a child molester. Walked right into the classroom and told all the kids to leave, then I closed the door and shot 'im. Called the police myself. Didn't run, y'know. He deserved it. That shit just ain't right.

"The second time," he says, "some guy was robbin' Enid. Nobody's gonna mess with my woman. I gutted 'im with his own knife. SWAT team come down here to get me—"

He breaks off the story, studies his bottle. "Y'know," he says then, "I'd kill 'em both again. My dad, he tol' me women and children's what makes this world beautiful. Gotta take care of 'em. Hell, if I ever raised my hand or voice to a woman, my dad, he'd come down from heaven and shoot me hisself."

houseplans

(**camp, early evening.**) The evening turns brisk. We forego a fire, crawl into the shelter, pile on the blankets, light a candle, eat a cold dinner. We're jotting down notes, hoping they'll make sense the next time we read them, when car doors slam. More volunteers. James wants to stay in bed, and I'm tempted, but at least one of us should go out of politeness. "My turn," I say, and I'm tying my shoelaces when Harold Martin's flashlight pokes in through our door. I ask him to please wait outside.

He's brought a group from a suburban church. The volunteers hand me two styrofoam boxes. James and I aren't hungry, but in this deep-freeze weather, food keeps.

Harold's excited. "We've gotta hut for ya," he says.

"Whaddya mean?" I say.

"We're buildin' ya a hut. We're gonna set it up for you guys next week."

Déjà vu. Last time I saw Harold, he was trying to give us a tent.

"Harold," I say, "please believe me, James and I are satisfied with our shelter. Give the hut to somebody else. Ask the Professor if he'd want it. He's livin' in a *refrigerator.*"

Harold persists. "We're gonna give ya a little heater, too," he says, and ignores my efforts to dissuade him. "We'll talk about it later," he states finally, and leaves.

Never thought I'd be working so hard, begging somebody *not* to help.

Back inside the shelter, James and I mull things over: When did we forfeit the right to choose our own home, the kind of place in which we'd like to live? When did we become subservient to the good will of others, compelled to accept whatever they want to give us, or do for us, or make of us?

"To stop this," I say to James, "maybe we're gonna have to lie."

James and I can hardly think of a time on the streets when we've told an outright lie about ourselves. Sometimes we've tweaked the truth a little, but mostly, till now, we've just allowed people the right to their own assumptions about who we are and why we're here. Considering the circumstances, though, we now need a story of our own—a story, as true as possible, that will help us deflect help we don't want in the direction of somebody else. Beginning, of course, with Harold's hut. By candlelight, James and I improvise, finally settling on a simple "come-up" tale, spun of just enough truth to salve our uneasy consciences. Since it's often presumed that, of the two of us, only James is seeking employment, we make him the hero:

"I have a line on some work up north. We'll prob'ly be leavin' soon, so please give the hut to somebody who can use it more."

We're agreed then. We'll tell the Martins our good news, next chance we get.

day 28: tuesday, march 16

hanging by a rope

(**riverbank, mid-morning.**) On our way to Grubb Street for lunch, James and I pass a crew of railroad men realigning a short section of rail. Though the change looks to be subtle, it's measured in straining muscles, groans and the gritting of teeth. Like one's life, this track, wherever it leads, demands not only maintenance but respect. Otherwise, disaster.

Further up, we cross a trestle over the river. On the south bank, suspended in a harness from a tree, a railroad man is using a chainsaw to lop off limbs grown too close to the bridge. James and I exchange a glance, recalling our first day on the streets, when city workers in Worthington were trimming saplings. That day we identified with the trees. Today we identify with the railroad man, hanging by a rope in mid-air over a swollen, muddy river, out here where nobody can see him. *What if you were to fall?*

gallery

(**downtown, mid-afternoon.**) Roaming back alleys, James comes to an abandoned warehouse, recently torched. The barred windows are ringed by soot. Peering into the building through a vent, he sees charred beams crisscrossing the floor, light spilling from holes in the roof. The way the stark light illuminates the space makes him want to take pictures. He shoulders his way in through a stubborn door.

Melting snow drips from jagged edges of roof, creates pools of liquid sunshine on the blackened floor. The reflected sky is brilliantly blue.

James's steps are measured and slow. Hardly a sound. Careful, he tells himself—you may not be alone.

A small room off to the side has been used as a shooting gallery. Syringes and crack pipes litter the floor; a tourniquet hangs off a wobbly table, like a dead man's arm off the side of a gurney.

149

Despite its scars, the place has an ethereal feel; captivating now, but dangerous after dark. James manages three photos before the shadows creep in on him, send him hurrying back out through that stubborn door.

busted

(**late afternoon.**) We take the tracks south, all the way out of the downtown, James shooting pictures on our way to camp. We're almost home when we spot Jake up ahead, waving his arms to get our attention—

"Hey guys, the railroad cop's comin'!"

James and I exchange an anxious glance. *There's a railroad cop?*

Jake points. We turn around to look. A white jeep is headed our way, slowly bumping along over the coarse gravel between two sets of tracks.

We step off the railroad bed and walk a little ways off, casually, pretending we're not scared of being busted. "What should we do?" I ask James.

"Don't know."

We smile and wave as the jeep rolls up. The cop waves back, drives right on by.

We look at Jake, relieved. Even at this distance we can see he's grinning, ear to ear.

"Yeah," he says when we catch up to him, "the railroad's got some cops. They drive through every so often, and if they see ya walkin' on the tracks, they can arrest ya, but usually they give ya a warnin' first. They 'specially don't like ya walkin' over that trestle to get to Grubb—I been busted there. Ya just gotta be careful. It's best to walk 'longside the tracks, if you're gonna walk 'em at all."

So much for the one place James and I felt totally free.

pick-up line

(**riverbank, late afternoon.**) James and I hitch along the tracks toward home. We're almost there when a vehicle approaches from behind, bumping along the gravelly railroad bed. With a low western sun glinting on glass and metal, we can't make out the driver till he's right on us—Harold Martin. Ada's in the passenger seat.

"Hey," Harold says, "ya'll wanna go somewhere, maybe chill outa little?"

Ada says, "We gotta house where we sometimes take people. Why don'tcha c'mon? You can getta bite to eat, clean up a little, watch some tv."

Dead tired, James and I hesitate.

"You guys can even take showers, if ya want," Ada says.

Showers? Hallelujah! We open a rear door and climb in.

150

Up top, Harold stops at a gas station. Now Ada turns around, says to us, "Oh, by the way, there's gonna be some tv people at the house. You don't have to talk to 'em if ya don't wanna."

Dread spills through my gut. "I really don't want to," I say, with an emphatic echo from James.

"That's okay," she reassures us. "I just wanted ya to know they're gonna be there."

Soon we're zipping through traffic. After ponderous weeks of walking, standing, sitting, lying down, I'm unprepared for speed. I grip the handle of my door, white-knuckled. Harold turns right, veers left, shoots into the far lane, then back across, and suddenly we're out on the freeway, headed east. I blink. How far are we going, anyway?

"Ya sure you don't wanna talk to the tv people?" Ada asks over her shoulder.

stories

"Where ya from?" Ada wants to know. "How long ya been on the streets? Are ya on welfare? SSI? Are ya lookin' for work? What kind?"

"Ada," I say, trying to change the subject, "how d'ya keep goin', with all this work you do?"

"Well," she says, "of course it's the Lord, it's *always* been the Lord, but—" and now Ada launches into the story of all she and Harold have accomplished the past seventeen years. Much of the story is familiar; articles have run in the paper, coverage has aired on the news, word gets around on the streets. It all started just before Thanksgiving, 1982, at a downtown skating rink that no longer exists. Harold spotted a homeless man stealing a skater's shoes, and he intervened, giving the man his own sneakers, socks and coat.

The Martins fed that man for several days. Then he disappeared. When they went looking for him, they didn't find him, but they found many other people in the same straits. Now, all these years later, they work with volunteers up to six nights a week, delivering food to homeless people in different areas of the city. They also collect toys for homeless kids, line up jobs for the unemployed, hold memorial services for people who have died on the streets, and run a halfway house that helps homeless people make a transition to stable housing. That house is apparently where we're headed.

"Homeless folks are *my* people," Ada says more than once. "They're my *family*. Harold and I, we don't make *any* judgments."

Harold, a factory worker, has been married to Ada, who's retired from civil service, for more than thirty years. He admits wishing sometimes that he and Ada could have more time alone, especially now that they both have serious health problems, or that they hadn't spent so much of their own money on homeless people. "But then," he says, "I'm always thinkin', 'What if *I* was homeless? What if it was *me*?'"

"By the way," Harold says to us after a while, "we're gonna get you guys a tv, hook it up to run off a car battery. We'll getcha all set up."

I look at James, he looks at me. "Thanks," I say to Harold, "but we don't wanna tv."

"Whaddya mean, *ya don't want no tv?*" He stares at us in his rearview mirror, shakes his head.

naked

Clear over on the east side of the city, in working-class Whitehall, Harold pulls into a driveway. The house itself scarcely makes an impression, I'm so anxious to be clean, but I do observe, thankfully, that we've arrived before the tv crew.

Once inside, James and I are introduced to Charles and Theo, two black men, formerly homeless, now residing at the house. Charles escorts me to an upstairs bathroom, where he provides me with a bar of hotel soap, shampoo and a towel before I finally, eagerly, close the door.

There's such relief in stripping off my dirty clothes, in standing naked in the heat of this room, I begin softly to cry. Nothing to hide here, and no need to hurry. I stand in front of the mirror: long straggly bangs, dark circles beneath my reddening eyes, face sunburned, windburned and pimpling, cheekbones starting to jut, lips chapped and peeling. . . . My vanity's shot to kingdom-come.

I lean into the glass, look closely. Scarcely any light in my eyes. That scares me a little.

I'm even thinner than I used to be; the mirror doesn't tell me this, but the vague way of my body in air. It feels light and empty, yet coarse, like a dusty burlap sack after its feed has been dumped in a hog trough.

Meanwhile, in a downstairs bathroom, James stands naked before a cracked mirror. He hasn't seen his skin in two weeks or more. His face is red from the elements, but the rest of his body is yellow gray.

He stinks. Bad.

He can hear my shower running upstairs. Reaching into the tub, he turns the water on hot, then grabs a bottle of Prell from the vanity. Peeling back the cheap shower curtain, he steps into steam.

The water pressure surges and sinks; the temperature runs cold, then hot. No washcloth, but the water, *oh, the water. . . .*

light lost from the eyes

practicalities

A knock on the bathroom door. Hurrying to dress, I open it to Theo, who holds out a pair of high-heeled boots, flare-legged jeans and a tight sweater, all suitable for a sorority girl. Wherever they came from, they'd be impractical for the streets. He frowns when I turn them down. "Don't worry," I tell him, laughing at my dirty clothes, "it's almost laundry day."

Downstairs, there are no towels. James squeegees his body with his hands. Then, still dripping, he leans down, picks up the fuzzy teal bath mat from the floor, begins to wipe. . . .

alias

Slowly I descend the stairs. Channel 4 News has arrived. In the adjacent living room, bright lights are being adjusted by a cameraman. Ada is talking in low tones to a woman, heavily made up, whom I recognize as a feature reporter. Instantly uneasy, I consider retreating to the second floor, but before I can make my escape the reporter spots me on the stairs. She walks over, says she wants to interview me on camera.

"I don't wanna be interviewed," I say. *So this is why the change of clothes. They want you to look more presentable. More stylish. More like a woman, for the camera.*

"This is *very* important," the reporter says, drawing me down the steps and into the living room. James, his hair and beard dripping wet, is already sitting on the couch. The reporter stands between us—classic "divide and conquer"—and says, "Don't you know why we're here?"

"I'm here to take a shower," I say.

"Well," she says, "let me tell you why we're doing this segment. We want to help Harold and Ada. They have to raise $40,000 in the next two weeks, or this house will be repossessed by HUD."

Ada is directly behind the reporter, her eyes wide open and fixed on me, palms pressed together as if beseeching the Lord Almighty. Please, please, please, she mouths. I understand her desperation, but James and I did tell her no interviews. Told her not once but twice.

"All we want the two of you to do," the reporter says, "is tell us how important this place is to you. What it means, knowing you can come here—"

"But we didn't even know this place existed," James says, "till a coupla hours ago—"

"More than two hundred people have lived here," Ada pipes in, as if prepping us. "We helped get 'em off the streets. Other folks come here, too, like you done tonight, just to chill."

"We *really* need you," the reporter coaxes.

James shoots me a *what-have-we-gotten-ourselves-into* look. I shoot it right back. If only the Martins had been straight with us. But then, we haven't exactly been straight with them. Maybe you reap what you sow.

Spirit does move in mysterious ways. Some good could yet come of this. I draw a deep breath. "Okay," I say, "I'll help, but on certain conditions. I don't want my face shown, I don't want my real name used, and I won't answer any questions about my past or my personal life. All I'll do is talk about what I know—that it felt great to come here tonight and take a shower."

The reporter agrees. Then she retrieves a memo pad and pen, wanting background. "Where are you from? Why are you on the streets? How long have you been out?" Amazed at the effrontery, I respond to her questions only vaguely, reminding her, more than once, that she agreed to respect my privacy.

"What's your name?" she says.

"Phyllis," I say, noticing that she hasn't bothered to introduce herself, "but like I told you, I don't want my real name used."

"What name should we use then?"

I smile to myself. Just this afternoon Jake had christened James and me "Mister and Missus Ingalls," after the characters on Little House on the Prairie. "That was one o' my favorite tv programs as a kid," he'd said. "Yeah, the *Ingalls*. Rooster and I thought that name fit, 'cause you guys don't smoke, ya don't drink, ya don't party—you're kinda, like, the *good* couple." The three of us had laughed.

"Use the name Ingalls," I tell the reporter. "Mary Ingalls."

lights

Harold escorts James into the kitchen. He sets out some chips and salsa, asks James if he'd like some soup. "Yeah, okay," James says weakly, wondering how I'm holding up on camera.

Harold opens a can of Campbell's chicken noodle, dumps it in a pan. Smoking a cigarette as the soup heats, he repeatedly begs James to do a straightforward interview. "Ya gotta let 'em see your face," he says, relentless as a spoiled youngster in a toy store. "Please show your face, man. *Please.* C'mon—"

James is beyond disturbed. Not that he doesn't want to help; he just feels pressured, and betrayed, as though the promise of a shower and all the goodnatured chitchat and now the food were just meant to buy him off. He protests, but Harold's not hearing him. Harold whines till James breaks down, sick at heart, and agrees to show his face on camera.

When the tv crew finishes with me, Harold ushers James back into the living room. Pulling his knit hat down over his eyebrows, James slumps on

155

show your face: James
(photo credit: Jihong Cole-Dai)

the sofa. "Call me Jonathan Ingalls," he tells the reporter. Every ounce of him wants to get up and walk out the door, but there's nowhere to go. On the verge of tears, he answers the questions put to him, never looking directly into the camera, tv lights hot on his flushed face.

The interview is a blur. Finally the reporter says, "We've got enough." She gets up, walks away, but the cameraman keeps rolling, pretending he's not.

News at eleven.

derailed

Around 10:00 p.m., more than four hours after they picked us up, the Martins drive us back to the riverbank. On the way across town Ada sermonizes about how she must be "faithful to the Lord" in her life and work in order to be successful; a bewildering comment to hear, after the events of this night. As James and I get out of the Blazer along the tracks, she reminds us that "we're family, and will always be family."

"Three hours ago," James mutters, as we stumble through the darkness toward camp, "those words meant something. Not now."

We fall into bed, totally spent. We feel like passengers on a train that derailed after somebody secretly switched the tracks.

The night is surprisingly warm. We open the plastic flaps over the shelter door, but the fresh air doesn't help us sleep. We're both restless. So many unresolved feelings: regret that we ever got into the Martins' vehicle; resentment, even anger, at being exploited; guilt over our own imposture; fear of being exposed; hope, despite everything, that these strange doings might yield some good. The showers we took are all but forgotten. The price we paid was too high.

Grown weary of tossing, I light a candle, pick up The Crucible where I'd left off. The curtain is about to fall on Act II. John Proctor is in a helpless rage. "We are only what we always were," he cries, "but naked now. Aye, naked! And the wind, God's icy wind, will blow!"

day 29: wednesday, march 17

kinship

(riverbank, early morning.) Walking alongside a train, just after dawn. It's coasting on the rails in the same direction I'm going, at the same unhurried pace, with scarcely a creak or groan. I feel an easy kinship with it that's getting harder to feel with people. Maybe a train is easier to trust.

157

history

(white castle.) 6:40 a.m. Take-out customers stand in a long line at the counter, street folks occupy a few scattered tables. In the booth next to mine, a wild-haired anglo wearing a ragged army coat is grumbling in an ugly tone, now to himself, sometimes to the rest of us. I've never seen him before.

I try to make small-talk with him, and gradually his tone begins to change, losing some of its hostility. Following his lead, we discuss American history since the Civil War, McCarthyism, recent discoveries in physics, Hillary Clinton's service as a KGB agent, how he'd like to hone his carpentry skills and move to Vermont, or go to Scotland and become a fisherman, or get lost in the heart of New Zealand. . . .

The man slips outside to smoke a cigarette. Soon he's in passionate conversation with the air.

There's an ongoing debate, a Dispatch article reports this morning, over how to deal with the city's "Homeless Problem." With the redevelopment taking place just west of downtown, certain shelters will have to be relocated, but nobody seems to want a new shelter established in their neighborhood. One Franklin County commissioner would like to give homeless people a choice: "Either get your act together, or we'll give you a bus ticket out of town."

From across the aisle a well-dressed black woman starts telling me about her husband of eighteen years. He lives on the streets now, she says; she can't remember the last time she saw him. Sometimes, when she has a free hour, she hangs around here, in case he might drift in. She sighs, says, "He's an alcoholic, and he uses drugs, but he raised all our kids before he left. He was a good father. He was *real* good about *that*."

I ask the man's name. *Who knows, our paths might cross.* "Name's Luther," she says, then adds, "He prob'ly goes by some other name now, but how would I ever know?"

bagpipes

(mid-morning.) Today, the Irishman reminds me, is St. Patrick's Day. He wants to see the downtown parade, scheduled to step off from St. Patrick's Church at 11:30 a.m. I don't have any blarney in my bones, but even I have an itch to hear some bagpipes. Somehow they'll match my mood after last night's fiasco with the Martins and Channel 4.

James's pace quickens as we near the crowded parade route. At the corner of Broad and High, he flops down on a spare patch of curb, a good Irishman looking for some better luck. Next to him, a young woman with a stroller.

The infant inside is wearing a green bonnet. James smiles at the child's bright blue eyes and rosy cheeks, till the woman notices and protectively turns the stroller away.

The parade approaches: the standard assortment of shamrocks and leprechauns, the slow march of pipes and drums. Bagpipes wail, echo. James rests his chin on his knees; his eyelids droop, close. For a few precious seconds, he doesn't feel a thing.

I may not be Irish like James, but I do know that St. Patrick's Day celebrates the life of a remarkable man. He didn't, despite the legends, drive all Irish snakes into the sea, and he wasn't the first to bring Christianity to the shores of the emerald isle, but he was the first person in recorded western history to condemn slavery, and he was also one of the few early church leaders who respected and upheld the dignity of women. He was a tireless prophet, demanding justice for all poor and disadvantaged people. So on this, the feast day of Patricius, the Brit who became patron saint of Ireland, I carry in my pocket a wee bit of kelly green, paper from somebody's trash.

anonymity

(mid-afternoon.) Our route out of the downtown takes us past the Columbus Health Department. Two staffers in neckties are smoking on the back stoop. They hail us, say, "You guys looked good on tv last night! That *was* you, wasn't it?"

So much for anonymity.

We find a payphone. I call Jihong. Yes, he says, James and I were on the eleven o'clock news last night. A few of our friends, most of whom rarely watch the Channel 4 broadcast, called to tell him they'd just happened to have it on.

Maybe the news segment will help Ada and Harold obtain the required funds. Maybe not. James and I hope for the best, but we aren't attached to the outcome. It isn't difficult to let go of something you weren't invested in from the start.

It's the questions we can't seem to let go of. Why us? Was our involvement in all this mere happenstance, or something more? Had the Martins, desperate for donations from a predominantly anglo viewing audience, drafted us because we're white? Is that why Harold had pressed James to show his face on tape? Is that why the reporter had chosen *not* to interview two black residents of the halfway house, and instead begged James and me for paper-thin testimonials?

Amid all the questions, only one thing is certain: last night's events would never have happened if James and I hadn't come out on the streets in the

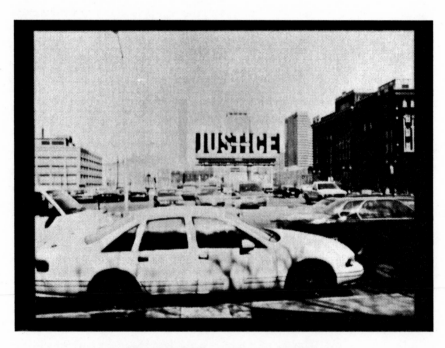

JUSTICE: billboard in the downtown

first place and kept our identities a secret. Who knows? Maybe all of us—including the Martins, including the reporter—were just doing the best we could.

day 30: thursday, march 18

home improvements

(camp, mid-morning.) We're always looking for ways to improve the shelter. James is especially creative. This morning, on the ground near a utility pole, he found a glass insulator; in the trash at the bottom of the bluff, a rusty bedspring. Now, back at camp, he stretches the bedspring into an inverted cone, sets the insulator upside-down into the coil, and hangs it from the ceiling. Perfect for holding a votive candle.

So often what helps best is humble.

lost

(holy family soup kitchen, lunchtime.) Still bleary-eyed after a tough night, James and I wait at a table for the serving line to open. Suddenly, a familiar voice—

Maddy. We're thrilled. We haven't seen her in weeks.

She tells us the cold and snow eventually got the better of her, and she gave up camping with Jeff. Luckily she got into a shelter, then into a short-term rehab program, hoping to detox.

You can see in her eyes she's not making it.

"It's hard, isn't it?" we say.

She nods, tearing up. "I wanna get straight," she says, looking broken, like the spine of a book too long mishandled. "I know what I gotta do, but I can't seem to do it. Sometimes I think knowin' you're a drunk is worse than bein' in denial."

She tells us for the first time about her children, who live hours away. She's lost custody. She doubts she'll ever see them again.

"Sometimes," she says, "I cut myself."

"You cut yourself?" I say, making sure I heard her right. She's beginning to mumble, as if drifting off to sleep. She nods, then mutters something about suicide. Stunned, James and I make her promise not to hurt herself, try to offer encouragement.

She begins to weep. "You two," she says weakly, "are my kinda people."

161

make believe

(**late afternoon.**) James and I pass by a German Village art gallery now closed for the day. On a table in the window, a slim gray tiger cat with white spots lounges in a last splotch of sunshine. Through the glass we scratch her forehead, tickle her paws. *Make believe.* She rolls over, exposing her belly, then jumps up and rubs against the pane. We stroke her back, gloves now off, smearing fingerprints. After a while she draws back on her haunches and stares at us, as if mystified. Finally she rises abruptly and butts her head hard against the window. She wants our touch as badly as we want to give it.

godparents

(**riverbank.**) Rooster and Jake surprise us with a strapping rottweiler pup, maybe three months old, a stray they've "rescued from the streets." She lies on her back, very calmly, in the cradle of Jake's arms, already his baby, trusting him completely. Her short black coat is soft and sleek, her body rippling muscle. Her paws, limp in air, fill the palms of our hands. She's absolutely adorable—no stray, of course, but James and I don't ask any questions. We're just grateful to touch her.

"I'm callin' `im Dog," says Rooster. "That's it. Just plain *Dog.*"

Jake says to James and me, "How 'bout you guys bein' godparents, just in case somethin' happens?"[16]

a single candle

(**st. mary's roman catholic church, late afternoon.**) James and I rest in a back pew. Parishioners straggle in and out. When the sanctuary finally empties, James lies down on the carpeted floor. This church is about the only good place he's found to do his yoga stretches, release some tension—lots of room, no guards, no snow, no cold, no dirt, no mud. . . .

I rise and go to a shrine. I light a candle for Elena, now disappeared ("I couldn't help `er," Blue said, "she liked the bottle too much"). I light a candle for Maddy, who feels so cut off from the world that she slices herself with razor blades. I light a candle for Enid, feet tiny as a ballerina's. I light a candle for Sweetness *(is she in her new apartment?)*, for Cindy *(may you soon be in Texas)*, for Toots *(know you're free)*, for so many women—

I make myself stop. If I keep on, there won't be a single candle left.

A small placard requests a donation. I offer my goodwill. Not everybody who needs to light a candle can afford one.

hausfrauen

(**riverbank, late afternoon.**) Walking along the tracks near camp, I come up behind our neighbor Enid, standing with her arms crossed, staring south as if expecting Yahweh himself to appear. Beyond a few bald facts (she was born in Germany seventy-six years ago, was once a nurse, is now a panhandler, is living in Rooster's tent), she's still a mystery. I've rarely seen her. We've never spoken.

"Guten abend," I say now as I pass, wishing her a good evening, my tongue testing my recollection of college German.

"Guten abend," Enid returns matter-of-factly, as if she and I were two hausfrauen meeting on a street corner in Berlin. Then, suddenly, she seems to realize where she is, and what's just happened—

"Guten abend!" she exclaims.

I smile at her over my shoulder. Her mouth is hanging open.

dust

Jihong once told me that the Chinese character for human being is 人, two lines supporting each other. In other words, no human being stands alone. Just as a house is made up of studs and joists, wiring and pipes, who we are as individuals is, in large part, constituted by a network of relations, both intimate and vast. Not only am I wife, daughter, sister, friend, neighbor, colleague; I'm also a conspiracy of sunshine and rain, soil and trees, gravity and genes. . . . On and on, out and out, down and down the web of relations goes, spun without beginning or end. By virtue of it, I'm located in space and time, and just as truly I'm blown away, a particle of dust. I'm everything, and nothing.

On the streets I have trouble sensing the intimacy, trusting the depth, of these relations. Most of the time I feel remote from them. The house is gone, you might say, and home with it: I seem to stand alone, a nobody, a match lit in breeze.

But then somebody sees me. Bothers to look, and sees me true. Their eyes penetrate mine with the recognition that I matter, and suddenly it washes over me, all that I've fallen out of touch with. In that instant, I feel restored. Significant.

walking the line

(**camp, evening.**) Per the usual schedule, James and I were expecting a visit tonight from Take It to the Streets, but nobody showed up. As we spoon down a little government peanut butter with cold canned salmon, we second-guess ourselves for not having packed out some provisions from a soup kitchen.

This night's hunger, though slight, is a good teacher, revealing just how much we now rely on the Martins and their volunteers. By stressing how happy they are to tend our needs, and at times even tending needs we don't have, they clearly invite this dependency, and from relief we've fallen right in. We're much more lax than we used to be in seeking food elsewhere.

The line between accepting somebody's help and becoming habituated to it is a fine one. When you're dead-tired and depressed, you walk that line like a drunk.

day 31: friday, march 19

grudge

(**downtown, late morning.**) Crusty snowdrifts are melting fast away, except on the north side of buildings, where they're out of the sun's reach. There the snow refuses to thaw, stubborn as an old, old grudge. In some places, despite the springlike days of this past week, it's still piled up to the eaves.

On busy Front Street Harold Martin drives past in a rusty red pickup. Seeing us, he brakes to a stop, backs up alongside the curb. "We'll be workin' hard on the hut today," he says hurriedly, holding up traffic. "Next week, it's all yours."

The hut. Of course. We'd forgotten all about it.

Harold's face is bright as he gives us a parting wave.

"Something's happened," I say to James, the truck sputtering off.

When we reach the Statehouse, shortly before noon, Jihong is waiting. Meeting us briefly in an out-of-the-way spot, he informs us that an anonymous donor has pledged to purchase the halfway house from HUD for $40,000, the exact amount needed. Channel 4 updated the story last night. Ada Martin was shown, live, receiving the good news from the same reporter who had taped the appeal.

James and I are pleased. We wonder, though, if the donor would have been as anxious to help if the halfway house were located in an upper-class suburb like Bexley instead of blue-collar Whitehall. According to the Dispatch, a recent effort to transform a three-story Bexley building into supervised housing for a dozen homeless men has met with strenuous neighborhood opposition.

feast day

(st. joseph cathedral, lunchtime.) St. Joseph, in Roman Catholic tradition, is the protector of anybody who calls on his name for help. Today is his feast day, and to honor the saint for his patronage, the cathedral is hosting a special luncheon for the homeless in its undercroft.

The dimly lit rooms of the undercroft, with their arched doorways, brick floors and stone walls, remind me of vaults in a mansion's wine cellar. In one room several tables have been spread with white linens and adorned with silver service. White tapers flicker in silver candelabra above crystal platters overflowing with homemade bread, chunky chicken salad, deli meats, cheeses, fresh fruit and sweets.

In an adjoining dining room James and I sling our filthy coats over the back of two chairs, feeling a little out of place. Only a half dozen of us among the twenty to thirty people present look remotely poor; the rest, dressed in Sunday finery, are chitchatting about church matters, family concerns and business affairs.

At the buffet table we're happy to run into Sam.

"Didya ever find what you—uh—*lost?*" I say, referring to the recent robbery, and Sam shakes his head.

James and I sit down with mounded plates. Against the far wall the mustached monsignor, dressed in a black double-breasted cassock and purple sash, stands stiff as starch, saying little, hands tightly clasped.

Another, older priest, sporting a collar but in casual clothes, hollers a greeting to us across the room. Last Sunday, I remember, he offered James and me donuts after mass. Now he compliments the size of my sandwich, chicken salad heaped high between two slabs of homemade bread. I laugh, making no apology.

After the tables begin to clear, somebody from the church remarks on how few homeless people showed up for the meal. Sam mentions that last year none came at all.

"The luncheon isn't advertised like it oughta be," says a streetwise anglo who often hands out the sandwiches at the rectory door. "Homeless people are just tryin' to make it from one day, or one hour, to the next. Ya can't just advertise a meal like this a whole month in advance and expect 'em to remember. They're not gonna be writin' it down in a datebook.

"Besides," he goes on, "who woulda known about the luncheon in the first place unless they read it in the church bulletin? We gotta do a better job gettin' the word out. We gotta think the way homeless people think. We gotta take the news to where they are."

freckles

(**deaf school park, mid-afternoon.**) James and I collapse spread-eagled on the ground, thrilling in the sun's warmth. Within a few minutes, a policewoman appears across the way, mounted on a magnificent chestnut horse with a braided tail. She snaps the reins, and the horse begins a slow saunter in our direction. Alarmed, I say to James, "We *are* allowed to lie on the grass, aren't we?" Asking the question seems absurd, yet necessary, considering all the anti-homeless laws on the books in this country. Besides, when you've been rousted as many times as we have, and can easily be charged with vagrancy by anybody not liking the looks of you, the absurd seems more possible than not.

The cop reins in just a few yards away. Deciding to take preemptive action, I jump up, I walk over to the officer like we're old friends and ask if I can pet the horse. "Sure," she says, smiling. "His name is Freckles."

all smiles

(**downtown, early afternoon.**) A woman in her twenties, with a full head of long, red curls, bounds out of a doorway to her car, parked curbside. "Nice hair," James says. "Thanks!" she replies, with spirit, turning to look him straight in the eye. Then, to us both, dirty and ugly as we are, "You guys have a *great* weekend!"

We're all smiles, ready to burst.

day 32: saturday, march 20

gravity

(**riverbank, mid-morning.**) In the field above camp I'm hailed by Rooster, standing at the edge of the woods near his campsite. On the ground at his feet an old man slumps, head bowed. "This is Joseph," Rooster says as I walk up. "Joseph, this is Phyllis, one of our neighbors."

Joseph stares vacantly at the ground.

"He's eighty-six years old," Rooster says, pride in his voice. "Full-blooded Indian. His picture used to be in all the papers, 'cause he'd lead all them big Indian dances, y'know, out west. That was a long time ago, now."

"How long?" I say, and Rooster gestures toward the woods, says, "Since those big trees were small."

The old man can't be warm, clad only in a thin shirt and a lightweight coat, zipper broken. Dried blood stains the front of his dirty khaki pants. Rooster says, "Ol' Joseph escaped from the hospital last night, and somehow he made it all the way out here. I let 'im spend the night in my tent, but he can't stay. Gotta get 'im some help."

He tells me Jake's gone off to retrieve a wheelbarrow from his shack. The old man won't be easy to move. He's big-framed, well over six feet tall, bloated from drink. Dead weight. I lean down, rest my hand on Joseph's shoulder. "Are ya warm enough?" I say, my face near his. "Needa drink of water?"

"Oh," Rooster cuts in, laughing, "Joseph only drinks alcohol. Says water rusts his pipes."

"What I could really use is a cigarette, if ya got any," Joseph says now, lifting his head for the first time. High, square cheekbones. Dark eyes, boring into mine.

"I'm sorry, Joseph. I don't have any."

His eyes soften, drift.

Jake's wheelbarrow is small and rusty, a flat tire wobbling loose on the rim—discouraging, but the best thing we have, probably better than nothing. Jake and Rooster get on either side of Joseph and hoist him off the ground with throaty grunts while I maneuver the wheelbarrow in behind him. I see now that the old man has soiled himself. I think again of the blood on his pants. *Why were you in the hospital last night? Why did you run away?*

Jake and Rooster lower Joseph as gently as they can into the wheelbarrow, but sometimes gravity is cruel, and at the end he drops hard, with a moan, onto the shabby lawn-chair cushion Jake's put in the bottom. I ease the back of the barrow down. Joseph's legs hang over the front, the tips of his shoes almost touching ground. Under his weight, the tire's splayed flat beneath the wheel's rim.

Jake says they'll haul Joseph south along the tracks. Once under the bridge, they'll go up top to call Netcare, an emergency service for persons with substance abuse or mental health problems. Once a squad arrives, Joseph can be carried up to street level on a stretcher, then transported to a hospital.

Joseph's muttering, trying to say something. Rooster kneels beside him. They old man draws a shuddering breath, says in barely a whisper, "Don't wanna go."

"Ya don't wanna go?" Rooster repeats.

Joseph shakes his head.

An awkward silence. Then Joseph says, "But guess I gotta."

Rooster gets to his feet, steps a short distance away, turns his back. Hands on hips, he digs at the ground with the toe of a boot. At last he tips his head back, as if staring straight up into his God's heaven, and doesn't move. Not for the longest time.

When finally he turns around again, his face is flushed deep red, and tears are streaming down his wind-burned cheeks. "Joseph," he says, his voice cracking, "I just can't take care of ya. Not like ya need. Not out here. Understand?" He wipes his cheeks on his sleeve. Joseph doesn't say a word.

Rooster circles behind the wheelbarrow, grabs the handles, lifts, and shoves. The wheel doesn't budge. The barrow teeters. Jake throws his weight against the side.

"She ain't gonna roll thru the field," Jake says. "We'll have to pull 'er."

"What can I do?" I ask.

"This ain't for you," Rooster says, not without kindness. "Jake and I'll manage."

Reluctantly I stand aside. "Okay," I say, "but if you guys get stuck and need another pair of hands, come get me. I'll be at camp."

They promise they will, but I know they won't; they're both protective of me, Jake in his sweet, almost brotherly way, and Rooster with a machismo that sometimes seems exaggerated for my benefit. "This is a good thing you're doin'," I say to them, as encouragement.

The guys each grab a wooden handle and at the count of three begin to drag the barrow behind them through the dead weeds. Momentum's slow to gather, the going clumsy, till finally they hit the smoother ground alongside the railroad bed. There they start to push. Joseph bumps along, chin resting almost on his chest, straight gray-black hair tumbling over his shoulders, shoestrings untied and dangling—

If only you'd had a cigarette.

James, returning to camp from up top, meets the wheelbarrow along the tracks. "You guys need help?" he says.

"Yeah," Jake says. "This here's Joseph. He ain't doin' so hot."

Joseph rolls his head toward James, opens one eye, says, "Hey, ya gotta cigarette?"

"Sorry, Joseph," James says, "I'm all out."

The three men take turns shoving the old man on the rim, all the way down to the south bridge. Sometimes the barrow gets bogged down in a dip, won't budge, and it takes all of them to lift. During a break, bent over, panting for breath, Rooster tries to lighten things, says to Joseph, "Ya big dummy, if ya didn't eat so much, you'd be able to get outa here on your own."

Meanwhile, back at camp, I yank off my coat, throw down my gloves. I pace, now and then kicking the ground. I pick up long sticks, smack them against trees till they're only stubs in my smarting hands. Finally, tears come, powerless, and angry—angry at Joseph for drinking himself down, angry that we couldn't have moved him with a little more dignity, angry that Jake and Rooster might end up just like him—

And yet, Jake and Rooster had bothered to do what they could, and for this I feel keen gratitude, and respect. There's joy, even, for those tears on Rooster's face (tears he'd wanted no one to see), and for that seedy cushion Jake thought to put in the bottom of the wheelbarrow—

Sometimes hope screams.

counting

(ohio statehouse, noon.) Occasionally during our noontime meditations at the Statehouse, James observes passersby stopping to contemplate the Statue of Peace. Some people, like this business suit wearing loafers shined to a high gloss, seem to be interested in the statue itself, while others are apparently more curious as to why two street people should be resting on the ground within the shadow of its wings. Whatever the reason, their gazing at the angel, their considering the word PEACE engraved below, always fills James with a quiet satisfaction.

But not today.

Today, after Joseph, the strain's too much—

You look at the angel, he says silently to the businessman, while all around you there are terrified human beings—can you bear to look at *them*? D'ya wanna know they're here? So many men and women, all around you, tryin' hard not to remember anything good that's ever happened to 'em, anybody who's ever been kind to 'em—They don't *dare* remember—Remembering just reminds 'em of what they don't have, and feel powerless to get, anymore—just makes 'em wanna tippa bottle—

So many people—without a home—afraid—grieving—downright lost—

Who keeps *those* statistics—

Who does the counting—

Who *counts*—

Who—wants to know—

letters home

(ohio statehouse, early afternoon.) On the east end of the Statehouse is the Ohio Veterans Plaza, dedicated in August of last year. Inscribed on limestone walls are excerpts from letters that soldiers scribbled home to their loved ones from trenches and jungles, foxholes and tents, hospital beds. This afternoon, while James is off shooting photographs, I linger on the plaza, reading the soldiers' words. I'm surprised sometimes to hear them speaking of things close to my own heart, here on the streets:

"The place I sleep is my home"—Brad, during the Gulf War. *The Professor, sleeping in his refrigerator.*

"Perhaps soon I can tell you just where I am. Even after I tell you, you probably won't know where I'm located"—Joe, war not specified. *Elena, whereabouts unknown.*

"I am really anxious to get out and get home and stay there and live like a human"—Clyde, writing from Japan, end of WW2. *Jake, wanting his own apartment, telling me, "A person just can't keep livin' like this."*

"How are we going to get home? Perhaps on the wings of angels"—Gail, the Gulf War. *Maddy, separated from her kids, fantasizing suicide.*

"We could not help but think of the ones who will never know the joys of this day. . . . They too dreamed of their homes"—Ralph, end of WW2, remembering his fallen buddies. *James and I, when we finally leave the streets, aware of those we're leaving behind.*

Life on the streets isn't war. But it *is* a pitched battle, waged against the elements, hostile powers, even your own body and mind. However you come to be on the streets, you won't leave them unscathed—that's guaranteed; and if you leave them alive, that'll be no proof you've survived. Veterans know: You can be dead and still be walking.

lifesavers

(**downtown, mid-afternoon.**) An anglo is digging feverishly in a small dumpster; at his feet, a growing pile of assorted snack goods, vending machine fare. Amazed at the man's luck, James walks over and peeks into his treasure chest.

"Mind if I grab some, too?" James asks, and the fellow says, "Yeah man, go ahead," then stuffs his haul into two grocery bags and leaves.

The guy was thorough. Any remaining goodies are now at the very bottom of the dumpster, and most appear to have been nibbled by mice. James leans over the edge of the bin, his feet sticking up in the air, and scavenges the only snacks whose wrappers are still intact: two granola bars, a pack of gum, a chocolate bar, a roll of Lifesavers.

Meanwhile, at a big dumpster behind an upscale bakery in the Short North, I smell the yeasty bread even before I lift the lid. The bin's empty except for a dozen or more large, golden loaves of bread, down in the smutty bottom; crusty Italian bread, unwrapped but relatively clean. I'm tempted to climb in and retrieve them—the bread we can't use our neighbors can—but without some trash to stand on, crawling back out of the bin with my bum knee would be a stern test. I shrug my shoulders, limp away.

In the very next dumpster I check, behind an apartment building, I find a single loaf of the exact same bread, fresh as you'd ever want to eat. Letting out a howl, I toss it into a Lazarus shopping bag and loop the handle over my wrist.

In another trash bin, not far away, are cosmetic cases containing a woman's toiletries. Lotions, tweezers, powders, lipsticks—did she move across the country and not bother to take them? Did a jilted lover throw them into the trash? I don't speculate long. I'm just happy now to have a few things, only a few, that used to be hers: aloe vera gel, sunblock and chapstick, for my sun- and windburned face, plus a small cardboard box, probably from her desk, chockful of pencils and pens. One of the pens is glittering gold, stout, inlaid with tiny diamond-shaped mirrors. In my grip it feels like affirmation.

witness

(capitol square, mid-afternoon.) I'm walking along Broad Street, opposite the statehouse, when a police car squeals to a stop in the far lane, lights flashing, right in front of the Statue of Peace. Two cops jump out in pursuit of a very tall, lanky black man, who is apparently unarmed, and barefoot, wearing only bib overalls. A white family, touring the capitol grounds in their heavy winter clothes, scurries out of harm's way as more cruisers scream up, killing their sirens. Six squad cars, by now. Mother and children huddle within the father's circling arms, gawking, as the cops quickly hem the black man in.

This being a weekend, the square is fairly empty of pedestrians. Something tells me to stay put and serve as a witness *(would anybody listen to* you?) in case the cops—at least ten of them, all white—should use excessive force on this black man. By now they've trapped the fellow on a wheelchair ramp near the Statue. He's immediately across the street from me, drumming the handrail as he fantasizes an escape, as if guns weren't trained on him from all sides. *Don't be foolish.* The cops tighten their noose, trying calmly to reason with him. *Please don't be foolish.* At last he tries to leap the railing and flee, but one of his gangly legs doesn't make it over, and he flops headfirst into low evergreens. Easily apprehended, he's frisked and cuffed and hustled into the back of a cruiser.

Across the way the white children stare.

waiting to be seen

(columbus community hospital, evening.) Tonight is the Take It to the Streets "solidarity camp-out" at Mad Dog's, up north along the tracks.

171

Wanting to avoid the news cameras we know will be there, James and I treat ourselves instead to a televised basketball game. March Madness is well underway, and the Ohio State men's team, after a rash of losing seasons, is in the midst of a surprising tournament run. Tonight OSU battles St. John's in a regional final.

The game is already on when we enter a waiting room adjacent to the emergency department. Feeling conspicuous at first, we soon relax; as usual, nobody's paying us any attention. Relatives and friends of patients brought in by squad shuffle in and out. Even the most distraught visitors watch a little of the game—a distraction; some of them admit they don't even like basketball—till finally white coats come to consult with them in hushed tones. Gradually the room empties.

After a couple of hours, a nurse walks in.

"Is anybody in here waiting to be seen?" she asks.

James and I exchange a smile. Waiting to be *seen*? If only she knew.

day 33: sunday, march 21

answers

(**white castle, early morning.**) James: "I dreamed that you and I were back home, and everybody was askin' us questions—'What's the solution to the Homeless Problem?' 'What should be done about overcrowded shelters?' 'How can you help people who won't help themselves?'. . . .

"We didn't know what to say. We didn't have any answers. We'd never been *lookin'* for answers—just came out here to *be*—and nobody could understand that. Questions flew at us from every direction till finally all we could give, in reply, were tears."

stinkin'

(**mid-morning.**) James and I are walking into the downtown for breakfast at Central Presbyterian Church. The Sunday morning streets are practically deserted, so we're surprised on the way to see a van, up in the next block, parked in the middle of the sidewalk, and an anglo climbing onto its roof from the rear. He aims a pressure washer at a store awning, starts hosing it down. Mist travels all the way down the street to greet us.

As we approach the van, the guy on its roof thoughtfully turns off the spray so as not to drench us. Smiling up at him, James yells, "Hey man, I needa shower. Can ya hook me up?" The man grins, playfully points the nozzle at him and says, "Sure, I'll getcha—"

We all laugh. Another guy sticks his head out the van window, driver's side, says with a wide, toothless smile, "We got *hot* water, too!"

All kidding aside, we do need showers. Bad. As James is so fond of saying, "There's nothin' wrong with stinkin'. The problem is when you know it's you."

tight shot

(riverbank, mid-afternoon.) Along the railroad tracks north of camp is a gigantic billboard, visible to the freeway—a tight shot of a white man's eyes, staring down. They're the kind of eyes you'd rather not have looking at you; the kind of eyes James and I see every day. Wanting to photograph them, James shinnies halfway up a utility pole with a pinhole camera. Hanging on as best he can, he squeezes the box between the post and his belly to keep it steady, then barely breathes through a roughly ninety-second exposure. He's climbing back down again when he notices a cluster of homeless people under a nearby overpass, huddled around a big bonfire, watching him like he was a circus act.

Uh-oh, he thinks. How'll you ever explain yourself?

Quickly slipping the camera into his duffel, James walks over to join two men and a woman, all anglos, their cheeks rosied by the heat of the fire. Amazingly, he's never seen any of these faces, despite passing through here practically every time we go to Grubb. The trio has seen James, though. "Almost every day," they say, "you walk by with your woman."

Initially guarded, the group soon starts to open up. The younger guy introduces himself as Don; the older man, Mad Dog; the middle-aged woman, Susan. They offer James potato chips left from last night's Take It to the Streets camp-out, held around this very fire. Lots of volunteers came, they say, and a tv crew from Channel 4, but only ten homeless people they can think of. Harold and Ada Martin hooked up a big-screen tv so they could all watch the OSU-St. John's game while eating burgers from White Castle.

Don jokes and raps with James as if they're old buddies. He's incredibly big, as is Susan; a rare sight on the streets. He brags about his weight, says he's around three hundred pounds. Susan, throwing more wood on the enormous fire, picks up the theme, says, "The first thirty days I was out, I had lotsa trouble findin' food. Dropped from two-hundred-fifty-six to a hundred-ninety-eight."

She says, "Where ya from, James?"

"New York."

173

**tracks that James and Phyllis walked almost every day, as did their
homeless neighbors, stared down by billboard eyes**

She says, "Me, too. I'm a tough girl from the Bronx. Used to own two construction companies. Then I gotta $3000-a-day dope habit and lost it all. Two times since then I almost starved to death, and once I almost froze. Those three times I broke the law to stay alive, and ended up in the state pen. I'm not a criminal. I just wanted to live."

The four of them talk for a good half hour. Nobody ever asks James what he was doing up the pole.

rap

(**riverbank, late afternoon.**) James is walking along the railroad tracks, just coming up to the bridge south of camp, when a chorus of "Hey yous" rains down. On the bridge are three young black boys on bikes.

"Hey, you poor?" they shout.

"Yeah."

"Where d'ya sleep?"

"In the woods."

"Where your mom and dad at?"

"Back east."

"You cold?"

"Not bad, today."

"Where ya goin'?"

"To hang out with a friend. Where you all goin'?"

"To jump our bikes in the park," they say. "D'ya ride trains?"

"If they're slow enough."

Excited, they talk among themselves, voices floating down. "I wanna ride some trains." "Me too, man." "Yeah, cool."

Maybe fifteen minutes later, James comes upon the same boys in the White Castle parking lot. They're all wearing football jackets—Ohio State, University of Miami, Dallas Cowboys. "Hey," they say, "you the dude we just saw down on the tracks. How'dya get up here?"

"I walked."

"You broke?"

"Yep."

"You don't have no money to getta drink or a cheeseburger?"

"No."

"Ya hungry?"

"No."

"Where d'ya eat?"

"Churches, soup kitchens, dumpsters."

"What'dya eat today?"

175

"Bologna sandwich for lunch, oatmeal and a biscuit for breakfast."

"*Big* bowla oatmeal?"

"Yeah."

The leader of the trio leans back on the seat of his bike, grinning. "Yummm, you makin' me hungry—we ain't been home *all day.*"

man of god (2)

(white castle, late afternoon.) Early on, the afternoon was sunny, breezy, temperature in the forties. Now, with the sun having disappeared behind ominous clouds, it's getting cold fast. I beg a cup of hot water and collapse in a corner booth, staring out the window at the darkening day, grateful finally to be out of the raw, bullying wind.

A few minutes later, Harold Martin, with a sack of burgers in his hand, rousts me from my reverie. "Ya need anything?" he says, pulling his wallet out of a hip pocket. "Wanna cuppa coffee? How 'bouta sandwich?"

"No thanks, Harold, I'm fine."

He flips a dollar bill onto the table. "There," he says. "Get somethin' for yourself."

He leaves. I stare at the bill for a minute, then pick it up with both hands and touch it to my forehead. "When a man of God tries to give ya somethin'," David said, that first night. . . .

Wind beats against the window.

staying (3)

(camp, evening.) "The Thing's got me," James says tonight, out of a long silence.

I wait for him to explain.

"To be honest, till these past few days, I think I've stayed on the streets not because I felt a deep sense of call, but because I had enough *reasons.* For one thing, I was searching for spiritual lessons, and I didn't wanna miss somethin' important by goin' home early. I'd also made a commitment, and I like to finish what I start. Then, well, y'know, I'd look weak if I went home early. If nothin' else, I did have my pride.

"But now the Thing's got me. Just when it got me, or how, I can't say exactly, but it has, and now all those old reasons don't matter so much anymore. Bein' here, stayin' here—it's not about reasons. It's about Joseph in that wheelbarrow. It's about Susan, Don and Mad Dog, huddled around that bonfire. It's about Maddy, missin' her kids. It's about those boys, ridin' their bikes. It's about—*presence.*"

day 34: monday, march 22

boldface

(**camp.**) Alone in early morning, James lies in bed, lazily browsing a recent issue of the New York Times, rescued yesterday from a German Village trash can. Nonchalantly he turns a page, and instantly bursts into laughter—
"ANALYZE THIS."

It's a movie title, printed in huge boldface letters on a full-page ad, but it might as well be heaven's idea of a bad joke: "Yeah, man, your bein' on the streets is absurd. Analyze it all you want, but you won't ever be able to explain it to anybody. Not really."

Still laughing, James props up the ad in plain view just outside the shelter door, then scrambles back into bed.

Some time later, I return from my morning toilet at White Castle. Spotting the ad, I chuckle, holler inside with heavy sarcasm, "Well, Irishman, I can tell *you're* in a fine mood this morning!"

We enjoy the levity while we can. It won't last. It never does. Out here, nothing's that funny. Laughter is just your soul struggling to survive. One minute you're rolling in a fit of hilarity; the next, you're spent, wanting to cry for no reason.

trespass

(**holy family soup kitchen, lunchtime.**) Before the serving line opens, a volunteer staffer usually leads everybody in the Lord's Prayer. The crowded room quiets. Voices join. Not the words we say, exactly, but the act of our saying them together, around these tables, creates some semblance of fellowship. That sense of fellowship may be fleeting, lasting little longer than the Amen, but it's worth something.

The Lord's Prayer is practically in my genes. The words have never resonated, though, like they do out here. Especially, "Give us this day our daily bread." Especially, "Forgive us our trespasses as we forgive," a petition so poignant on the streets, where NO TRESPASSING signs glare at you from chainlink fences, utility poles, dumpsters, doors; where you have no claim to the trash you're digging in, to the land you're squatting on, to the money you're begging; where just your standing on the street, if not your very existence, is an offense to many. . . .

zippers

(downtown, mid-afternoon.) The zipper is working loose from James's coat. Zipping and unzipping is an exercise in mindfulness; if he's the least bit careless, he widens the tear. To ease the stress on the remaining stitches, he carries less in his pockets. On warmer days he lets the coat hang open. Not today.

As the stitching unravels, so does his mind. Hallucinations, now. Seeing things that aren't there. Not seeing things that *are* there—or, at least, not being certain they're real. Delirium without the fever.

Uneasiness comes and goes in waves, prompted by nothing specific. One minute he's fine, the next he's full of anxiety and confused emotions, his insides rushing and churning like whitewater. In such moments, faith disappears. He feels utterly alone, unable to cope. He forgets to ask for help, almost as if he never knew how.

Sometimes the spell passes quickly.

luck

(downtown, mid-afternoon.) The last few days have yielded more than our share of lucky pennies. The thing about lucky pennies is, they show up when you're not especially looking for them. Else they wouldn't be lucky, I suppose; just found. That's the secret: Don't try to find them—they'll find you, so long as your eyes are open.

Sometimes, though, you forget what you know. Just now, I had my eyes glued to the sidewalk along State Street, searching for lost change, and I walked smack into a low-hanging tree limb.

motherlode

(downtown, mid-afternoon.) In an industrial-sized dumpster next to a derelict gas station, James hits the motherlode: some photographer has apparently cleaned house. Excited, James picks through outdated darkroom equipment and other spoils, packing a few things into his duffel: a Polaroid camera (maybe it still works); some American Photo magazines (for evening reading); a portfolio of black and white pictures (for browsing); and a smudge stick, still in the wrapper (for this, special plans).

Rummaging further, he uncovers a box containing a hundred or more lightproof photo bags. Amazing. James has been storing his photographic exposures in bags like these, then passing them on to his darkroom assistants, but his supply was nearly depleted. Now, more bags than he'll ever be able to use.

178

day 35: tuesday, march 23

neanderthal

(white castle.) 4:35 a.m. Terrible night. For the first few hours, the most peaceful sleep I've had in weeks. Then, out of nowhere, a panic attack. Instantly awake, I fled out the shelter door, stood staring up at the dark, empty sky. At that moment, it would have been so easy to end it, so easy to quit and go home—if only the Thing had given me up.

City lights were reflecting off the clouds, making it difficult to judge the time. Surely, though, it was almost daybreak. *Go up top, wash your hair, wait for dawn, you always feel better at dawn.*

When I got here, the clock read 4:20.

Now, hair dripping dry, I sip hot water, exhausted but relieved to be out of the shelter. I'm amazed at how neanderthal the mind can be; how in dark, close places it can twist and wring your perceptions till you cry out and run. No matter how you try, you can't reason away the fright.

Never in my life have I felt so powerless.

The attacks of fear are more severe when I'm in pain—this I've begun to notice. Limping up to eight miles a day on concrete and asphalt, my legs ache almost constantly, and my bad knee burns. By nightfall, muscles are knots, from hip to ankle. As soon as I lie down in bed, they start to throb, then to scream for space, for stretching out, and there's no room; there's just the dark, clutching in from all sides, and then the cramps, and finally a mind crazy for escape—

Gotta stay awake. Gotta keep your head up off the table, or you'll get rousted.

At the counter, a few people straggle in to carry out. Most of the business is drive-through, though. Odds on a newspaper are slim to none.

A while ago a Dispatch delivery truck dropped a stack of papers at a store cross the street. The store's still closed. The bundle sits innocently on the stoop. *Who'd know if you took a copy? Who'd it hurt—*

No. Sleep is what I need. Maybe I should go back to camp.

Maybe you could go to St. Mary's, lie down on a pew. It's a long way over there, and the doors might be locked, but maybe you could break in—

That homeless woman James met under the overpass—what was her name?—she said she'd only commit a crime if her life depended on it—

But the church would be so warm—

This is crazy. Since when do I think about stealing newspapers and breaking into buildings?

179

Since when can't you spell? Since when can't you do simple math? Since when can't you talk without mixing up your words or losing your train of thought? Since when can't you walk down the street without forgetting where you're going? Since when do you get urges for whiskey, or pills, anything to get you through the night—

But none of that is me—

Maybe it is you, sunk low. Broken.

"It takes alotta courage when faith is hard to find"—a line from the middle of some love song, radio music, piped in. Funny what you hear, sometimes, when you don't know you're listening.

disappeared

(5:00 a.m.) Traffic on the streets is picking up a little. Out on the curb sits a young man who looks homeless. Maybe he just walked up from the riverbank. Is he anxious for this night to end, too? What is he waiting for, out there in the cold, at this hour?

An elderly couple settles in at the table next to mine. There's comfort, for me, in their being here, starting their day. The man looks like a farmer; he and the woman remind me of my grandparents sitting in a small-town diner. I'm happy not to be alone in the tables.

The young man—gone now from the curb. *How quickly you can disappear.*

lines and circles

(5:30 a.m.) A line of carry-out customers, now. A black cop. A jaundiced old white woman, hair in bristly curlers. Delivery men. A latino cab driver. City of Columbus employees, in pairs. A black security guard. Another white woman in curlers, around my mother's age. A homeless anglo, gaunt, wearing a pony tail, counting out change, coin by coin. A construction worker in Carhartt overalls.

Some of the customers greet each other by first name. Men shake hands, slap each other's backs, ask after wives and work, tell bad jokes, gripe about the government, the war. Most of the women quickly leave.

Outside my window, it seems darker than it did. Dawn's on its way but so, I suspect, is bad weather. I shiver in a draft from a ceiling vent.

James shows up now, dark circles under his eyes. Water he just splashed on his face in the restroom drips from his unkempt beard onto the tabletop. "Guess I'm rubbin' off on you," I say. "You're never up this early."

Wearily he flashes that Irish grin. "If I start menstruating, too," he says, "I'm goin' home for sure."

footprint and handprints near a manhole cover

woe

(6:15 a.m.) We decide to spend 50¢ on a Dispatch. Today's edition is woefully thin, but it'll occupy us till the sun comes up. "Kosovo Still A Stalemate," the front-page headline blares, as a band of refugee children—toddler to maybe ten years old—walks hand in hand away from the violence, no adults in frame.

Sometimes you're so alone. . . .

signs of trouble

(riverbank, mid-morning.) We run into Jake and Sarge, headed, as we are, for Grubb Street. Hands buried in pockets, the four of us walk the tracks together, the pace slow, no reason to hurry.

Sarge doesn't have much to say. He rarely does, especially when Jake's around and in the mood to gab, as he is now, confessing that one of Enid's social security checks was to have paid his and Rooster's way to Florida. Another check was to have set him and Rooster up in an apartment here in town. Somehow neither scheme had worked out. "I'm not proud of takin' the ol' woman's money," Jake admits, "but that's what we were gonna do."

Will James and I ever properly meet Enid, our tiny neighbor from Germany? Now and then we catch glimpses of her, but only rarely have our paths crossed, in such bad weather nobody wanted to stop and get better acquainted.

As Jake tells it, Enid used to be a nurse. Over the years she'd accumulated a nice little nest-egg, even owned her own home, but then somehow she met Rooster, and now he's conning her, love for money. Rooster's spent nearly every penny she had on booze and crack, and sweet-talked her into living out here on the riverbank, at her age, in a leaky tent. She spends her days panhandling at the top of a freeway exit ramp. "Riches to rags," Jake says. "That's what it is, for her."

As for Rooster and him, Jake says now, they've had a falling out. There are signs of serious trouble. "I gotta get away from 'im," Jake says. "He's crazy. Gonna bring down the heat. Wouldn't be surprised if he don't kill somebody out here."

elderly

(schiller park, late afternoon.) The day's an ugly duckling turned swan, sunny now and calm, temperature in the high forties. For many people here in German Village, the workday is over; infected by spring, they gather in the park, warming to the lazy breeze.

Dogs freed of their leashes chase preening ducks off the banks into the fishpond; collies stop at water's edge, retrievers leap in headlong. Toddlers, watching the action within quick reach of their parents, prance and squeal. On the sidewalk, bicycles whizz by, roller blades whir. Not far away, on a blanket spread over grass, a middle-aged man and woman kiss. Lips linger. A hint of smoke wafts from a distant cigarette.

I take my shoes off. Then, on impulse, I peel my many socks off, too. The pale skin of my feet, exposed to sunlight, is tinged yellow gray, like that of a new corpse.

I feel old. Feeble as a tottery grandmother. But why should this surprise me? Life on the streets forces you to contend with many demons faced by old people—physical deterioration, lack of mobility, loss of self-sufficiency, weariness, loneliness, a sense of not being needed, of no longer being somebody who matters; fear of the unknown. Little things now seem big, nothing works well, everything's an effort—

You suffer. Even being here by choice, you suffer.

Still, as many elderly people will say, there's also a part of you that can detach from your body, from your suffering. It can watch from down deep, or hover above you, serving as impartial witness to whatever's hurting in you, and changing, passing away piecemeal. That part of you, I suspect, you mustn't lose. If you do, the light fades in your eyes, and once it's completely gone, even the greatest of loves may not be able to bring it back.

gone

(**camp, evening.**) James has been quieter these past few days than I've ever seen him. Tonight he seems especially far away. I ask him where he's gone. "Not sure," he says, but the words aren't quite true. He knows exactly where he's gone. He just doesn't know how to tell me.

Where he's gone is deep into desolation. He feels completely self-absorbed, utterly collapsed upon the ruins of what he'd thought himself to be. This is his hell, an ice-cold pit of self-pity; the longer he stays in it, the more normal it seems, and the harder it is to try and pull himself out.

day 36: wednesday, march 24

missing

(**white castle, early morning.**) There's a spot up top, overlooking the tracks, where homeless men often sit together, drinking beer. Last night,

Bobby was up there, drinking alone. White, in his mid-fifties, he lives in a tent camp somewhere downstream. Calls himself a river rat. Almost every morning I see him at White Castle with his sister Jan, a farmwife who drives into the city to eat breakfast with him.

Last night I was walking the tracks when Bobby hollered down at me from the lookout, said, "See ya *early* in the morning."

"Why's that?" I shouted back.

"It's gonna be *cold,* girl. Cold and rainy. Big storm's comin'."

"Maybe it'll go around us."

"Yeah, maybe." He laughed. "I'll see ya *early.*"

Now it's shortly after 7:00 a.m. Bobby should be here by now. He's always here, by now. Up at the counter, there's brisk business. Across the aisle from my table, his sister Jan says to a friend, "I've gotta bad feelin' about this."

My old paper-buddy, the black gentleman of the meticulous folds, is back this morning; a long time since I've seen him. Patiently I wait. Finally he folds his newspaper, pulls on his coat, dons his hat. Crossing the room, he makes a hand delivery to my table, a slight smile creasing his lips. He never says a word, isn't interested in my thanks.

A song lyric plays over the radio: "I believe in you / and all I wanna do is help you / believe in you—"

"I've gotta *really* bad feelin' about this," Jan says again.

I share her anxious vigil from behind the pages of the Dispatch. In Kosovo, NATO has ordered airstrikes. An estimated 25,000 ethnic Albanians have fled their homes in the past few days. *25,000.* Foxes have holes, and birds have nests, but the children of God have nowhere safe to lay their heads—

"I'm worried someday they'll find Bobby face-down in the mud," Jan says, absently stirring her coffee. "He takes coumadin, y'know. Bloodthinner. Could easily freeze to death. That's why he has to have a heater in his tent, despite the risk of fire."

An hour drags by, maybe more. Another homeless man, a friend of Bobby's, comes into the restaurant, tells Jan there was some fighting along the river last night, down near Bobby's camp.

"I *knew* it!" she cries. "I could *feel* it!" She buries her head in her arms. The man tries to console her, says surely he would have heard by now if "anything bad" had happened.

We wait. After another hour, Bobby's still awol. Reluctantly I rise from my seat. I have to head back to camp. It's almost time to leave with James for Grubb Street.

When the door closes behind me, Jan's pacing around empty tables.

friends

(**holy family soup kitchen, lunchtime.**) Aaron, our friend who was hit by a car some weeks back, hobbles up like a saddlesore cowboy. He seems somewhat stronger, more centered, than the last time we saw him, but he's obviously still suffering with his injuries, and now he has a bad cough as well. When I reach out to shake his hand, he warns me off, says, "Better not—I don't wantcha catchin' nothin'." I offer him the baggie of vitamin C tablets I always carry in my coat. Tomorrow, I promise him, I'll bring a bottle of 250 pills. Take It to the Streets brings both James and me a bottle, every week.

James tells Aaron that he'd like to visit him at the men's shelter later in the afternoon. "Good," Aaron says, smiling.

(**volunteers of america, early afternoon.**) An obliging staffer lets James have a used copy of The Big Book. He removes its torn dust jacket, then opens the hardcover, scrawls inside, "To Aaron, One day at a time. Your friend, James."

(**men's shelter in "the bottoms," late afternoon.**) Aaron's shelter is in a tough neighborhood. Right now, on the corner just outside the building, twenty or more residents are mingling with drug dealers. Just as James reaches the crowd, a dust devil swirls up, forcing everybody to shield their eyes. Wearing engineer shades that he found along the railroad tracks, James is the only man unaffected. He walks straight through the parted sea of crack, goes inside. There he finds Aaron sitting at a cardtable, staring into space.

Aaron smiles, pulls out a chair, offers James a smoke.

He smells of liquor. Half buzzed, he looks James straight in the eye, says, "You're my friend, y'know."

"Yes, Aaron, I know. You're my friend, too."

"I been drinkin', James," he says. "There's only so long I can stand it, sittin' 'round here doin' nothin'. Some guy tells me he's goin' to the store, and my mouth starts to water. I think, 'One little drink won't hurt'. Once I start, I can't stop."

"I've been there, Aaron. I know whatcha mean."

He says, "Friends are hard to come by out here. You're my friend, James."

"You too, Aaron."

He says, "Y'know, I went to church yesterday. I'm not right with God yet, but I'm workin' on it. I've gotta start crawlin before I start walkin'."

He shifts in his chair, then leans in close. "That's a cop out, y'know," he says. "I gotta get on the right path *now!*"

185

James places The Big Book in Aaron's hands. Aaron brightens, says in amazement, "You *told* me you'd get me a book, and ya did." He smiles a broken, buzzed smile. "It'll go in my locker, with a lock," he says. "James, we're the same kinda people, you and me. I wish ya could meet my son—he's a good kid."

"Maybe someday, Aaron, but I'll be movin' north in a coupla weeks to find some work."

"Sorry to hear you'll be leavin'," he says. "Friends are hard to come by."

keeping watch

(camp, late afternoon.) Jake stops by, needing some candles. I pull a box of six white tapers from our stash; the volunteers have been generous.

Jake's in a chatty mood. I invite him to sit with me by the fire, but he stands a short distance away, dodging woodsmoke. He tells me he's landed a temp job, starting Monday. "Last job, I blew it. Drank too damn much. But I haven't hadda drink in two days now. Just water. Lotsa water.

"Y'know," he says, "I really gotta slow down, change my life. If I don't, one day I'll be an ol' man walkin' around with a bottle. Gotta stay away from the crack, too. I like the stuff, but ya gotta know your limits.

"I really made a mistake, fallin' in with Rooster," he says, talking to the ground. "He's dangerous, y'know, 'specially when he's been drinkin' or doin' crack. Gets real mean. Ya never know what he's gonna do."

The fire pops. Jake raises his eyes, says, "He won't bother *you* guys, though."

"How can we be sure?"

He shrugs. "You just bein' who you are."

Jake says Rooster's dealing drugs now, and leaning hard on him to sell. "I won't lie to ya," he says. "I was at a crackhouse with 'im, night 'fore last. I like my crack now and then. But I don't wanna be sellin'."

With his new job, Jake says, he'll be just a few paychecks from moving into the YMCA. Maybe he'll even take Sarge along, if he wants to go.

"By the way," Jake grins, "Sarge wants you guys to have this—" He hands me a digital watch-face, scratched and battered. "You guys were sayin' how ya don't have a way to tell the time. Well, this ain't no Rolex, but it should do the trick. It's yours to keep."

callus

(camp, evening.) Scrap of paper. Pencil stub. *What happened today? What can you say that will help you remember?*

186

Memory continues to atrophy. James and I are losing any sense of continuity with even the recent past. Today must be written tonight; tomorrow may be too late. Yesterday seems little more than heavy mist; we reach out for it, and our hands come back wet but empty. We feel cut off. Less than human.

What if you got used to feeling this way?

What if you gave up wanting to remember?

By candlelight James examines one of the American Photo magazines he found recently in a dumpster. This issue contains "The Most Powerful Photographs of 1993"—images of war, flight, famine, poverty. . . . The editor believes these photographs will break through "the emotional callus" of whoever looks at them, making him or her less numb, less indifferent to the world.

"That's what I want my photography to do," James tells me. "Help break through the callus. My own, especially."

day 37: thursday, march 25

offensive

(white castle, early morning.) Today we're bombing Yugoslavia.

trapped

(riverbank, mid-morning.) Jeff, walking the tracks with us toward Grubb Street, urges us to "try and hold our heads high." "It's hard," he says, "but ya gotta hold onto your pride. Sometimes ya feel trapped. I know *I* do. When you've gotta past, it keeps catchin' up with ya when you're lookin' for a job."

He's worked low-paying temp jobs for more than a year, and he isn't making it. He wants steadier, more gainful employment. Wants to sober up, too. "I work as hard as I can, but I drink more. Can't seem to stop. Wish I could."

dictatorship

(holy family soup kitchen, lunchtime.) The volunteer in charge of today's kitchen crew is short. In inches. On kindness and patience. It isn't that he's having a bad day, unless every Thursday (his usual shift) is a bad day; either his heart isn't in the work, or he's afraid to let it show. In my private world I call him—rather meanly, I'm sorry to say—the little dictator. Bespectacled, he always wears a carefully pressed off-white business shirt and bland brown tie, and a full apron, tied just so. His manner reminds me of an accountant who lives for his books, whose entire universe is arranging numbers and justifying columns and decimal points. We're his pennies and nickels, and he wants us in perfect order.

Now, in condescending tone, he instructs the room on procedure. "There will be a prayer. After the prayer the line will form, numbers one to seven. I repeat, one to seven, *not* one to ten. You will proceed to the line by sevens, *not* tens, when your number is called by the gentleman with the megaphone. You will take no more food than you can eat. You will carry your tray to the back of the room to collect your drink and your dessert—you will not be served drinks or desserts without a tray. When you have finished eating, you will push your chair back into position before leaving the table. You will walk to the service window at the front of the room, toss your trash and empty your garbage into the can, then pass your dishes through to the volunteer. You will exit in orderly fashion. . . ."

The speech ends, the prayer begins. Foregoing the customary Lord's Prayer, the man invites us into a time of silence, then concludes with a prepared text: "Let us be thankful for those who donated this food, for those who delivered the food to this kitchen, for those who have prepared the food, and for those who now serve it. And Lord, please forgive those who sin, for they are only human—"

I feel slapped. No need, apparently, to be thankful for those who will *eat* the food; for them, a need only to plead forgiveness.

I peek at James across the table. His face is screwed into a scowl.

"In Jesus' name we ask it—"

On the Amen, chairs scrape back. One to seven dash into line. "It's gonna go slow today," James says, "counting by sevens—"

Suddenly there's an eruption of noise, and a surging mass of bodies, up toward the front of the room. A volunteer standing nearby freezes, says, in understatement, "Hey, we've gotta problem—"

A brawl—women on women, men on men, everybody else up and trying to see, tense, the whole room could explode, the fight's spreading, nobody's moving to intervene, the servers are still scooping green beans and doling out chicken thighs like nothing's happening—

Adrenaline rushes the room like a tidal wave. A guy in front of us yells, "Hey, not in a church!" and though this isn't a church, exactly, he's got the idea, if only somebody would listen. The little dictator reaches out for a tray, ladles some noodles, hands the tray along, takes another, sneaks a look at the brawl, ladles noodles, the swarm's out of control—*God, let there not be knives,*

188

let there not be guns—somebody do something —somebody—

Men shout, "Call 9-1-1!" James thinks of crawling under a table, just in case, then decides to hang with me near a door to the hallway—

A few down-on-their-luck middle-aged men, employed part-time to run the line, throw themselves into the fray. Finally they manage to break it up. As they escort the toughs out of the cafeteria, the air curdles with obscenities and threats.

Crisis resolved, people return to the business of eating. Cops eventually appear in the hall. I toy with my food, not hungry, now. One of our friends at the table complains about the lack of security, says, "I don't wanna be afraid to come here."

James and I, when we speak again, wonder aloud if the fight would have broken out, had the prayer not ended as it did.

privilege

(**camp, evening.**) Every day James and I experience a profusion of moods. All of them pass, except for gratitude. Always gratitude.

Clearly we're on a downhill slide; we keep hoping for the ground to level off, but the grade only seems to steepen. Despite our best efforts, we can't get our bodies to feel better, our minds to think better, our spirits to lift.

As the days pass, and the streets become more familiar, we want to find more meaning than we have, but we can't. We want to feel some semblance of progress, something more than the mere march of time, but we're left disappointed. We want to stop the endless parade of people we're meeting *(all the faces you see, all the voices you hear in your sleep)*, but there aren't enough boundaries to keep them away. In the end, I suspect, we'll want closure, only to be denied. Meaning, progress, boundaries, closure: these seem to be privileges we have only when suffering is past, or when we choose to stand apart from it; when we're in the midst of it, the privilege is survival, without the loss of our humanity.

day 38: friday, march 26

arms

(**white castle, early morning.**) Three days. Three terrible days. Jan pulls her river-rat brother Bobby into a long, tight hug, then pushes him away, bawls him out.

189

hostilities

(6:45 a.m.) The right side of Jake's jaw is swollen, and an ugly purple bruise is raised on his cheek, but otherwise he's unhurt. He and Sarge were attacked at their camp around 3:00 a.m.—the sound of it jolted me from an uncommonly sound sleep. A flurry of sharp cracks and dull pops. James was already awake, and nervous, convinced that at least some of the sounds, obviously coming from Jake and Sarge's place, were gunshots. I wasn't sure. Finally, after much listening, we decided that somebody was throwing things, mightily hard, against the shack, all the while screaming a blue streak. We recognized the voice.

Jake and Sarge tell me they were fast asleep when Rooster burst in, armed with a big stick. He slammed it against their stove, their chairs, their walls. Then he lit into Jake, first with the stick, then with his fists. "We were *sleepin'*, for Godsake," Jake says in a painful mumble. "I was *in bed*—penned in. Couldn't defend myself. He was crazy, screamin'. Said I was tellin' people he's smokin' crack. Hell, missus Ingalls, the only people I really talk to is you and James.

"It ain't safe for me to be out here anymore," he says, shaking his head. "Maybe I'll call Harold and Ada, see if they can help me leave. I told 'em the other day, 'It's gettin' crazy down here, I need to get off the riverbank.'"

"Can you *believe*," Sarge says emphatically, his eyes wide, "Rooster *apologized*, to *me*, 'fore he left? 'Got no quarrel with *you*, Sarge,' he says. 'Sorry to wake ya up!' *Hell!* Y'know, I think he's tryin' to drive us off 'cause he wants our shack. Well, he ain't gonna get it! I'll burn it down first!"

smolderings

(camp, mid-morning.) James greets me outside the shelter with a birthday present. Thirty-seven years. With all the hostilities, I'd forgotten.

"Stand here," he directs. "Close your eyes."

I hear him strike a match. Now smoke wafts up; sweet, sweet smoke, tickling my nostrils. Breathing it in, I begin to smile. By some miracle, James has conjured up some dried sage. He passes the smoldering herb around my head, my torso, my legs, smudging my bundled body.

"Take off your gloves. Hold out your arms."

His voice is quiet but firm. I obey like a child. Soon the air is full of the heady fragrance. I feel clean, new as rain.

When James finishes the smudge, the woods are still but for birdsong. I listen a while before opening my eyes. Then I bow deeply to James, palms together as if in prayer, and take the smudge stick from his hand. The bundle of dried white sage leaves is as big around as a fist. Wherever did he find it?

"Close your eyes," I say.

Not a breeze stirs. The sage smoke hangs in the air, wispy as floss silk. For a few minutes, I don't think of the feud between Rooster and Jake. I don't think of the bombing in Yugoslavia, the atrocities in Kosovo. I don't think of homeless people, of refugees, of victims. For these few minutes, the world has righted itself. Fanning the sage lightly with my free hand, I weave the smoke around James's lanky body.

James says that he found the smudge stick at the bottom of a dumpster, still packaged in crinkly plastic. Indigenous cultures around the world commonly use white sage for rituals of purification and blessing. For me, today, it also serves as evocation, summoning up memories of home, of writing at my desk, wrapped in the fragrant smoke of braided incense from Nepal—

I stub out the still-smoldering stick. The rest we must save for Easter.

maneuvers

Jake stops by, carrying two duffel bags and a sleeping bag, says he'll see us around. He intends to set up a new camp, somewhere along the river where Rooster won't find him. "I won't be tellin' you guys where I've moved to. Rooster might lean on ya to say."

Wherever Jake ends up, may he be warm. May he be dry. May he be safe.

exposed

("the bottoms," mid-afternoon.) James hides behind a stack of railroad ties to change photo paper, working quickly, feeling exposed. At least the area isn't busy at the moment; just some kids playing on the other side of the street.

Up to his elbows in the sleeves of the lightproof bag, he has finished changing his first camera and started in on the second when suddenly a white man and a black woman appear around the piling. Their eyes look like pinwheels. Obviously they're high, and jonesing for more.

"Shit!" they say. "Somebody's here, too!"

"Hey, I'm leavin' in a sec," James says, his blind fingers fumbling in the bag.

They have no idea what he's doing, and obviously couldn't care less. "Naw," they say, "you don't have to leave. You straight. You was here first."

The couple light up some crack in a pipe only a few feet away.

Surreal, James thinks, groping.

arms (2)

(**mid-afternoon.**) Behind Holy Family Church, a shrine to the virgin Mary. Mary's outstretched arms are welcoming. James clears away dead pine needles from the walkway, sits down cross-legged amidst bird droppings. Being here is a comfort, like being hugged by a woman.

Though raised Roman Catholic, only once before has James felt a powerful connection to Mary—several years ago, in a chapel in Medjugorje, a small village in Bosnia-Herzegovina where almost daily since 1981 people have reported seeing apparitions of her. That day, a special worship service for children and young people had been led by a visionary named Ivan, one of several villagers to whom Mary regularly appeared. When after the service Ivan led the worshipers out of the chapel, James lingered, not yet ready to leave. He went up to the front of the shrine, stood near the queen of peace. The energy of the place was intense, healing.

Suddenly, a touch on his shoulder—Ivan. The two men's eyes locked for an intense, otherworldly minute. Finally Ivan smiled, said, "It's time to go." Afterwards James couldn't stop crying, and didn't know why.

That day in Medjugorje, Mary had been to James a heavenly, angelic figure. "Don't be afraid," she seemed to say. "Open your heart."

Today, in this place, Mary is mother, arms ready to gather him in. "Rest," she says simply. "Rest."

home front

(**sarge's shack, late afternoon.**) "You gonna stay on?" we say to Sarge. He's camped with Jake a long time and (being "a bit slow," as he puts it) very much depends on him, tagging along like a little tyke after a brother he adores.

Sarge shrugs, says he thinks his wife may have lifted the restraining order against him; if she'll let him, maybe he'll just go home. "I wasn't allowed to be around there for awhile," he says, "'cause I didn't like the neighbors. Made some threats and stuff. Stupid. I really miss my kids."

negotiations

(**riverbank, late afternoon.**) I run into Rooster along the tracks. He looks bloated, jaundiced. His appearance has deteriorated profoundly these past weeks.

"Sorry if all the ruckus kept you guys up last night," he says with a grin. "It's all on Jake's head. He come over to my place yesterday when I wasn't there and cussed out my ol' lady. Just ain't right. Nobody gotta right to talk

Mary, queen of peace

to 'er like that.

"Now you tell me," he says, wagging a finger in my face, "wasn't I right to stick up for 'er?"

I say nothing.

"Well, *wasn't* I?"

"I'm not your judge," I say, watching him carefully, afraid he might come unhinged. Then, on impulse, I say, "But to be honest, Rooster, when all that fightin' was goin' on last night, James and I were afraid you'd be comin' after us next—"

"No *way!*" he says, stepping back as if I'd thrown a punch. "I like the *heck* outa you guys! You're damn straight. *Damn* straight! No need to worry."

He holds out his hand, and I grasp it, somewhat relieved. But now he doesn't let go. I feel his grip tighten. *You know what he told James. He thinks you're an ex-con, likes you because you're tough.* I tug my hand hard. *You know what he said to you, that one time in the woods—"You can trust me, I'm not tryin' to get into your pants."* I tug harder, and he's still not letting go—

But now, here comes Sarge up the tracks. Rooster sees him, too, and abruptly drops my hand, struts off in the opposite direction.

day 39: saturday, march 27

public relations

(**riverbank, mid-morning.**) Along the tracks James and I run into our reclusive neighbor Calvin, the old white man who lives in the next camp north. He surprises us by initiating a conversation, or, more accurately, a monologue. Obviously he's eager to talk when he chooses.

Calvin is a very proud man. Proud of his strict moral code. Proud of his camp, so neat and clean. Proud of his ability to keep himself going, doing the best he can.

He's deeply resentful of Take It to the Streets. This is easy to understand, given not only his pride but his fear. Whether or not he's clinically paranoid, as James and I suspect, he's deeply suspicious, easily frightened, and extremely protective of his camp. How must he feel when six carloads of volunteers (and he does keep count) suddenly converge on his camp in the darkness? Recently, he says, he told the Martins that he wants to be left alone, and since then things have been somewhat better: a single volunteer delivers his rations while Calvin hides inside his tent.

Calvin worries that somebody from the Martins' organization will either put his picture in the newspaper or videotape him for the news. "I know they gotta have publicity to get money, to do what they do," he says. "But lotta times they don't getta person's permission. I know that for a fact. If they ever use *me* that way, I tell ya, I'll *sue* 'em. You can understand, prob'ly. Somebody might see ya, and recognize ya from the paper, and then they'd know ya was homeless. It'd be *embarrassin'*."

open window

The other day, upon returning from a Twelve-Step meeting, James told me that somebody had defined forgiveness as the letting go of the wish that the past had been other than it was. When I think of the Martins and Channel 4, I try to practice this letting go. Instantly my attention boomerangs to the present, and my spirit lightens, for a while. I'm no saint—forgiveness is often a struggle—but my sense of indignation is slowly receding. It'll just take time.

Sometimes when a wild bird is in the house, swooping room to room, you can chase it through an open window with a broom. But sometimes it's best to put the broom down, let the bird find its own way out, in its own time. Just keep the window open wide, for however long it takes.

hit

(deaf school park, early afternoon.) James sits quietly at a picnic table. Nearby, three gang members are hanging out. Wind brings him snatches of their rap. One of their homies is missing; they haven't seen him in days; they're afraid he's been hit by a rival gang. "Hey, I'm tellin' ya, man," the loudest guy says, "if them badasses gets mad at you, ya just disappear. Don't *nobody* ever know what happened."

Suddenly James sees it—a woman's face, staring up at him from the weathered gray wood of the tabletop. Drawn in black drymarker, her features are soft as charcoal, faded by the sun. He almost missed her.

Lying atop another table, I laze in a patch of sunshine. With the arrival of more favorable weather, I'm suddenly a person of leisure, relatively speaking. Coping takes less planning, less effort, less energy; a good thing, since I have no reserves left. I can't imagine trying to hold down a job while living this way.

The top of this picnic table is my chaise lounge. I sink, begin to relax, my body warm, slackening.

Suddenly, just at the edge of sleep, I don't like the feel of it. Beneath the easing tension, there's no contentment—just pain—vulnerability—a distress I can't name. I yank myself out of it, sit up straight, heart racing—

I'd rather have winter.[17]

195

neutrality

(**riverbank.**) Around 9:00 p.m. Headlights from half a dozen vehicles spray across the scruffy field above the woods. James and I, just returning from the laundromat, drop into a crouch beside the railroad tracks, concealed by darkness, listening to the shouts, watching the wagging flashlights. Tonight we'd prefer not to deal with volunteers from Take It to the Streets. Grateful as we are for their help, it does get a little tiresome, twenty or thirty people showing up at your house two or three nights each week, sometimes unannounced, maybe even with a videocamera. You begin to feel they own you.

Spotting several flashlights down by Calvin's camp, I wonder what he's thinking, holed up in his tent. Then, suddenly, I'm wondering, too, if my wanting to write down something of his life, tell something of his feelings, to bear him witness, isn't also an intrusion.

James and I finally tire of waiting for the volunteers to leave. We stand up, walk into headlights. At our approach, Sabrina Martin hurries up to greet us, making sure we're safe. She laments the feuding between Jake and Rooster. "This is a war zone now," she says. "At least you seem to be in neutral territory."

She's just come from Rooster's camp, where she left some rations. "Even them that's causin' the trouble's gotta eat," she says.

Now a woman hails us from a mini-van. "It must take lots of strength to stay out here," she says, through a window half rolled down, "especially with the bad weather we've been having. I admire you two for your strength."

"You're helpin' us be however strong we are," we say.

Long after the volunteers drive off, the woman's words keep rising in James's mind like a mirror in the hand, reflecting the image of what, not so very long ago, he desperately thought he needed to be: Strong. Unbreakable. A rock.

No more.

Now he knows: he doesn't need to be strong. He needs only to be who he is. Who, after all, can be more?

end

times

day 40: palm sunday, march 28

tie that binds

(**early morning**.) I'm sleepwalking up an alley when my wedding ring and amulets spill with a clatter onto the pavement. I've been wearing them on a cord around my neck ever since I left home. Now, after all this time, with only a week left on the streets, the knot in the cord has come untied. It almost feels like a sign.

fit

(**white castle, early morning**.) James: "I dreamed that Dad and I were spendin' Lent homeless in New York City. The two of us were sittin' at a table in a deli, starin' at each other over cups of hot water. Suddenly Dad broke down, started screamin', 'I can't take it anymore! Gimme some money! I wanna buy some bacon and eggs, rye toast!'

"For some reason I hadda bank card in my hand. Dad snatched it away from me and ran outside to an ATM, but instead of withdrawing money, he stopped short, squatted down on the sidewalk. Suddenly now he was holding my tool kit (credit-card-sized, y'know). The little tools were scattered all around him on the pavement. One by one he picked them up, tried to return them to their proper places in the case, but every tool was twisted, bent. He groaned. Nothing fit like it used to."

doomed

(**central presbyterian church, mid-morning**.) James and I settle with our trays at an empty table. Before long, a barrel-chested, thick-necked anglo sits down in the chair across from James, sizes him up, mumbles a few words. James smiles, says to him, "I'm sorry, I didn't hear—what'dya say?"

The man glares, works his thick lower lip. His brow creases. The lip starts to tremble. Then an animal growl issues from his belly. Elbow on table, he points a stubby finger directly at James's nose. Doesn't say a word, just points. James looks like a mountain climber who's seen the start of an avalanche a thousand feet above him. Doomed.

You saw this man just yesterday. He walked past you into the library, with A History of the American People tucked under one arm—

James takes several deep breaths and lowers his gaze to his plate. Intense minutes pass. The man still doesn't move. James glances sidelong at me.

"Don't say a word," my eyes warn. He forks up more biscuit.

Finally the man starts wolfing down his food. James relaxes a little. Eyebrows arched, he shoots me an incredulous look.

"Y'know," the man says suddenly to James, his voice now friendly as a distant cousin's, "all that coke they found is comin' outa Haiti. Twenty-four pounds."

"Really," James says, clueless.

"Yeah," the man says. "That's somethin', huh?"

The man is no longer eating. His eyes dart all around, as if watching a swarm of insects. Finally, he seems to remember his food. One big hand starts spooning furiously.

"We've only got eight months left, y'know," he says after a while, sounding now like a scared little boy. "Governor Taft said in the paper he's gonna live in a bunker when Y2K comes. Don't know what the hell *I'm* gonna do."

the city

(**late morning.**) For Palm Sunday mass, James and I walk way north to St. Patrick's Church on E. Naghten; an old church, built by the Dominicans in 1852.

The nave is abuzz. Unlike at St. Joe's, where you whisper, if you say anything at all, as you slide into a pew, here you can speak in normal tones, laugh without apology. No elegance to be maintained; this is a working-class church with a neighborhood feel. Fathers carry young children high on their shoulders, mothers reach up and wipe a last bit of breakfast from the corners of jabbering mouths. Elderly men snore or stare at their bulletins, waiting for mass to start; elderly women dig into purses for a mint, wave white-gloved hands at friends across the aisle. In the back, just inside the sanctuary doors, a big, bearded Dominican gives final instructions to two altar boys.

The church is packed. There's a rare empty seat beside James, right along the aisle. Several times a parishioner starts to sit down, only to notice him, back away and awkwardly retreat to the back of the sanctuary. Standing Room Only.

The Palm Sunday procession finally begins, recalling Jesus' triumphal entry into Jerusalem shortly before he was killed. The priest sprinkles holy water, swinging the pot from side to side as he plods up the aisle, while we in the congregation wave palm fronds with (feeble) shouts of Hosanna.

"As Jesus came near and saw the city, he wept over it, saying, 'If you, even you, had only recognized the things that make for peace. . . .'"

trial

This old church, we discover after mass, houses a humble shrine devoted to the Blessed Margaret Castello. Margaret, we learn from a brochure, was born in 1287, a child of Italian nobility, but her life was hardly one of luxury and ease. She was a midget, a hunchback scarcely able to walk, and totally blind. Her parents, so the story goes, were so ashamed of her physical impairments that when she was only six years old, they locked her up in a cell adjoining a chapel; for the next fourteen years, they allowed her out only to attend mass and receive the sacraments. Finally, as a last resort, they packed her off to a shrine in a distant city, where they prayed for a cure. When the miracle wasn't forthcoming, they abandoned her to the streets. Margaret remained homeless till some Dominican laywomen kindly took her in.

Margaret spent the remainder of her life ministering to the imprisoned, the sick and the dying. She died in 1320, at the age of thirty-three. In Roman Catholic belief, she continues even today to intercede for the poor, the disabled, the rejected—and the homeless.

I dip my fingers in her holy water, touch them to my forehead.

The artist who sculpted the statue of Margaret for this shrine apparently didn't know her story. Or maybe he meant to suggest that true beauty is an attribute of the spirit. Whatever the reason, the lovely woman who gazes down at me, arms full of red roses, shows no sign at all of infirmity.

Scripted in red above Margaret's statue: "If you are willing to serenely bear the trial of being displeasing to yourself, then you will be for Jesus a pleasant place of shelter."

palm

(**ohio statehouse, noon.**) At the base of the Statue of Peace, a palm frond. Settling in for meditation, James and I stare at it with wonder. Who could have laid it there?

When our period of silence ends, James says that he'd like to come back in a few hours when the sun is softer and photograph the frond. In the meantime, he suggests, we should hide it from the blustery wind.

I carry the frond to a flowerbed, some distance away, and delicately push it down among blooming daffodils.

The day's good for taking pictures, sunny with occasional billows of clouds; a full spectrum of light, from bright to shade, with which to work. For more than two hours we walk the railroad tracks that cross beneath High Street, James looking for shots among the solid concrete pillars and screaming graffiti.

Spraypainted on a cement wall: HAROLD FOR PRESIDENT. Harold Martin, maybe?

Nearby, a double mattress on springs, neatly made, covered with colorful children's comforters. Some things, James tells himself, you don't take pictures of.

altar

(**ohio statehouse, mid-afternoon.**) "No way!" I exclaim.

"What?"

"It's *gone!*" My hands probe gently among the flowers, but the palm frond isn't there.

"Maybe the wind got it?" James ventures.

"Not down in there. *Couldn't* have!"

Suddenly James grabs my arm, says, "You're not gonna believe this. *Look—*"

The palm frond is back at the Statue of Peace, exactly where we first saw it, now held in place by a beautiful yellow apple. Lying beside it, a yellow daffodil. Offerings on an altar.

relics

(**camp, late afternoon.**) Lately, when I'm alone, I've been working on Easter gifts. Large gift-boxes of gratitude: for Jihong, so unwavering; for James, and his companionship on the journey. For others, smaller tokens of appreciation, like the bookmarks I'm making now, cut from dried river reeds, pressed between bricks, inscribed with a line by W.S. Merwin: "I will take with me the emptiness of my hands / What you do not have you find everywhere."

The impulse to give gifts in exchange for favors and kindnesses rendered is probably very middle-class. Gift-giving helps not only to express gratitude but also to assuage a sense of indebtedness; generally speaking, bourgeoisie don't like feeling beholden. But while something of this middle-class civility may have prompted my desire to give gifts as I leave the streets on Easter, the gifts themselves—recycled from dumpsters, scavenged from sidewalks, scrounged from the riverbank, transformed by hand—will speak, I hope, of something more than blushing courtesy.

There are also a few objects that I intend to keep for myself when I go, chief among them the golden pen with which I've been writing lately, and a tin candleholder, stashed each night with a book of matches within easy reach. The urge to keep these things feels almost primal. I read once about

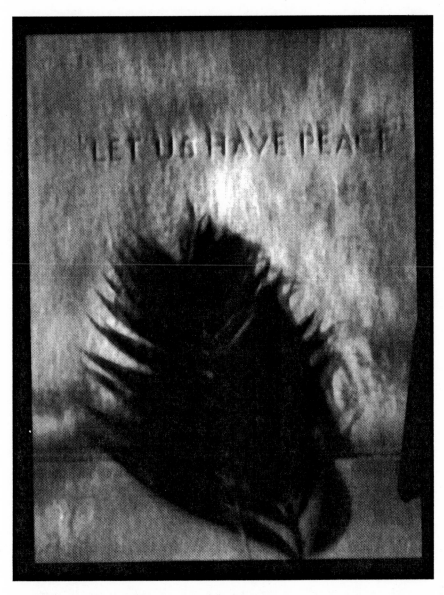

palm frond at the base of the Statue of Peace on Palm Sunday

civilian survivors of war who keep in their homes certain relics of that terrible time, not to honor it, but to domesticate its savage memory. In this way they manage to make life in peacetime more livable. I remember reading this, and not understanding. Perhaps I still don't understand fully, but somehow the candleholder and the golden pen—these I must take home with me when I leave the streets. Not for forever. Just for long enough.

world away

(**high street phone booth, late evening.**) In the darkness James hears Phoebe ask, from a world away, how he's doing. He tells her this happened, that happened. "Yeah," she says, "but how do you *feel*?"

He almost buckles beneath her question. He has no idea how to answer, where to even start. "I feel *everything*," he says, beginning to cry. "Everything *at once*—"

His body convulses. He hears his own sobs as if they were somebody else's.

People say, with a dismissive air, "Why can't homeless people just go get help from their families?"

God, James thinks, they don't know what they're asking—

day 41: monday, march 29

truce

(**white castle.**) 6:40 a.m. Jake shows up out of nowhere. Three days have passed since he moved out of the shack, trying to avoid more fighting with Rooster. He tells me that he's pitched camp in a remote part of the woods.

Things have been quiet between him and Rooster; a temporary truce, but Jake doesn't trust it. Word is, Rooster's easing up on him so he'll let down his guard. "Then," Jake says, "he's gonna kill me. Gut me on the tracks. That's what he's been sayin'."

Across the aisle a few men over sixty are debating the war. One of them, redfaced with fury, talks the others down, says, "If you're gonna help another country, at least help somebody who's gonna help ya back, *goddammit.*"

Jake shakes his head, says, "I got in with Rooster for the wrong reasons. When somebody's buyin' ya smokes and liquor and food, it's easy to be their friend. You don't realize there's gonna be a price to pay in the end."

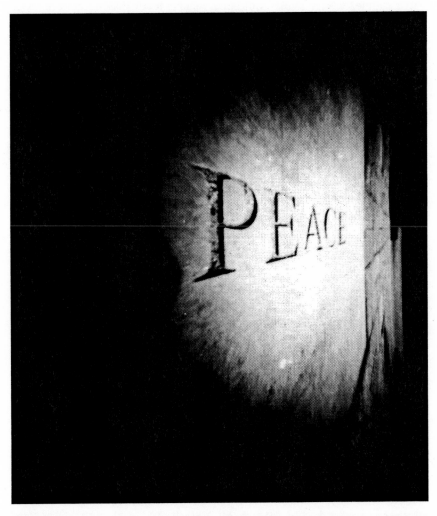

PEACE: engraving on the sidewalk outside the downtown YWCA

names

I'm into the entertainment section of the newspaper when Jake tells me his real name, given *and* family, for the first time. At least he *says* it's his real name, and today I believe him. His revelation is entirely unexpected. Out here, people use first names, sometimes nicknames or aliases—no more—not wanting to know, or be known, too much; a matter of survival, just like not asking, not answering, too many questions.

He tells me that he's forty-three years old, and has never had a real home. Born to a fourteen year-old girl, at once he became a ward of the state. He spent his childhood in a blur of orphanages and foster homes. "No wonder I been a drifter all my life," he says. "A modern-day hobo. I work when I can and lay my head where I will."

"Speakin' of work," I break in, "didn't you tell me you were startin' a new job today?"

He stares into his coffee cup.

"I'm sorry, Jake. Didn't mean to butt into your business."

"It ain't that," he says.

I wait. He rubs his forehead.

"Look, Missus Ingalls," he says finally, "I ain't gonna lie to ya. There never was a new job. I just said that, tryin' to give myself a little hope."

He looks me straight in the eye, now. I smile a little, say, "It's okay, Jake. We're straight."

Jake, I call him. Not his real name, but Jake.

star trek

Jake's a trekkie, though he rarely sees an episode these days. "I 'specially like the Voyager series," he says.

"Why's that?" I ask him.

"I don't really know."

"What's it about?"

"The starship Voyager is lost, eons and *eons* from home, and Captain Janeway—she's a woman, y'know—she's tryin' to get 'em all back to where they came from." Suddenly his face lights up. "It's the *theme*!" he cries. "It's the *theme* that makes that show! It's all about *goin' home*!"

revelation

From behind the metro section of his newspaper, Jake asks if I'm religious. "I'm interested in the spiritual life."

206

He lowers his paper. "What's that mean?"

"I believe there's a little truth, a little wisdom, in every religion. Outside religion, too. I'm interested in whatever opens the mind and heart, regardless of where it's found."

Jake says that he once attended seminary, but he had a crisis of faith and dropped out. "That's a story for another time," he says with a sigh, "but I was wonderin'—you ever read the Book of Revelation?"

I nod.

"Well, Revelation and the teachings of Nostradamus—if ya believe what they're sayin', things are comin' to a head. We're comin' to the *end*."

I sip my water, say, "Y'know, Jake, I'm not gonna worry 'bout that."

He deliberates a moment, then says, "Y'know, I'm not gonna worry either. I believe if ya try to do the right thing, and ya say a prayer sometimes, and ya do the best ya can, God'll see you. He's all the time *seein'* you."

The air between us feels suddenly charged; the moment delicate, like a bubble floating on breeze. I lean forward, elbows on the table, look directly into his eyes.

"It feels good to be seen, doesn't it, Jake?" I say softly.

"Yeah," his voice almost a whisper, a tear in his reddened eyes, "it does."

fences

(camp.) 8:00 a.m. James and I lounge outside the shelter, soaking up sunshine, our fuel for the day. I'm screwing open a can of sliced government peaches, the perfect accompaniment to stale dumpster bagels, when a City of Columbus truck brakes to a stop across the chainlink fence separating our little strip of woods from the water treatment plant.

This has never happened before.

Despite our feeble attempts at camouflage, our camp has always been in clear view of the plant. The tall fence around the city's property is a mere thirty feet away, the gravel drive to the plant maybe another ten feet beyond that. For weeks now James and I have watched city trucks come and go. Early on, whenever a truck showed up, we'd hide, afraid of being reported; a futile exercise, since our shelter was still plainly visible, but we were acting on instinct, not reason. As time went by, and no police materialized to roust us, James and I began to feel more secure. Bold, even. Sometimes when a truck appeared, we'd wave at its occupants. Nobody ever responded in kind. These days, when a truck arrives, we scarcely pay attention.

But this truck has stopped. The guy on the passenger side rolls down his window. "Hey, you guys wanna cuppa coffee?"

James and I exchange a look, dumbfounded. The moment is downright historic. Whether or not we actually want coffee, there's no way we're turning it down. "Sure," we say, "that'd be great. Thanks!"

"You drink it black?" the guy yells as the truck lurches forward. "Cream and sugar?"

In a short while the city men are back from White Castle. The guy on the passenger side jumps out of the cab, quickly hands two bags over the fence to James, climbs back in. The truck drives off.

In the bags are two large coffees, a handful of creamers, and two sausage-egg sandwiches. Manna in the wilderness.

Beneath our feet is a carpet of woods flowers, purple and pink. They just poked up overnight.

fools

(**camp, late afternoon.**) I'm sitting on my favorite tree stump, munching on dumpster popcorn, when a white van lurches into the field. A rangy sandy-haired anglo jumps out from behind the wheel and struts off toward Sarge's shack, obviously annoyed. Soon I hear him hollering, first for Jake, then for Sarge. There's no reply. Before long, the guy is back at his van, hands on hips, glaring at the woods.

Here in the thicket, tree branches only beginning to bud, my bright green coat is hardly inconspicuous. When the guy catches sight of me, he comes striding down the path toward camp.

I watch him come. I don't trust him. Not at all.

"Where's Jake?" the guy barks.

"Dunno," I say, stupidly, chomping away on my popcorn. *Let him think you're a fool.*

"Seen Sarge today?"

"Nope."

"Were they around yesterday?"

"Couldn't tell ya."

He cusses under his breath. I glance up at the van. A young black man is standing there now, watching us, holding an empty trash-bag. I recognize him. He's been staying at Rooster's. Word is, they're both dealing crack. Word is, maybe Jake's dealing, too.

"When will ya be seein' Jake again?"

"No idea."

More obscenities. The guy glares. "When ya do see 'im, tell 'im I was here lookin' for 'im."

"And you are—?"

"*He'll* know."

trains and rails

(**riverbank, late afternoon.**) Near the city junkyard north of camp stands a lonely railroad car. Crawling under, James lies down and nestles his cheek against a cold rail, carefully positioning his pinhole camera to photograph one of the wheels on the steel track. A strange shot, maybe, but it's his way of paying homage to the railroad. The trains, out here, have been an inspiration to us both. There's something reassuring about how they follow the tracks beyond where you can see, with a strong surety; something beautiful in the fit between their wheels and the rails. Rail gives, wheel receives: a powerful, steady exchange, made possible by the emptiness of the groove.

James peels back the shutter-tape over the pinhole, exposing the photo paper inside the camera. Waiting for the shot to take, he recalls an early morning in Bexley when he'd sneaked off to a park instead of loitering with the guys at the bus stop. He was breaking the rules—homeless men were strictly forbidden to enter that park—but he didn't care. He needed to be alone.

A cop car had turned into the park on routine patrol. James dodged its headlights, scrambled for cover. Once the squad drove off again, he explored a little, eventually climbing up onto a frostbitten railroad bed to wait for sunup, hands and feet already numb, temperature in the teens.

Maybe an hour later, a train far down the tracks had blasted its horn, approaching from the south as a bright sun mounted the eastern horizon. Motionless, he watched it come. The train finally passed only a few feet from where he stood, the orange rust on its cars blazoned by dawn. His lonely shadow had run with the cars, going nowhere.

The memory brings tears.

He closes the shutter.

gourmet

(**camp, early evening.**) Dinnertime. James is in the mood to cook. With misgivings I watch him improvise a recipe from our meager store of food. First, he sets out a package of flour tortillas recently dug from a dumpster. Next, he dumps a can of fatty government shredded pork into the metal bowl we've been using as a cookpot, combines it with a can of government spinach, and tosses in some sliced jalapeño peppers from Grubb Street. After heating the concoction over a small fire, he rolls up some of the runny green mess in a couple of stale tortillas. Keeping one tortilla for himself, he offers the other to me.

I take it half-heartedly. "Grateful, grateful," I say, praying the simple

train wheel on railroad track

prayer that has become our custom. James smiles, suspecting sarcasm.

Warily we each take a bite.

Make a face.

Laugh out loud.

Eat the whole nasty potful.

charged

(camp, late evening.) Eudora Welty, quoted in American Photo, read aloud now by James: "Insight doesn't happen often in the click of a moment, like a lucky snapshot, but comes in its own time and more slowly and from nowhere but within. The sharpest recognition is surely that which is charged with sympathy as well as shock—it is a form of human vision."

day 42: tuesday, march 30

rapid-fire

(ohio statehouse, early afternoon.) James and I are conversing on a bench when a woman in high heels scurries by so briskly that we both stop talking, watch her all the way up the sidewalk, then all the way up the steep capitol steps on rapid-fire tip-toes. "Y`know," I say to James when she hits the top, "I couldn't walk that fast now even if I tried. Besides, I don't think I *want* to walk that fast, ever again."

James nods. He knows.

We walk slow, slow, now. We joke that we only have one gear left, the rest stripped.

In our other life, time squirts like thin ketchup from a bottle, and somebody or something always seems to be squeezing, pressuring us to speed up the pace, to crowd the day's schedule, to accelerate the plan. But time on the streets is thick. It oozes. Out here, we walk slow as the day.

space

(st. joseph cathedral, late afternoon.) I sit in the dimly lit quiet, writing on the back of spacewalking astronauts; they float above an earth muddied by photocopy grays. Around me, the church is trimmed in yellows, golds, virginal white, as if for an elegant, and lavish, wedding. Up in the loft, an organist begins practicing for Easter. A disciplined piece of music, a fugue, resoundingly triumphant. I close my eyes. The pew vibrates with sound.

"Hey, you got some money ya can gimme?"

I look up. The voice belongs to a wild-eyed anglo. His clothes are clean, his beard a day old. I shake my head.

The man sidles back out the pew, then strides up the aisle toward the only other person in the nave, a woman kneeling at a shrine up front. She's been kneeling there, head bent over clasped hands, ever since I arrived. Under my breath I plead with the guy to let her be, but he's too bold, or too desperate, for such delicacy; he interrupts her prayers with a brassy voice that echoes all the way back to my ears: "I want some money—"

"This is too much," I mutter.

The woman's purse is resting on the floor beside the kneeler. The man pleads and pleads. She tries to ignore him, then finally snaps, scolds. In that instant I fear for her safety, but the man turns on his heel and strides back down the aisle, slams through the door. Shortly after, the woman crosses herself, rises slowly and leaves.

My anger remains, without an object.

Not long after, James joins me, weary after an afternoon of shooting photographs. He lies down on a pew not far away, adjusts his body to its hard wooden curve. Soon he's drifting in thought and prayer—

Suddenly his feet are shoved violently off the pew. His sore ankle strikes the kneeler. Across the space between us, I hear him groan.

"No sleeping!" our old friend Sam says sharply, glaring down at him. "Sit up!"

"I wasn't sleepin'," James says, grimacing. "Sometimes I just pray better lyin' down—"

"Not in *this* church!" Sam says.

Turning on his heel, Sam marches down the side aisle. Before he exits the sanctuary, he kneels, genuflects before a statue of the crucified Christ.

face

(camp, early evening.) The reclusive Calvin pays us a visit. James and I are delighted. Though oft invited, this is the first time Calvin has come to our camp. Sitting with us by a slow-burning fire, he's jumpy but eager to talk.

"Heckuva basketball game last night," he says, referring to UConn's national championship win over Duke. "Yes, sir, I listened to it on my transistor." Calvin gives us an amazing play-by-play, practically a re-broadcast, of the last few minutes of the hard-fought contest. "Woulda liked to heard the whole game," he says, "but had to save my batteries. Batteries cost plenty.

Nobody'll bring me none either.

"Last fall," he says, "them Take It to the Streets people wanted to put my picture in the paper. No way I was gonna do that. Now, *some* people—and I ain't gonna say who—they agreed to have their pictures taken, and they get alot more stuff now. *Alot* more `n *I* do." His eyes, when they land on you, are piercing.

"Sometimes," he says, "I've asked them people for stuff, like batteries, or a kerosene heater, or some laundry detergent, some aspirin. They always tell me they'll bring it, and they never do. They just lie to ya. *Lie* to ya, just `cause ya won't agree to bein' in the paper."

"Don't get me wrong," he says. "I can get along just fine *without* `em. They bring me gobsa stuff I don't need. I mean, who can use a whole bottle of vitamins every single week? Whatcha s'posed to do with a dozen toothbrushes? They tell ya, `Just pass `em on if you don't need `em.' Well, I don't have nobody to pass `em on to."

Some volunteers, in my presence, have referred to Calvin as the "mean guy," the "crazy old man." "He's not crazy," I've tried to tell them. "He just gets scared. He likes to keep to himself."

The other day, Calvin says, he was over at Sarge's, and he spotted a wooden cross the volunteers had given him in celebration of Holy Week. "Nobody brought *me* no cross," he says. "I woulda liked to had one o' those."

James and I trade glances. Ever practical, we'd used our crosses for kindling. They burned like glory.

"Y'know," says Calvin, after a moment, "them people's linin' their own pockets. It's the same with the shelters—they don't really help homeless people. Nothin' changes for *nobody*, not *really*. They're just keepin' their own people employed, that's all."

Calvin stands up as if to go, then says, "How long you two been out?"

"A little over six weeks," James says.

"Why, that's not long at all. Not *a*-tall. Bobby tol' me he'd seen ya out here a coupla years ago."

"Wasn't us."

"Y'know," he says, sitting down again, "I'm worried `bout Sarge. Since Jake's moved out he's started to fall in with Rooster. Rooster's buyin' `im liquor, feedin' `im steak, just like he did Jake, at first. . . ."

For a recluse, Calvin seems to be remarkably well-informed about his neighbors on the riverbank, and now that he's trusting James and me a little, he gives us a full reporting. Listening to him prattle on, I begin to suspect that gossip, for him, is more than just a way of connecting with us; it's also a way of facing, sidelong, some of his greatest fears. If this is true, maybe his worst fear of all is dying a death you're driven to, and dying that death alone—so I gather when he tells us, at the very last, about the homeless man who sat down on the railroad tracks in front of an oncoming train, and the woman who jumped not long ago from the south bridge. He doesn't know who those people were, only that they died—alone.

Calvin's stories are frightened slivers of lives. They cut. His face is crisscrossed with lines.

custom

In my other life, the question "What do you do?" often breaks the ice between strangers. That, and "Where do you live?" and "Are you married— any kids?" First exchanges so commonly revolve around job, house, and family that two people, upon being introduced, can almost predict the course of their conversation.

On the streets, such questions are rare. "Don't ask, don't tell" is the unspoken rule. Take our neighbors: even after a month, James and I know little, if anything, about where they came from, or why they're homeless, or how long they've been on the riverbank. Withholding information, like manufacturing lies, is wisdom on the streets, a strategy for survival. As it turns out, James and I, in deliberately disclosing little about ourselves, are only following custom.

What James and I try to offer in place of particulars is presence. We've stripped ourselves to the essentials: Here we are, and this little light, this little fire we have, we'll share with you till there's no more wood. When it dies out, we'll shiver with you in the dark.

day 43: wednesday, march 31

bag of bagels

(**riverbank, mid-morning.**) A few days ago, returning to camp in late afternoon, James and I had swung by Einstein Bros. and rescued another full trash-bag of day-old bagels from the dumpster. After taking out a week's supply for ourselves, we'd abandoned the bag by the railroad tracks, out in plain view, hoping they wouldn't go to waste. We were simply too beat to make deliveries to our neighbors.

By the next morning, the bag of bagels was gone. From that we took not a little satisfaction.

Now, though, we run into Calvin along the tracks. "Y'know," he says, "the other day I found a whole bagga bagels, dozens of 'em, right by the tracks. I took 'em over and dumped 'em in the weeds. Somebody mighta seen 'em, come snoopin' around, lookin' for whoever mighta put 'em there."

goodbye

(**holy family soup kitchen, lunchtime.**) Eating lunch alone, James off to join Aaron at another soup kitchen out east, I catch a glimpse of Jake across the crowded cafeteria, give him a wave. Already finished with his meal, he soon comes by my table. His face is sallow, his eye sockets sunken and dark. "I'm goin' into a treatment program this afternoon," he says, his voice dead. "Gotta get myself cleaned up."

Please be tellin' me the truth, I say to him silently, standing up to give him a hug. I wish him well, warning him, whatever he does, to steer clear of Rooster. "I saw Calvin early this morning. Rooster charged into his camp late last night, lookin' for ya. Calvin told 'im to go away, told 'im you weren't stayin' with 'im. Told 'im he oughta leave ya be."

Jake stares, doesn't say a word. Another hug goodbye, weaker this time, and now he's walking away.

You'll never see him again.

friends are far

James stuffs his hat into a pocket and unzips his sweatshirt. The temperature must be around sixty. On his way to meet Aaron at a Parsons Avenue soup kitchen, he's enjoying the warmth, and the walk. This part of town is new to him.

After a half hour's hike through mostly poor, tumbledown neighborhoods, James sees a man two blocks up, staggering on the sidewalk. A sick gnawing in the pit of his stomach tells him it's Aaron, but the man disappears before he can be sure.

Just before he reaches Parsons Avenue, James turns his head to look down an alley, and there's Aaron, staring straight at him. James goes to join him. Aaron reaches out to shake hands, keeping a tight grip on his bottle. "Mornin', James," he slurs loudly. "You're my friend."

He's far gone.

Inwardly grieving, James tries to keep his voice light. "Hey Aaron, how's it goin'? Ready to eat?"

"Naw, this is my seconda these," he says, holding up his bottle. "I ain'ta bit hungry yet."

Together they shuffle up the alley. "Aaron," James says finally, "I could use some food."

"Well, Parsons ain't open yet," Aaron says roughly, "and I need to sit down!" He flips an abandoned shopping cart onto its side for a seat, motions for James to join him, says loudly, "C'mon! You're my friend! Sit with me!"

James sits down to appease him. This isn't the Aaron he knows.

Aaron takes a few swigs of his Strawberry Cisco. "Liquid crack," he says, "that's what this is."

Nearby is a dirty yellow metal shack, maybe ten feet square. The Golden Goat, reads a rusty sign across the top. A very short anglo is feeding one of its machines soda cans for dimes.

"That's Carl," Aaron says, and the man looks at James with sunken eyes, his face haunted, like that of a man who's been terrorized. "He showed me a way to get a dime with four cans 'steada ten." Aaron brightens, telling this, as if it were remarkably fortunate.

"Where'dya sleep last night, Aaron?" James asks.

"Down 'round here. I got kicked outa the shelter causa my drinkin'."

"You know this part of town?"

"Yeah, my sister used to have a place near here. Last year I slept under her old pool when I didn't have nowhere else to go. The house is abandoned now, but I climbed the fence last night, and sure 'nough, the pool's still there."

Suddenly he grows quiet. "James, this liquid shit has got me. If only. . . . Friends are far, James."

"No, they're not, Aaron. I'm your friend, right?"

"If—yeah—but friends are—friends are—*far*. . . ."

He drifts. For a while he sits with James in silence. Then suddenly, like a hellfire preacher, he roars, "Let's pray! *Pray* with me, James!" James closes his eyes, and Aaron rambles on, talking to Jesus about wanting to do right, get himself saved. When he finishes, Carl is still feeding cans to the Goat.

"I still got that book ya gave me," Aaron says now, in a voice loud enough to be heard a block away.

"I'm glad, Aaron. Check it out sometime, okay?"

"I will, James," he nods, staring at the ground. "You my friend, James."

Now a rangy black man shows up. He flaunts his height over the five-foot Carl, trying to provoke him. Carl doesn't take the bait, but Aaron, not very tall himself, rises up on his feet, sticks out his skinny chest and screams, "What the hell ya doin'?"

"*You* talkin' to *me*?" the black man says menacingly, squaring up to Aaron, and James thinks, Oh *God*. The two men yell at each other, bumping chests. Aaron raises his bottle as if to strike—

Suddenly, laughter. The black man throws an affectionate arm around Aaron's neck, and the two men start jiving. Aaron says to James, "This here's

Frank—"

Relieved, and exasperated, James gets up to go. "Aaron, I gotta eat. I'll see ya at the soup kitchen."

"Yeah, man," Frank says. "We'll be there after this bottle."

"Don't go, James," Aaron begs, as loudly as before. "James! *James*—"

(ohio statehouse, noon.) Under a bleached-blue sky, and a glorious sun, every bench on the capitol grounds is full of people on lunch break. To James's surprise, sitting a short distance from the Statue of Peace are his friends Tyler and Marela, both from out of town. The sight of them brings tears. Tyler has traveled all the way from Maine, just to be here.

Aaron, James says to himself, if only you had friends like these. . . .

hope

(white castle, late afternoon.) Jake had agreed to meet Sarge here at 4:00 p.m. "He's an hour late," Sarge whines. "It's not like `im, not to show up. Maybe it's true—maybe Rooster beat him up. That's what Rooster's been sayin'. Said he hurt Jake *bad*."

"When?"

"Last night."

I smile. "Sarge, I saw Jake today at Grubb Street, and he was okay, far as I could tell. Said he was goin' into a treatment program this afternoon."

Sarge's face lightens. "That makes sense," he says. "I went by Jake's place earlier, and all his stuff was gone.

"Y'know," he says, "I was drinkin' with Rooster last night. Don't remember much. Passed out. I shouldn't drink with that guy. He's too dangerous. You wake up, and there he is, ready to beat your face in.

"So," he says, eyes locked on mine like I'm his last hope, "you *really* think Jake's okay?"

day 44: holy thursday, april 1

a place at the table

During the night, a Holy Thursday dream: In the middle of a wild forest, you happen upon a farm, generations old. There's a three-story brick house, a huge red barn, and a cluster of outbuildings, all carefully maintained and abundantly full. The mow is stacked high with hay, the stalls and pens are

217

fat with animals, the smokehouse is crowded with hams and sides of beef, the root cellar's crates and burlap bags are bulging with apples and pears and potatoes and onions. . . . Surely more bounty is here than could ever be raised on a farm in the heart of a forest, but you accept what you see without question, as you're apt to do in dreams.

You step up onto the front porch of the house and open the door. Walking inside, you find the rooms unremarkable, except for the fact that each is a garden plot. Corn stalks, vining cucumbers, melons and squash, stands of lavender, bushes of basil, rows of beans and peas and pepper plants are growing out of the floor. A man whose age you can't guess is tending the plots, pruning here, harvesting there.

Finally you enter what can properly be called, despite its rich vegetation, a dining room, since it's filled with tables covered with starched white linens. The sight of the tables stuns you. Suddenly, you're aware that there's a multitude who must be fed, an invisible throng of fellow travelers—

Now a woman appears, elderly but by no means frail. She hands you a tall stack of bread plates. Everyday dishes, showing signs of wear. Without needing to be asked, you begin setting them around the tables, which all at once are overflowing with platters of fried chicken and roast beef, tureens of different kinds of soup, bowls of mashed potatoes and creamed spinach and corn, brimming gravy boats, pans of fruit cobbler, filled pies—so much food, more than any holiday meal you've ever seen. As you try to squeeze in the bread plates among the serving dishes, you ask over your shoulder, "Will there be enough room for everybody?"

"Of course," the old woman says matter-of-factly, as if she's been asked this question every day for the last hundred years. "Not everyone will be fed here—there are thousands and thousands of rooms—but *everybody* has a place at the table."

hard time

Another dream, from James: After serving a prison sentence, hard time, you're riding on a bus full of new parolees, about to be released in the city. When the bus finally pulls over to the curb, you all get off, stand there looking at each other, bewildered. Where do you go from here?

staying (4)

April Fool's Day.
The first day of Passover, when the Hebrews were delivered from slavery in Egypt.

218

Holy Thursday, when Jesus, the Jew, took the unleavened bread of Passover in his hands, and blessed it, and broke it, in the presence of somebody he loved—somebody he knew was about to betray him.

It's wisdom to know that loving is never easy; folly, many believe, to love anyway.

In this morning's Dispatch, a photograph: a teenage girl from Kosovo wiping away the tears of her young sister, the two of them finally safe but all alone in a Macedonian refugee camp. I look closely at the teenager, and know nothing: not her name, or whose eyes she has, or the lullabies she heard as a baby, her favorite color, the childhood toy she'd kept hidden away while pretending to be all grown up, what she wants to be someday, or will she always be mother, now, to this crying little girl. . . ?

Grief is heavy in these last days. The many people James and I have come to know a little and care for, here on the riverbank, at Grubb Street, other places—when will *they* make their way home, and how? As if by agreement, James and I don't speak of this. In the same way, we don't speak anymore of going home early, even though there seems no real reason to stay for just a few more days—

No reason but Easter itself—

We stay on the streets for those who feel trapped here. We stay for those who can't leave.

mantra

(**lunchtime.**) James and I trudge through cool gray mist to the soup kitchen, arriving before the line opens. This being Thursday, the little dictator is on duty. In a brief interval of silence as he begins his prayer, we hear a radio playing out in the hall. Some lyrics reach our ears, faint but clear: "If you feel like lovin' me / when you get the notion / I second that emotion. . . ."

"Sounds like a mantra for the streets," James whispers.

Almost every day the same woman is stationed at the bread and dessert table. James and I don't know her name. She's in her sixties, at least, and can barely speak or understand English. If you ask for a cookie, she may shingle six of them across your plate, despite your protests; if you ask for a slice of brown bread, she may toss on a muffin and a slice of white as well. Language difficulties alone can't account for her behavior. It's more, we suspect, the gift of generosity, well concealed beneath a dour, tough veneer that sometimes puts you off, makes you feel you're a bother.

Last week we tried to talk to this volunteer a little, and she made us understand, finally, that she immigrated to this country, years ago, from Hungary. We asked her how to say "Good day!" in Hungarian. She taught us syllable by syllable, drilling us to her satisfaction.

Today, as we're leaving, we pass by her table. "Jona-pot-kiva-nok," we stammer, as best we can remember. "Oh, jó napot kívánok!"[18] she cries, laughing, pressing one veiny hand to her ample bosom. Beside her, two girls in prep school uniforms, also volunteers, shoot her a quizzical look.

"It is *Hungarian!*" the old woman brags, absolutely beaming.

thirst

(**camp, early evening.**) Sarge drops by as the sun's going down. Never before has he ventured into our camp without Jake.

"You guys mind if I sit with ya for a spell?" Sarge says, his hand gripping a liter bottle of water. Not beer, but water.

Back when Jake was around, Sarge never had much to say. Tonight, though, he practically tells us his life story. Says his father was an alcoholic, and he's been an "alky," too, since he was thirteen years old. As a youth he'd run off and joined the Marines, become a machine gunner. At the end of his stint, he wanted to re-up, but since he was a "non-reader," the brass wouldn't let him. "Never learned to read," he says, "'cause I didn't like school much. I was the only white kid in my class. Didn't fit in. Finally I just dropped out."

After the service, Sarge got married, worked construction, had four kids. "Then there was the drinkin'," he says, "and the thing with the neighbors, and the restrainin' order. Don't know how to go home now. Don't know how I can face my kids. Really miss 'em though. Y'know, some people's got kids, and don't have no feelin' for 'em at all. Rooster, that's the way he is. That ain't natural. I ain't like that.

"I'm thinkin' 'bout goin' into rehab," he says. "If Jake's really gonna do it, I could do it with 'im. He prob'ly checked into Maryhaven. Gotta use the phone, though, to get into them kinda places. I'm not too much on usin' the phone."

Realizing he probably can't read a phone book, I say to him, "Sarge, if ya want me to, I could go up top, call Harold and Ada, tell 'em ya need some help gettin' into a program. They do that sorta thing."

He mulls it over. "Maybe tomorrow," he says, finally. "I gotta do *somethin'*. I need to get off the riverbank. I'm spendin' too much time with Rooster. Keeps givin' me liquor, y'know. But not the crack—I *don't* smoke crack. Jake, he'd get crazy on the stuff."

He says, "Y'know, one time some cops was hasslin' me in United Dairy Farmers. But one o' the guys workin' the counter stuck up for me, said to the cops, 'Look, Sarge is a nice guy, he don't bother nobody'—and I *don't*, y'know. I don't mean nothin'.

"Guys," he says now, "I *really* needa drink. Wouldya mind if I went and gotta forty, brought it back and drank it, here in your camp?"

conquerors

Long into evening, a hot-rod pickup pulls into the field above camp. James and I go to greet the volunteers while Sarge stays on his log by the fire, clutching his brownbagged forty. He doesn't want them to see him drinking.

Two anglo couples climb out of the truck, all wearing black leather jackets. A guy with a mustache crawls into the back, which is crowded with coolers and picnic baskets and water jugs, and starts filling large styrofoam containers with food. James and I try to say that while we're very grateful, we aren't at all hungry, having already eaten our dinner, and their food, which is no doubt excellent, won't keep in this warmer weather—but nobody's listening. Eventually we give in with powerless shrugs, watch them spoon up huge mounds of mashed potatoes and top them with thick brown gravy. A woman hands me two gallons of water, then loads James's arms with loose soda cans.

The quartet follows us back to camp, each carrying two big bags of foodstuff, which they deposit at Sarge's feet. An awkward pause, then the mustached man starts in preaching. Says he's a biker; nearly got killed in a bad accident a while back. "God knocked me off my bike, and that's how I found Jesus," he says. "We all come to 'im in our own way, don't we?"

He wants us to know that Jesus will save us, too, if we let Him. He recites, in dramatic fashion, his favorite passage of scripture, the last few verses of Romans 8: "Who shall separate us from the love of Christ? Shall tribulation, or distress, or persecution, or famine, or nakedness, or peril, or sword? As it is written, 'For thy sake we are being killed all the day long; we are regarded as sheep to be slaughtered—'"

Sarge slumps lower on his log. The fire's dying. I give it a poke—

"No, in all these things we are more than conquerors through him who loved us. . . ."

plush

One of the biker women, hanging back as the others leave, presents me with a gift bag containing several sets of stationery, a book of stamps, three expensive pens, an address book, and last but not least, a variety of Clinique cosmetics and beauty aids. Then she hands me a cosmetics storage box, in which I discover two plush handtowels and washcloths, and a polished brass hand mirror sheathed in burgundy velveteen. I sigh. The woman leans in, murmurs in my ear, "I just don't know how you do it. I know *I* couldn't. Guess I wouldn't make a very good pioneer."

nobody there

By the time the bikers drive off, our tiny camp is cluttered with eleven bags of food, more than a dozen soda cans, and several gallons of water. Wearily James and I sort out a stash to send home with Sarge, who by now is far gone; the remainder, we'll worry about tomorrow. If nothing else, we'll lug the supplies up to Grubb Street, or the Salvation Army, or Volunteers of America. We've done it often enough.

We sit with Sarge by the fire till there's nothing left but coals. Again and again, he thanks us for letting him drink in our camp. Again and again, he thinks he sees people sneaking around in the night woods, up to no good. "Who *was* that?" he says, panicked, pointing into the darkness. "Didya see 'em? Tell me—didn'tcha *see* 'em?"

Nobody's ever there.

day 45: good friday, april 2

bare hands

A Good Friday dream: You're planting trees in the downtown in memory of all the homeless people who have died, and are dying now—so many people, so many trees, there's not enough room for them all, so like a giant you begin knocking down skyscrapers, angrily tearing them apart with your bare hands, making room for the planting. . . .

life for life

(**early morning.**) James and I walk the tracks toward White Castle. Between us and the path up top, a train is stalled. It may not move for an hour.

"My bowels can't wait," James says. He drops on all fours, starts to crawl under a coupling.

Suddenly the train lunges. Terrified, James scoots through to the other side, just as the train groans, begins to roll forward.

Now he feels the pain. A bloody slice across his palm, cut by a broken forty.

222

Today is Good Friday. A day of crowing cocks and betrayals; of false accusations, illegal interrogations, rigged trials; of riotous crowds, and unbearable silence; of portentous dreams, ignored, because dreamed by a woman; of handwashings, and the trading of life for life; of floggings, mockery and spit, of nakedness and thorny branches twisted into a crown; of crude wooden crosses, too heavy to bear, borne to the Place of a Skull—

A day of darkness, descending on the land in the middle of the afternoon—

The agonizing cries of a dying man—

Earth shaking—rocks splitting—wails rending air—

How much time had to pass before somebody began to call this day *good?*

refugees

(white castle.) On the front page of the Dispatch: Thousands of refugees walking the railroad tracks through winter mountains, approaching the Macedonian border. A long, long human line. I can imagine, better now after these weeks of walking the railroad toward Grubb, how the tracks might feel beneath their slow feet. At the very front of the line, a man assists an elderly woman *(is she your mother?)*, hand gripping her elbow, his body ready to bear her up. These two carry nothing; behind them, other refugees are bent beneath bundles of possessions.

What would you choose to take with you if you had to leave behind the life you'd always lived, and all you could take with you is what you could carry?

Perhaps what is truly yours, to keep and to give, can't be carried at all. . . .

names (2)

James returns to camp. Not long after, Sarge sits down at my table. "Thanks again," he says, "for lettin' me come over last night, lettin' me drink in your camp. I really needed to talk to somebody."

A homeless black man is begging quarters from the customers. I wave him over, give him 30¢.

"Rooster was pickin' on me this mornin'," Sarge says, his voice grim. "I'm scared, man. Never got hold of my wife. Gonna try to get in touch with my sister; maybe she'll let me come over. I gotta get outa here."

Now, for the first time, Sarge tells me his name. A name of many names, each of them delivered with emphasis. He laughs at the expression on my face, says, "Oh, it's a good Irish Catholic name." I'm touched by his trust, and amazed that he should make this personal revelation only days after Jake had done the same.

Bobby's sister Jan is sipping coffee at the table across the aisle. Once Sarge leaves, she leans my way, says softly, "He's lost without Jake. He's absolutely *lost* without Jake."

kinda crazy

I nearly collide with Rooster on my way out of the restaurant. He's hopping mad at Sarge, threatening to beat him up. "I'll *get* `im, goddammit! Put him in the hospital, just like I did Jake!"

A flicker of dismay must show on my face, because suddenly Rooster calms down a little, gives me a thoughtful look. "Hope you guys ain't gonna leave," he says. "I know things are kinda crazy `round here right now, but—"

"We'll be leavin' soon," I say firmly.

His face reddens. He rubs at his eyes, doesn't say a word. *What'll become of you, Rooster?*

"Hey," I say, remembering the wheelbarrow episode, "any word on Joseph?"

"Oh, Joseph, he's back sleepin' in his dumpster, up behind the Starlight pub."

spikes

(**riverbank, mid-morning.**) Up and down the railroad bed, old spikes lie scattered in the gravel. Once upon a time they held the crossties in place; rusty now, some of them bent and twisted, you don't think of them as all that substantial, till you pick one up and feel its weight, so solid, in your hand.

James and I begin collecting spikes, tossing them into piles along the tracks. It's a task we've saved till today; appropriate, somehow, for Good Friday, when Jesus the Nazarene was nailed to a Roman cross. We want to take the spikes home with us—relics again; one by one, we want to give them away as reminders of how every human being, homeless or otherwise, must inevitably suffer; and how no human being, homeless or otherwise, can endure that suffering without love, without compassion. Love and compassion: These two—our wish for another's happiness, and our wish for their anguish to end—are the strength of us; like old railroad spikes, they may not be perfect, but they can endure.

Sun's just broken through the clouds. Blue sky opens. As we walk along two different sets of tracks, a short, skinny anglo, apparently drunk, waggles toward James pushing a rickety bike, fishing pole in hand. "Whatcha doin', man?" he slurs.

"Gatherin' spikes," James says matter-of-factly, as if it were the most natural thing in the world to do.

"Oh," the man says. "Need some help?"

"Sure," James says with a grin.

The fellow lays his bike on the ground. Stumbling up the tracks, head bent low, he finds two or three spikes before losing his enthusiasm.

"Have a good day, man," James calls, as the guy totters back to his bike. "Good luck with the fishin'."

"Yeah, you too," the man says, in a bewildered tone. Then he leans into his bike, wobbles on up the tracks.[19]

walking away

("the bottoms," lunchtime.) Behind a warehouse on Church Street, two black men stand smoking and drinking. Between them, lounging on the loading dock, is Aaron, entertaining them with stupor humor. Catching sight of James and me, Aaron waves us over. "Hey, where ya goin'?" he shouts, as if we were a world away.

"Grubb Street," we say.

Aaron tries to stand up, teeters, falls off the dock, his buddies and James managing to catch him before he hits the ground. "Naw," he whines loudly, "you guys don't wanna go there. Let's go get some hot dogs and ice cream."

"We don't have any money, Aaron."

"I'll treatcha," he says, as if flush with cash. "What the hell time is it anyway? One o'clock?"

"Around ten," James says, looking at me helplessly. Seeing Aaron this way is painful, but there's nothing we can do. We back away. "Aaron," James says, "we'll see ya over at Grubb—"

"James—no, c'mon! Sit down with me here—let's bullshit—*c'mon*, man!"

James and I turn around, start walking. We force ourselves not to look back, not even when we hear Aaron fall down, trying to follow us, keep us from leaving. He shouts after James all the way down the street. "Hey, James!—*James!*—c'mon back, man! You my *friend!*"

We keep walking. A block away, our eyes full of tears, we can still hear him yelling. Neither of us can say a word.

rain

(holy family soup kitchen, lunchtime.) Morris, the graybeard who once propositioned me, is ahead of us in line. I greet him with a cool nod, wishing to discourage further overtures.

"How's it goin'?" James says to him.

"Oh, okay, James," Morris replies wistfully, remembering James's name for the first time. "But you know, don'tcha, it's gonna rain today. Around two or three o'clock."

"Why's that?" James says, baffled, remembering the brilliant blue of the sky after the morning murk had burned off.

"Why, it's Good Friday," Morris says.[20]

black box

James and I seat ourselves at a table at the very front of the cafeteria. Nonchalantly James removes a camera from his duffel and places it between our two food trays, aiming the pinhole at the serving line and the painting of da Vinci's Last Supper hanging above. The light in the room is poor; the exposure will take at least an hour—a true shot in the dark, but James wants to try. He peels back the shutter-tape, hoping for the best.

Before long, a weatherbeaten anglo sits down at the head of the table, right in the camera's eye. No worry; with so long an exposure, his presence probably won't even register on the photo paper.

"What's that, your lunch box?" the guy says with his mouth full, pointing at the camera.

"Yeah," James says.

For a moment the man studies it, a battered box covered with black tape, then shrugs. "I don't eat here much," he says then, glancing around nervously as he slurps and chews. "You can't trust anybody. There's some people in here that shouldn't be, even though they've got security cameras—they watch everybody who comes in here. 'Specially when they're havin' a summit. Coupla weeks ago, all the world leaders were here. They kept real close watch. I don't like bein' watched. Not at all."[21]

wine to blood

(**downtown.**) Having left Grubb Street, James and I are walking east along Broad, headed for the Statue of Peace, when James suddenly grabs my arm. "Is that *Maddy*?" he says, sounding stunned.

I follow his gaze. On the other side of the busy four-lane street, a woman lies on the sidewalk, her shoulders propped up against a building. I stare, trying to convince myself it's not Maddy, but now she waves a bony arm at us, removing all doubt.

She's drunk. We can tell from here.

The last time we talked to Jeff, a week or so ago, he hadn't known where Maddy was. She'd disappeared on a binge. "I don't know how to help 'er," he said. "Maybe I *can't.*

"She misses her kids, y'know," he'd told us. "Especially when school starts, and holidays. With Easter comin', she just lost it."

Now, across Broad Street traffic, James and I wave back at her. "What can we do?" I say, heartbroken.

"Nothing," James says. "Not really."

First Aaron, now Maddy. Crucifixion. Bodies, spirits, broken.

"Takes on a whole other meaning, doesn't it," James says, "'wine turning to blood'?"

pedestrian

(downtown, mid-afternoon.) I'm standing on the corner near St. Joe's, waiting for the streetlight to change. A Good Friday mass has just let out. Worshipers spill out the cathedral doors, turn pedestrian. An older man and what appears to be his grandson, six or seven years old, walk up next to me, hand in hand, dressed in their Sunday suits. I glance down at the boy and drop a smile. He presses closer to his grandfather.

Compliments of the Hungarian lady at Grubb Street, I'm toting a grocery bag filled with all kinds of cookies, clearly seen through the plastic. The man, whose features look Mediterranean, points at my bag, laughing. "She has many cookies, no?" he says to the boy, his accent delightfully rich.

"D'ya want one?" I ask the little guy, lifting my bag high to show off its bulge, and his grandfather laughs again, from down in his belly.

"I'm gonna have a *donut!*" the boy says with great seriousness, staring straight ahead.

"That's where we are going," his grandfather explains to me. "To get a donut."

I glance across the street. Don't Walk, in red neon.

"Now," says the man to the boy, "why don't you ask the nice woman if maybe *she* would like a donut?"

The boy stares up at me with a forlorn expression, chews on his lip. For all the world he doesn't want to ask me, but he doesn't want to disobey either. I smile at him again, say, "Thanks anyway, but I'd better eat my cookies."

"Okay," the boy says, obviously relieved.

"Happy Easter!" I say to them both.

"Same to you!" exclaims the man. "Yes, happy, *happy* Easter!"

227

receiving

(**downtown, late afternoon.**) At the Columbus Dispatch loading dock, a sign reads RECEIVING MONDAY–FRIDAY, 7AM–4 PM. Taking a photograph of this sign, one of the last pictures he'll take on the streets, makes James smile. When he and I first came out, we had difficulty accepting the kindness of others. We wanted to put limits on their help, and on our own requests for help. But now—well, let's just say we're trying to be receptive, every hour of every day.

last things

(**camp, late evening.**) It isn't till we're preparing for bed that James and I realize we've visited Grubb Street for the last time, the soup kitchen being closed on weekends. These last things are hard to register at the moment they're happening. A sense of finality requires a feel for the future, and we don't seem to have much of that anymore. Time has shrunk, the world with it, and so, it feels, has my flagging spirit. Every day I feel smaller, more shriveled, more self-absorbed. Easter is only two days away. What will be left by then?

When I was a child, being tucked into bed on the eve of a much anticipated day (my birthday, maybe, or the first day of school), my mother would always tell me, "The faster you go to sleep, the faster tomorrow will come. . . ."

Only two more days.

I snuff the candle, pull the blankets in tight.

day 46: saturday, april 3

strangers

(**white castle.**) 7:00 a.m. A rough night, though warm; extreme leg pain. Just have to make it through one more night.[22]

The high temperature today is supposed to be near eighty. T-shirt weather. I can't wait to strip down.

How typical of central Ohio to pretty much skip spring and head from winter directly into summer, but I'm not complaining. The grass, greening fast, is looking almost Irish. Down in our neck of the woods, a squabbling, twittering parliament of birds has returned from midwinter recess. Chipmunks

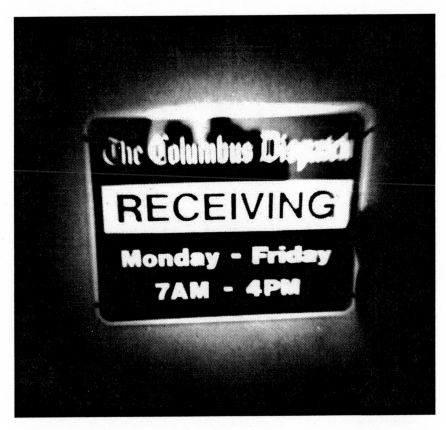

RECEIVING: hours posted at the *Columbus Dispatch* loading dock dart. Squirrels chatter and scold, contending for grazing rights at the bags of dumpster cereal we've hung in a sapling. The flat, bare ground between the field and the railroad bed has become a thoroughfare for cottontails. Soft anthills are swelling. Sometimes weeds and wildflowers rustle when there isn't a breeze, and you say hello, out loud, to the tiny critter that would rather be heard than seen.

There's more human activity in the neighborhood, too. Strangers (men mostly, but occasionally a woman) are walking the tracks and poking around in the woods, maybe scouting places to set up fair-weather camps. Their presence adds to the already mounting tensions on the riverbank. James and I have confessed to each other: "It's good, for us, that we're leavin' tomorrow."

My friend who wears the army coat and argues with himself about very important things (I call him the Philosopher) is back in White Castle this morning, after a long absence. He's shaved off his beard. Another sign of spring.

No sign of Sarge. Did he call his sister? Did she take him in? *Will you see him again before you go?*

So much will end tomorrow. So much begin.

passing on

This morning I feel much in common with certain elderly folks I know who, coming to the end of their lives, say they now understand a little better what's truly been theirs. Not their money or property, not their personalities or talents or successes, not even their loved ones—all these have a place, but in the end they're transitory. They don't survive.

What's mattered most, these people say, and what will endure, are the endowments of the heart, which across a lifetime they've had endless opportunities to develop:

Their capacity for love, and for giving themselves to another person—

For feeling another's suffering, and doing something about it—

For embracing change, even if it means a sacrifice—

For rejoicing—

For exercising faith—

For making peace—

For having visions that are beautiful and just and true, and finding the courage to speak of them, and to somehow try to give them flesh—

Capacities such as these will survive because they belong to us all. They're powers we human beings possess in common, a shared plot of fertile land that mustn't lie fallow for long.

empty pockets

(the agora, lunchtime.) James and I return to the Agora, where, shell-shocked on our second day out, we'd taken refuge for an afternoon. While James had slept fitfully on his cot, I'd wandered the building restlessly, finally ending up here, in the Five Loaves café. At one of these tables I'd been told stories, been offered food, by people who bothered to care.

Now, for our last lunch on the streets, James and I order a turkey club sandwich, a bowl of chicken noodle soup and a chocolate pastry, all to split between us. Then we deposit all of our remaining money on the counter— several crinkled dollar bills, a sweaty five, and a pocketful of street change. "Put it all in the till," we say to the server.

"But that's way too much," she says, looking us up and down. "Are you sure you don't need it?"

We smile, walk our tray of food over to a table. Any profit the café goes to support the Agora's socially concerned ministries in the Bottoms. Empty pockets never felt so good.

postlude

(riverbank, late afternoon.) If you cock your ear, you can hear Guitar Man, under the bridge north of camp, singing a ballad in falsetto. His lyrics make no sense, but his plaintive strumming, and his voice—they cling. I've never known Guitar Man to be down in these parts.

I've never met Guitar Man, and till now I've never heard him play, but I've been aware of him from my first day on the streets. That afternoon I saw him on the third floor of the library, leafing through an art book, the neck of his guitar resting against table's edge. The thought never occurred to me then that he might be homeless; I guess he didn't fit the profile. His guitar, though, made him a marked man, and after that day I was always seeing him, if only from a distance. Across the street, across the soup kitchen, across the park, across a crowded McDonald's. Always, it seemed, he was alone, except for an invisible, talkative muse.

His playing is beautiful as home.

remembrances

(camp, early evening.) After dinner it begins to rain. James and I scramble into our shelter, where we exchange humble gifts; a gesture of gratitude, and remembrance. My favorite of the gifts he gives me is an 8"x10" photograph from a downtown dumpster: a black and white close-up of two white girls, five or six years old, standing along a neighborhood street. A photo taken in the seventies, maybe. Whoever did the developing applied just a hint of blush to the cheeks.

The girl on the right glowers into the lens. Something has rankled her. Or maybe it's sadness, rather than temper, that tugs her eyebrows down. Her eyes are sober and testy, her hair unkempt, her mouth a frown.

Meanwhile, the girl on the left is laughing hard at the camera, nose wrinkled in glee, her short hair in angelic wisps around her face. She holds her cheeks between her pudgy little hands as if otherwise her face might bust—

Two realities, in the same frame.

"Pain and Wonder, remember?" James says.

fire

The rain has stopped, at least for now, and the sun's almost down. With wet wood James and I struggle to start a smoldering fire in the firepit. Our last fire, here.

Back on Ash Wednesday, as we were about to leave home, we felt the need for ritual—the imposition of ashes; now, as we prepare to leave the streets, we feel it once again. Beginnings and endings seem to demand some semblance of ceremony—some sort of container bigger than we are, capable of holding the strong emotions that might otherwise overwhelm us.

James and I place our metal bowl, our cookpot, between us. We fill it with white sand, dirty and damp, scraped up from the ground in front of our shelter. Then we remove twenty-four birthday candles from their little box—these, a token from Jihong, discreetly given on my birthday, bless him, along with a package of cupcakes I'd not had the heart to refuse. James and I saved the candles for a more practical use. Now we stick them, one by one, into the sand.

Each of us lights a slender taper, 18" long (found in German Village trash). James touches his taper to the wick of a birthday candle, says, "I light this candle for Jake."

"I light this candle for Sarge," I say, taking his lead.

"For Aaron."

"For Maddy."

"Jeff."

"Joseph."

"Rooster."

"Enid."

"The Professor."

"Calvin."

232

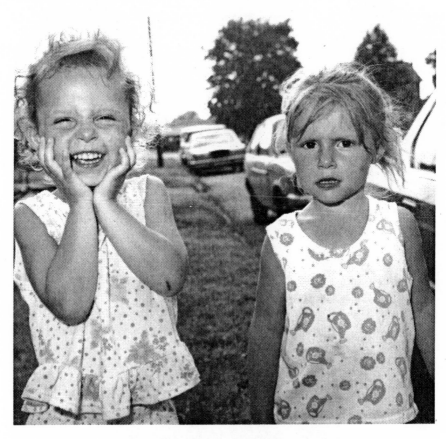

**"pain and wonder": a gift from James,
the photograph scavenged from a dumpster**
(photo credit: unknown)

"Blue."

"Elena."

"Morris."

"Sweetness."

"Manuel."

"Grace. . . ."

On and on the names, as by turns James and I light candles for every homeless person we've known or met on the streets. As the names keep coming, fire begins to leap between wicks—there's a flap of air as each wick ignites—and we watch the flame spread, till all the candles are melting down into a fiery pool of wax. Still the names, and tears too, now, as the wax suddenly blazes up with a quiet roar, then slackens, burns itself out.

Rain begins to sprinkle again. A breeze kicks up.

We huddle closer over the cookpot. We press our lit tapers into the sand. We cup our hands around their two flames, still naming names, using descriptions when names are unknown, till finally no more can be said. . . .

Our voices now silent, the tapers continue to burn, drops of wax sliding down their sides like tears. The candlewicks sizzle and spit, rain dripping on them through the trees. We can't protect them enough.

In the distance, the bells of St. Mary's.

Blessings come now, and thanksgivings too, for everybody who has helped us during these forty-seven days—for all the people who have taught us by their kindness, or their ignorance, or their hardness of heart; for all the places we've found rest, and smiles, and warmth, and food, the humblest of amenities. . . .

At last, James and I are spent. Silence again. A few minutes more, and we can bear to look each other in the eye.

a good thing

(**late evening.**) Sabrina Martin shows up with three carloads of volunteers on Saturday night rounds. We draw Sabrina aside for a private word. "We'll be leavin' soon," James tells her quietly, avoiding specifics. "I've got some work. So don't be worried if ya come out next week and find us gone."

Tears spill down Sabrina's cheeks. "You *leavin'* me?" she exclaims, throwing her arms around us both, pulling us close. "I don't wantcha to go!"

Her reaction startles us. "Sabrina," we say, "this is a *good* thing. We've got work, a place to stay—"

"Where ya goin'?"

"Up north," we hedge. "Don't worry 'bout us. We'll be fine. We're *happy* to be goin'. This is a *good* thing."

Sabrina sniffs, wipes her eyes, rubs the tears off her face. "Will you guys promise me somethin'? Will ya promise me if ya ever need a place to stay, you'll call me? You can even stay with me awhile, if ya need to. You got my number, *right?*"

day 47: easter sunday, april 4

provisions

(camp, early morning.) To bed last night at 11:30, but not to sleep—there was no sleep, for either James or me, all night long. Too much pent-up anxiety. *How to end things, here. How to start again, once you're home.* Too much, too much.

I remember a Columbus cop who, back in January, as a favor to a mutual friend, tried to dissuade me from the streets. "What'll ya do," he said, making one last appeal, "if you like it so much out there, you don't wanna come home?"

Yeah, right.

The time now is 6:10 a.m. In less than an hour, Jihong and Ron, my old friend, will be meeting us with a truck behind a dilapidated office building, a quarter-mile north of camp. How ironic that, having left home with little more than the clothes on our backs, James and I should now need a pickup to pack out all the stuff we've accumulated.

As James fumbles in the dark, packing up his pinhole cameras and other gear, I begin to stuff our bedding and clothing into McDonald's trash-bags (one last courtesy of Iris). I save out two blankets, the best we can offer, and the piece of foam rubber James has been using as a pillow; these we'll leave behind on our makeshift mattress. Now that the weather's warm, the rest of the bedding would just be in the way of whoever might move into camp. Besides, the bedding's not smelling so good. We'll take it home, wash it up, and donate it to Take It to the Streets.

James wants his wool pants to go to Jake, somehow. "Woolies," Jake always called them, with envy in his eye. Once they're clean, maybe the Martins can pass them on.

A variety of nonperishable supplies we stow in two boxes just inside the shelter door. The camp will be relatively well-stocked: some government canned goods, a full bottle of vitamin C (*Calvin: "Who can use a whole bottle every week?"*), matches and lighter, candles and candle holders (*"a different kinda light"*), Sarge's watch face (*"no Rolex"*), Repel bug spray (*volunteers*

235

brought it last night, just in time), sodas, two gallon jugs of water (*"Don't ever drink from the river"*), a few toiletries, several rolls of toilet paper, flashlight (*dead*), small metal bowl (*your cookpot*), plastic forks and spoons, plastic containers for food storage (*Grubb Street carry-out*), several sticks of Big Red gum, masking tape, scissors, pens and scratch paper (*will you be able to write? what might you want to say?*), a few photography magazines (*what will you look like?*), grocery bags for all sorts of uses, clean white socks, a sturdy pair of men's shoes (*if you're a woman, wear thick socks and stuff the toes*), winter coat (*just in case the weather turns*), safety pins, rope and wire (*shelter repair*), and our last lucky penny (*left for you to find when you're not looking*).

The little perishable food we have left we load into grocery bags to take home; we'll either return it to the Martins or donate it to a city shelter. We'll do the same with various other supplies that either were given to us in exorbitant quantities or were simply too impractical for camp life.

We pile extra kindling next to our meager stack of firewood and cover all of it with plastic. We rinse out the bucket that served as our toilet, turn it upside-down. We dump the ashes from the grill and replace the lid.

Jihong and Ron arrive with the truck, right on schedule. No time for sentiment. We have to hurry. The sun is up, bright and warm; the heavy morning mist is lifting. An early-bird neighbor might see us. James and I scuttle back and forth between truck and camp, loaded down with boxes and bags.

Over the next month or so, James and I hope to visit the Martins, Sam at St. Joe's, and other people who have helped us on the streets. We want to tell them who we are, what actually brought us here, and what their assistance meant to us. More than anybody, though, we'd like to reveal ourselves to the people we've known here on the riverbank, especially our near neighbors. Sadly, that can never happen. Jake has disappeared into treatment. Sarge is gone, too, apparently. Rooster we can't trust; he's too volatile. As for the reclusive Calvin, our confession would do him no good.

No, it's over now. There's no way to say goodbye.

We hurry.[23]

sage

The truck drives off, completely full. James and I return to camp. There's little time. We have to leave soon for center city. Our morning is booked solid: breakfast as usual at Central Presbyterian; Easter mass at St. Joe's, joined by Jihong and Phoebe, who's driven down from Connecticut; a final noon at the Statehouse, where we'll each lay a crooked spike at the Statue of Peace—

Then, at last, the going home.

James picks up the smudge stick saved from my birthday. He flicks the lighter, kindles the bottom of the herbs, blowing gently to encourage the burn. Then he crawls inside the shelter. One last ritual. As the scent of sage wafts faintly out the door, a feeling I can't name rises in my throat.

How inseparable are Lent and Easter, one requiring the other, like winter needing spring. In winter the old world gives itself up, lays itself down to die; in spring a whole new world strides forth from the grave, starts dancing to a penny-whistler's jig. This is the nature, the rhythm, of things. This is the way. Sometimes our lives are nothing but ash, other times they're butterflies and lilies—

Often, as now, they're everything—*everything at once*—

silence

He backs out of the shelter on his knees, as you've seen him do a hundred times, shoulders hunched so he won't hit his head on the ceiling. He reaches back, hands you the smudge.

You circle the shelter slowly, trailing smoke. The air is still as death, or grace. No birds. No noisy hum from the treatment plant. No sirens. No planes. Only light freeway traffic, dimly heard, and the snap of a twig underfoot, the brush of a dewy branch against your shoulder—

Little remains now. You stub out the smudge stick, scatter the charred leaves over the damp ground.

One last time, he lowers the plastic flaps over the shelter door, anchors them with full water jugs. By tomorrow night, probably, somebody else will be living here. The tomb's not empty. Not yet.[24]

No words now—they'd just slip between worlds, disappear. Only a glance between you, then you together walk up the path and out of the woods, through the field. Hands empty, you cut one last time across the tracks, high-stepping the rails.

Somewhere, not so far away, a lone bird is singing now. Whistling, right through you.

railroad switch, north of camp

James and Phyllis: Ash Wednesday morning (*above*),
Easter Sunday (*below*)

endnotes

prologue

1. National Coalition for the Homeless, "Why Are People Homeless?", Fact Sheet #1, June, 1999.
2. Barbara Poppe in Alice Thomas, "Study on Homeless Families Goes Beyond Obvious," *The Columbus Dispatch*, March 11, 1999.
3. A finding of the National Law Center on Homelessness and Poverty, 1999, cited in National Coalition for the Homeless, "How Many People Experience Homelessness?", Fact Sheet #2, February, 1999.
4. Philadelphia, 1,478, 002; Boston, 558, 394 (1996 figures).
5. 27% of homeless people are children (U.S. Conference of Mayors statistic).
6. Thomas, "Study on Homeless Families. . . ."
7. The chronically homeless are described as spending more than 160 days over a two-year period without a home. They tend to be older than other homeless persons, and are approximately 86% male *(Comprehensive Community Needs Assessment*, Columbus Community Shelter Board, January, 1998).
8. The following information on the criminalization of homelessness is based primarily on a study by the National Law Center on Homelessness and Poverty, dated March 17, 1997.

the emptiness of our hands

1. Pronounced YAH-sheer KO-ock; Hebrew for "Grow in strength." Some weeks before hitting the streets, James and I had received in the mail the well wishes of a Jewish friend, who concluded his note with this blessing. It became our traditional way to end each day.
2. Some weeks after leaving the streets, I revisited the café, told the employees who I was and paid this young man back. He was dumbfounded. When I apologized for having deceived him, he said, graciously, "The greater deception would have been if you'd never come back. Besides, you know what the Bible says—show hospitality to strangers, for you might be entertaining angels unaware." It turns out the man had once been homeless himself.
3. Mardi Gras: "Fat Tuesday," or Shrove Tuesday, is the day before Ash Wednesday. Traditionally, it's the last day of merrymaking and indulgence before Lenten fasting begins.
4. Families comprise around 40% of the nation's homeless

241

population. An estimated 1300 homeless children, elementary-school age or younger, live in the Columbus metropolitan area. No information was found on older children and youths.

5. Do you speak Spanish?

6. A little.

7. James and I had asked concerned family and friends not to bring us food, blankets, extra clothes, money or other forms of help.

8. After a few days, Dog disappeared. Jake and Rooster "just couldn't keep it."

9. After we came off the streets, James and I were both diagnosed with post-traumatic stress disorder and received counseling to alleviate panic attacks. Now, fortunately, most of those difficulties have passed.

10. Approximate pronunciation: yō NAW-pōt KEE-vah-nōk.

11. Little more than a month after James and I came off the streets, a shanty fire along the railroad tracks claimed the life of an unidentified homeless man. Given the location, we were almost certain the victim was our neighbor Blue until a well-placed friend called a contact in the coroner's office. From him we learned that the approximate height, weight, and race of the victim's body, which had been badly burned, didn't resemble Blue at all. The description matched only one person we'd met on the riverbank: the short, skinny anglo with the fishing pole. Since James and I never knew that fellow by name, we couldn't confirm our suspicions once the body was positively identified.
The fire's cause was never determined. The death was ruled accidental. In a December, 1999, issue of *Columbus Alive,* the associate director of a homeless shelter claimed that in recent years, railroad police have been regularly burning encampments alongside the tracks. A spokesperson for the railroad company said in response that while he wasn't certain the charge was true, taking such action wouldn't be "unreasonable."

12. Apparently referring to the storm that, in gospel accounts, blew up at the time of Jesus' death.

13. Perhaps fittingly, this photograph didn't turn out.

14. My knee required surgery. Eventually, my back would as well.

15. When James and I revealed ourselves to the Martins a few weeks after leaving the streets, we learned that Jake had in fact entered a rehabilitation program. Sarge had taken up residence in his sister's backyard, somewhere in Columbus. Rooster had been arrested, charge unknown. Calvin was still in his tent camp, doing fine, for him. Astonished at our self-disclosure, a speechless Harold and Ada greeted us with laughter, tears and hugs. During a two-hour reunion, James and I were able to explain to them what had led us to the streets, express our

immense gratitude for their help, and also discuss matters about which we felt ambivalent. The Martins' goodwill was remarkable. Parting was sweet.

Ada Martin died of kidney failure on July 29, 2000. She was 51. She is missed. Her spirit endures.

As this edition goes to print, Take It to the Streets is struggling financially to survive. According to an article in the 4/6/04 *Columbus Dispatch*, the "family charity is hurting." Harold Martin, with serious heart problems, has largely removed himself from the work. Sabrina Martin has left the organization, reportedly due to differences with her sister, Rhonda Martin-Cage, who now runs the grass-roots charity from the basement of the First Congregational Church, 444 E. Broad St.

16. The Martins told us that the Professor moved in almost immediately after our departure.

yashir koach

Printed in the United States
25894LVS00001B/207

9 781418 433291